Rodale's Book of

Hints, Tips & Everyday Wisdom

Copy Editor: Judy Camarda
Designer: Karen A. Schell
Illustrator: John Carlance

Major Contributors:

Joanne Brader	Judith Benn Hurley	Jill Polk
Dawn Cirocco	Debra Deis Johnston	Carole Rapp
Tawna Clelan	Rudy Keller	Dave Sellers
Holly Clemson	Dennis Kline	Marguerite Smolen
Budd Coates	John Kline	C. E. Spaulding
Rhonda Diehl	Felicia Knerr	Jackie Spaulding
Suzanne Ebbert	Angus Laidlaw	Paul Strassels
William Fisher	Gail Luttmann	Susan Weaver
Phil Gehret	Gene Mater	Fran Wilson
Linda C. Gilbert	Fred Matlack	Harry Wohlbach
Marie Harrington	Susan Nastasee	Sarah Wolfgang
Susan Hercek	Tom Ney	Martin Wood
Anita Hirsch	Penny Paquette	*Old House Journal*

Rodale's Book of

Hints, Tips & Everyday Wisdom

**Edited by Carol Hupping,
Cheryl Winters Tetreau, and Roger B. Yepsen, Jr.,
with special assistance by
Bobbie Wanamaker**

 Rodale Press, Emmaus, Pa.

Printed in the United States of America on recycled paper containing a
high percentage of de-inked fiber.

Library of Congress Cataloging in Publication Data
Main entry under title:

Rodale's book of hints, tips, and everyday wisdom.

    Includes index.
    1. Home economics. 2. Gardening. 3. Health. 4. Domestic
animals. I. Hupping, Carol. II. Tetreau, Cheryl Winters. III. Yepsen,
Roger B. IV. Title: Book of hints, tips, and everyday wisdom.
TX158.R63   1985   640'.2   85-10897
ISBN   0-87857-578-2   hardcover

  4 6 8 10 9 7 5 3   hardcover

Contents

4 The Well-Maintained Home

5 Home Energy

6 Safe and Sound

7 Mind Your Money

8 Gardening Indoors and Out

9 Yard and Patio

10 Auto Advice

11 Here's to Your Health

12 Look and Feel Your Best

13 Keeping Fit

14 Pets and Backyard Livestock

Introduction

It has been said that many a good idea is born during the pleasant, idle conversation that often accompanies a meal. Being a great lover of food who has spent many happy hours over meals, I know how true that statement is. Although I can recall several such mealtime instances, I am thinking of one in particular at the moment. The meal was lunch and the idea was, well, this book.

"I wish you could hear yourselves talk," said a friend to a fellow editor and myself one day at Rodale's cafeteria. "If you could, I think you'd be as amused as I am. In the last 20 minutes you've brought up a whole lot of what could be called Rodale trivia, and I don't think you even realize it. We've been talking about colds, this being the season for them. And so far I've learned how one of you has managed to keep from getting a cold for the last three years by taking vitamin C, I've picked up a remedy a book reader sent in for relieving hacking coughs, and I've gained a tea recipe for cold sufferers that the Test Kitchens have developed. The last time the three of us got together you were talking about pointers the coach at the Rodale fitness center gave you.

"I see you're both smiling as I say this, but it's true. And what amuses me most is that you seem to take all this sort of information for granted. There must be a gold mine of such trivia around here."

We were smiling because he was right. And we were as amused by his comments as he was by our conversation because we never thought of ourselves, really, as repositories of such information. We certainly were acquainted with a lot of people—Rodale staffers and writers, and authors who published with Rodale—who knew a lot more about a given subject than we did. But we got his point. If we put together all the useful trivia that each of us knew, we'd wind up with an enormous amount.

"What you ought to do," he said, "is write a book filled with just this sort of thing. I suspect that I'm not the only one who'd like to have one book filled with succinct bits of information that Rodale is so knowledgeable about, with Rodale's particular point of view."

Well, the lunch hour ended, but the idea didn't. We did a little brainstorming with a few others in the Book Division and came away with a list of people at the Press who knew at least one specific subject well: an *Organic Gardening* editor, a Reader Service correspondent from *Prevention,* the home economist in our Test Kitchen, an engineer in Product Testing, a writer at *New Shelter* . . . and we began to see the idea take shape.

Here it is, two years later: a collection of "Rodale trivia," perhaps better described as a family encyclopedia of practical, everyday information. Most of it is so everyday, in fact, that it appears to be little more than good common sense. And it is, but it's common sense only when you've lived long enough and done enough to have discovered all these little hints and tips for yourself, and used them long enough so that they're now second nature to you.

You'd have to have lived very long and done many things, though, before you'd find all the hints here second nature to you.

For instance, do you know this baking shortcut?

> To make quick biscuits that are almost as fluffy as real yeast biscuits that take time to rise, substitute a teaspoon of baking soda and an equal amount of powdered vitamin C (ascorbic acid) for the yeast.

And what about this energy- and money-saving piece of advice?

> Bigger isn't necessarily better. A fan placed on a low ceiling that moves air at a rate of only 200 cubic feet per minute—just 2¼ mph—can make torrid 87°F air feel like it's a comfortable 77°F. Higher speed fans are less efficient coolers; they increase velocity but do not appreciably increase comfort. And high-speed fans use more energy and make more noise than low-speed fans.

Or this first-aid tip?

> If you hit your thumb accidentally when driving a nail, immerse it right away in cold water. The coldness of the water eases the pain almost instantly and helps to prevent swelling, soreness, and a nasty black nail.

Or this idea for keeping garden tools?

> Use a pail of clean, dry sand as a storage place for small garden tools. Put them into the sand when you're not using them and they will stay rust-free and clean.

If you bother to count them, you'll find that there are about 1,000 more such pieces of advice in the pages that follow. And they sweep over a broad range of subjects: preparing and preserving foods, running your house smoothly and safely, managing finances, keeping yourself in good shape, caring for pets and livestock, growing vegetables and fruits . . . and the list goes on.

Rodale's Book of Hints, Tips, and Everyday Wisdom represents the combined experiences of a great many people: our magazine and book readers (if you sent us a hint in response to our magazine and book club members' announcements, you might be one of them); book editors; horticultural experts at our farm and on the staff of *Organic Gardening*; researchers from *Prevention, New Shelter,* and *Bicycling* magazines, and Executive Fitness Newsletter; and some of our favorite authors and consultants. All these hints have seen many pairs of eyes. Once collected and edited for a first time, they were sent to Rodale staffers expert in a given area for review. Those that we had questions about were tested and checked out. Then they were all edited once again before they made their way into print.

So, here it is. We hope you use it often and that it serves you well. And we'd love to know what you think of the book. Write us and tell us how you like it and what other kinds of "Rodale trivia" you're interested in. Who knows? Maybe we can be talked into doing a second volume of more hints, tips, and everyday wisdom.

Carol Hupping

1 Kitchen Wisdom

Baked Goods

Breads

For a Lighter Whole Wheat Bread

To make a whole wheat bread rise higher and feel lighter, add 1 tablespoon of lemon juice to the dough as you're mixing it. This will add lightness but will not influence the taste.

For Good Freezer Breads

If you want to make a bread that keeps well at room temperature or in the freezer, look for a recipe that contains dried fruit, honey, potatoes, or potato water. Or substitute any one of these for like ingredients in a given recipe.

For a Moister Bread

When making a whole grain bread, add as little flour as possible to the dough. Whole grains absorb water more slowly than refined flour and therefore become dry as the dough rises. The best way to deal with this problem is to use a "sponge," which gives the bread an extra rising. (A sponge is a soupy batter made with the liquid, yeast, and some of the flour that is allowed to rise once before the remaining ingredients are added.) The extra rising does not add too much more time because the last rising is very fast.

The Proper Flour

For whole grain yeast bread, try to get special bread flour. You'll probably have more luck finding it in a natural foods store than in a supermarket.

Measuring Guidelines for Flours

Flour	Unit	Vol.
Corn	2 lb.	8 cups
Rye	2 lb.	
light, sifted		10 cups
dark, sifted		7 cups
Soy	2 lb.	
full-fat, sifted		15 cups
low-fat		11 cups
Wheat, all-purpose	2 lb.	
sifted		8 cups
unsifted, spooned		7 cups
instant		7¼ cups
Whole wheat	2 lb.	6⅔ cups

This flour is milled from hard wheat, which is high in gluten, the stretchy substance that traps the air bubbles that make the bread rise.

Storing Flour

Store ground whole grain flour in the refrigerator or freezer if you'll be keeping it for more than a few months.

Let flour that's been in the refrigerator or freezer warm up before using it with yeast. Otherwise, you could chill and inactivate the yeast.

A Sweetener-Free Bread

To make a sweetener-free bread, omit all honey and sugar from the recipe and add 1 teaspoon of malt for every tablespoon of yeast called for. The malt provides the food that enables the yeast to grow.

Keeping Hands Clean When Kneading

Keep a plastic bag nearby when you're kneading bread or making pastry or pasta. Then when the phone rings or you have to reach for a clean bowl, you can slip the bag over your messy hand and not spread the flour around the kitchen.

Easier Kneading

Put a wet towel under your bread board when kneading or rolling dough so that the board won't move.

Taming the Dough Hook

Lightly oil the dough hook on your heavy-duty mixer before kneading your bread. The oil will keep the dough from "climbing" and will make cleaning up easier.

The Rising

To provide a warm place for bread to rise, place a pan of hot water in the oven. (Do not turn the oven on.) You can keep the pan of water in the oven while the bread is baking, too, if you like a crisp crust.

For Crisp Crusts

No need to go out and buy a fancy baking tile to produce a crisp bottom on your pizza and French bread. An unglazed terra-cotta tile purchased from a flooring or tile store can just as easily substitute.

Even Baking

For more even baking of bread, remove the bread from its loaf pan 10 minutes before it is finished baking and place it directly on the oven rack. Not only will the bread bake more evenly, but you'll also be able to test it for doneness more easily by tapping on its bottom.

Cooling

Cool baked goods in draft-free places because drafts tend to cause shrinkage.

Cool before Wrapping

Breads intended for storage should be cooled completely before being wrapped. Otherwise, they will release water vapor that will condense on the inside of the wrappings as they cool.

Freezing before Baking

You can freeze bread before it's baked so that you have just-baked bread whenever you want it. Make you bread dough as usual and let it rise once. Then punch it down and shape it into a loaf no more than 2 inches high so that later it will thaw quickly. Thaw the dough in a 250°F oven for 45 minutes (during which time it will rise), then reset the oven at the normal baking temperature and bake as usual.

Freezing before Completely Baked

To have quick, fresh-from-the-oven breads anytime, bake your bread for approximately two-thirds of the required time at whatever temperature your recipe says, or to within 10 minutes of completion. Remove the loaves from the oven at this point, take them out of the pan, and cool. Put the loaves in plastic bags and freeze until ready to use. (It's best not to keep them in the freezer for more than three weeks.) When you are ready to use the bread, thaw it and bake in a 350°F oven for about 20 minutes.

Thawing

Breads should be eaten soon after thawing, because thawed breads dry out quickly.

Rx for Dried-Out Breads

When your bread or rolls start to dry out, sprinkle a little water on them and heat them briefly in the oven.

Another way to moisten stale bread or rolls is to lay a strainer over a pot of boiling water or cooking vegetables and place your bread or rolls in the strainer. Put a lid over them so that the steam rising from the pot will moisten and warm them.

Homemade Bread Crumbs

Any bread can be made into crumbs, then toasted and added to the dough of fresh bread, a technique commonly used in many Russian peasant loaves.

Steaming Breads

To save time, steamed breads can be made in a pressure cooker. Just put the dough into coffee cans, filling them two-thirds full, place the cans in the pressure cooker, and cook at 15 psi for 30 minutes.

Quick but Fluffy Biscuits

To make quick biscuits that are almost as fluffy as real yeast biscuits, substitute a teaspoon of baking soda and an equal amount of powdered vitamin C (ascorbic acid) for the yeast. The soda, which is an alkali, reacts with the acidic vitamin C to form sodium ascorbate and carbon dioxide gas, the same gas that yeast forms to make a dough rise. No need to let the dough rise before you put it in the oven. You'll have fluffy, nutritious biscuits in the time it takes to bake them.

Cookies

Roll Out on Baking Sheet

When making rolled cookies or crackers, roll and cut out your dough directly on the baking sheet. This will save you time and cleanup.

Sugar Substitutes

Grind up puffed rice and use it instead of sugar to sprinkle on cookies or pastries.

Or try a light sprinkling of ground almonds.

Cooling Cookies

If you have no wire or wooden racks on which to cool cookies, or not enough of them when making large batches, cool cookies on cotton dish towels or on a large cotton tablecloth folded in half.

Keeping Cookies Moist

A piece of bread in the cookie jar keeps soft cookies from hardening.

Pies and Pastry

Our Best Whole Wheat Piecrust

For a single whole wheat piecrust, use 1⅔ cups of whole wheat pastry flour, ½ cup of butter, and 2 to 5 tablespoons of liquid. Two tablespoons of the butter can be replaced with oil. This recipe works well for pies but is too delicate for turnovers. For a sturdier dough, decrease the butter by 2 tablespoons, and add extra liquid as necessary.

Flavorful Pastry

To add flavor to whole wheat piecrusts, replace some wheat flour with other grains. For ¼ cup of whole wheat flour, substitute oat, soy, or millet flour, or even oatmeal.

Flaky Pastry

For a flaky piecrust, use sour cream or yogurt for the liquid.

Rx for a Too-Moist Pastry Dough

If you accidentally add too much liquid to a pie dough, don't try to work in more flour or the crust will toughen. Instead, sandwich the dough between two sheets of wax paper, flatten it to a thickness of about 1 inch, and place it in the freezer until firm. Then you will be able to roll it out easily.

Keep Things Cool

For better piecrusts, be sure all the ingredients are very cold, and be careful not to overwork the dough. Cover the dough and chill it in the refrigerator before rolling it out.

Marble pastry boards and rolling pins are always cool to the touch and help keep the dough cool as it is rolled out.

Rolling with Cornstarch

When you're rolling out dough, instead of flouring the pastry cloth or board, use a light dusting of cornstarch. It actually works better than flour, it leaves no starchy aftertaste, and it cleans up easier, too.

Frozen Instant Pastry Topping

Save leftover pie dough and freeze it into a ball. When you need an instant topping for baked fruit dishes, such as cobblers, just grate the frozen dough on top.

Proper Pans for Acidic Fruit Pies

Use glass or ceramic pans when baking apple or cherry pies; the acid of the fruit can react with metal and turn the pie grey.

Shiny Pastry

For a shiny crust on pastry, brush with milk or beaten egg about 5 minutes before the end of baking time.

Sealing a Prebaked Piecrust

To help seal a prebaked piecrust intended for a custard pie, save a tablespoon of egg (white or yolk) from the recipe, and brush the crust with it before baking. Crusts intended for savory pies, like quiches, can be brushed with mustard instead.

Coconut for Apple Pies

To add flavor to apple pie, sprinkle a cup of coconut over the apples before covering them with the top crust.

No Overbrowning

To protect the edges of a piecrust from overbrowning while it is baking, cut the center out of a 10-inch disposable aluminum pie plate, leaving a 2-inch-wide ring. Place this ring upside down on a 9-inch piecrust. You'll find that it does the trick and that it can be washed and used again and again.

General Baking

Oil before Honey, Eggs before Oil

When measuring oil and honey for a recipe, measure the oil first so that it coats the spoon or cup, making the honey that's measured next slide out easily.

When you're baking with oil and eggs, crack your eggs in a measuring cup first and then pour them into your mixing bowl. The eggs will coat the measuring cup so that when you measure the oil it will slide out easily, leaving no oil behind in the cup.

Dust with Carob Powder

Dust buttered pans with carob powder instead of flour to keep dark cakes brown and beautiful.

Lifting Baked Goods

The serrated, slightly curved grapefruit knife does more than just separate grapefruit segments; it is ideal for lifting baked goods and cakes that don't want to leave their pans.

Fat-Free Pan Lining

Parchment paper can be used to line baking pans so that you don't need to oil or butter the pans. This saves calories and also saves cleanup.

Substituting Baking Powder for Baking Soda

If you do not want to use baking soda in a recipe that calls for it, you must also eliminate the acid ingredient, which is usually sour milk. The rule to remember is that 2 teaspoons of baking soda to 1 cup of sour milk equals ½ teaspoon of baking powder to 1 cup of sweet milk.

Substituting Baking Soda for Baking Powder

To substitute baking soda for baking powder, for every teaspoon of baking powder use instead ¼ teaspoon of baking soda plus ⅜ teaspoon of cream of tartar.

Storing Baking Powder

Don't keep baking powder for more than one year, as it loses its potency. To check whether your baking powder is still usable, add 1 teaspoon of it to ⅓ cup of hot tap water. The mixture should bubble vigorously.

Cutting Down on Sweetener

To cut down on sweetener, you can use homemade sugar-free applesauce as a substitute for the honey in a recipe.

If you want to convert a favorite recipe that calls for sugar to honey, use half the amount of honey as you would sugar. For example, in place of 1 cup of sugar, use ½ cup of honey. Remember to adjust your recipe's dry ingredients by increasing them a little to compensate for the liquid honey.

Greasing Pans

Save margarine and butter wrappers. They make handy "disposable wipes" for greasing baking pans.

Beverages

Keeping Them Warm

To keep mulled cider or any warm party beverage hot, serve it from a Crock Pot.

That Last Bit of Honey

A good way to use up the last drops of honey in the container is to add a

Does Your Tap Water Smell of Chlorine?

You can get rid of the chlorine by using one of these tips:

- Fill a wide-mouthed pitcher with water and let it stand overnight. Because gas is volatile, the chlorine will escape into the air.

- If you're in a hurry, beat the chlorine out by whirling the water in a blender for about 15 minutes.

- Add a scant pinch of vitamin C powder or a piece of a vitamin C tablet to a glass of water immediately before drinking it. The taste and odor of chlorine will disappear because the acidic vitamin combines with the basic chlorine to form a harmless, bland salt.

cup of boiling water to the jar. Then add your favorite tea bag, let it steep, and treat yourself to a relaxing break.

No More Coffee Filters?

When you run out of coffee filters, try heavyweight paper napkins or a double thickness of paper towels instead.

Instead of Coffee Lighteners

Forget about those nondairy creamers that are filled with a laboratory's worth of chemicals. If you run out of fresh milk, just use a teaspoon of nonfat dry milk.

Raspberry Tea

It's not just the fruit that your raspberry bush has to offer. Pick the leaves when they are fresh and green and freeze them on baking sheets. Once they're frozen, store them in plastic bags. Steep a handful in near-boiling water in a small teapot for a lovely, light caffeine-free tea.

Grape "Cubes" for Your Punch

Freeze clusters of grapes to float in punches. They keep the punch cold and add a lovely garnish, too.

Dairy Foods

Butter

Better Than Butter

Make a butter spread with less saturated fat by mixing together equal parts of melted butter and a polyunsaturated vegetable oil.

For another healthful spread, beat together equal parts of softened butter, mayonnaise, and low-fat yogurt.

Sautéing with Butter

The salt in regular butter separates out when the butter melts and can make delicate sautéed foods slightly bitter. It's better to use unsalted butter for sautéing.

When sautéing with butter, add a little vegetable oil to the pan to keep the butter from burning.

Cheeses

For Longer Keeping

No more moldy cheese in the refrigerator: Moisten a paper towel with a bit of cider vinegar and wrap it around your wedge of cheese; then place the wrapped cheese in a plastic bag and seal. The acid in the vinegar will keep mold away. If the paper towel dries out, moisten it with a bit of water-vinegar solution.

To prevent cheese from drying out in the refrigerator, wrap a moistened paper towel around it, and then cover it with a plastic bag and tie it shut. Moisten the towel, if necessary, each time you cut a piece of cheese.

Ricotta and cottage cheeses will store longer in the refrigerator once they've been opened if you turn the reclosed container upside down, thereby forcing some of the air out of the container. You can get the same results by taking the cheese out of its original container and storing it in a smaller glass jar.

Bring Out the Cheese

A bit of Parmesan cheese added to a blander cheese called for in a recipe will accentuate the cheesy flavor in the finished dish.

Eggs

Small or Large Eggs?

If the difference in price between large and small eggs is 8¢ or less per dozen, the larger eggs are the better buy.

If You Find a Crack

You don't have to throw away the cracked raw eggs you find in the carton; use them, but only for egg dishes that are thoroughly cooked, such as hard-cooked eggs, or in baked goods.

Checking for Freshness

You can tell whether eggs are fresh or not by placing them in a deep pan of water. Any floaters should be thrown away; as an egg gets old it shrinks, and air fills the pocket that's been left, enabling the egg to float. The eggs lying on the bottom are fine to use.

Storing

When you need to store raw eggs without the help of a refrigerator, such as during a camping trip, coat the eggs with shortening. It will help to preserve them longer by sealing out air.

Never wash eggs before storing them; you'll wash off their natural protective coating.

To preserve leftover egg yolks for future use, place them in a small bowl and cover them with about 2 tablespoons of vegetable oil. Make sure they are completely covered with oil. Egg yolks can be kept this way for a few days in the refrigerator.

Freezing

Eggs can be frozen, but not in their shells, which would crack. If you want to freeze eggs, remove them from their shells and scramble them with 1 teaspoon of salt or 1 teaspoon of honey for each cup (about 5 eggs) to stabilize the yolks and prevent them from getting pasty after thawing.

You can pack scrambled eggs for the freezer together in one container or individually in ice cube trays. Three tablespoons of scrambled egg equals one whole egg.

Directions for a No-Fault Hard-Cooked Egg

Place a large egg in a pot, cover with cold tap water, and bring the water to a boil over high heat. When the water reaches a rolling boil, turn the heat off, leaving the pot in place. Allow the egg to cook for 17 minutes. Cool the egg by placing it in a bowl of cold tap water for 5 minutes, then peel and serve. The shell will not crack, but the egg will peel easily. The egg will be perfectly cooked, without the ugly dark ring caused by the separation of sulfur from the egg yolk when the egg is overcooked or not cooked quickly enough.

How to Avoid Cracking Eggs

To prevent an egg from cracking while you're hard-cooking it, prick a small hole with a needle in one end so that air can escape.

Add a little vinegar to the water if an egg cracks during boiling. It will help seal the egg.

Telling the Fresh Eggs from the Hard-Cooked Ones

To code hard-cooked eggs so that they are distinguishable from the raw ones, just add a few yellow onion skins to the water while simmering; they will color the shells.

A Free Egg Poacher

An egg poacher or fried egg mold can be made by removing the top and bottom of a clean tuna can.

More from Beaten Eggs

Get more volume from beaten eggs by letting them stand at room temperature for about an hour before you beat them.

No-Fail Way to Separate Eggs

If you have the patience, a slow but easy way to separate eggs is to break them one at a time into a small funnel over a cup. The white will pass through into the cup, and the yolk will be left behind in the funnel.

Other Dairy Foods

Smoother Homemade Ice Cream

To prevent homemade ice cream from crystallizing, add one envelope of gelatin for every 1½ quarts of liquid in the recipe. Just heat some of the liquid and dissolve the gelatin in it; then add it to the other ingredients.

Dry Milk as a Backup

Always keep dry milk on hand in your pantry to have ready if you run out of fresh milk.

Salvage the Sour Milk (or Cream)

Should your milk or cream sour before you have a chance to finish it up, use it in any quick bread recipe in place of fresh milk, and substitute baking soda for some of the baking powder called for. Don't keep it long without using it, however. If it's moldy, throw it away.

Sour Cream Substitutes

You can have "sour cream" on your baked potatoes without the extra calories by using cottage cheese instead. Run it through a blender or food processor to smooth it out, and flavor it with chives. Plain yogurt is a good sour cream substitute, too, and it comes smooth right from the container.

Cooking with Yogurt

To prevent yogurt from separating when cooking with it, first add one slightly beaten egg white, 1 tablespoon of cornstarch, or 1 tablespoon of whole wheat flour per quart.

Fruits

Apples

Baking Apples

To keep apple skins from cracking while they bake, pare a 1-inch band around each apple's center.

Avocados

Ripening Avocados

An avocado will ripen faster if placed in a plastic bag with a piece of banana peel.

Keeping Them Longer

To keep refrigerated avocado dip or half a sliced avocado from turning dark quickly, place the avocado pit in the center and wrap to form an airtight seal.

Bananas

Freezing

Extra bananas? You can freeze them either peeled or unpeeled, cut into chunks or mashed, depending on what you plan to do with them.

Frozen Banana Snacks

Here's another wonderful use for ripe bananas: Slice the fruit, place the slices on a baking sheet, and freeze them until firm. Roll each slice in honey and then in your favorite topping, such as chopped nuts, coconut, or crushed rice puffs. Return them to the freezer and when frozen solid, put them into plastic bags and seal. These make wonderful frozen candy snacks.

Pureed Bananas

Pureed bananas can be used in breads and cakes. Overripe bananas— too ripe to eat raw—are particularly good because they're so sweet.

Keeping Bananas Safely

If you bring home a big bunch of bananas that you know you'll be separating and using singly, separate them right away by cutting off the "knob" that joins them all together. Make sure that you cut them so that a 1-inch tip is left on each. This tip will dry up and seal itself in a day or two. Then, when you are ready to use the bananas, you won't have to bother breaking off one at a time, which can often result in splitting the top skin of several and exposing the open parts to bacteria.

Grapes

A Frozen Natural Snack

Frozen grapes make a fine natural snack: Just lay them out on a baking sheet in the freezer so that they freeze separately, and then bag them for snacking later.

Lemons and Limes

More Juice

You will get almost twice the amount of juice out of a lemon or lime if you drop it into hot water for a few minutes before you squeeze it. Heating the fruit breaks down the inner membranes so that they release more juice. Or instead of heating the fruit, try rolling it on a hard surface to break down those membranes.

For a Few Drops at a Time

If you want just a few drops of lemon juice, poke a hole in one end of the fruit with a toothpick. Squeeze the desired amount from the hole, replace the toothpick, and store the lemon in a plastic bag in the refrigerator for future use.

Grating

Grate your citrus rind over wax paper or foil to make pouring it into a measuring cup or mixing bowl easy.

Use a pastry brush to remove the citrus rind (or onion, carrot, or whatever) that is stuck in the holes of the grater.

Pineapple

Homemade Juice

They may be messy and prickly, but pineapple trimmings can make great pineapple juice. Pineapple processing plants use this trick all the time. Put the trimmings and even the core into a blender with just enough water for processing and grind them up; then strain the juice through a very fine sieve or cheesecloth-lined strainer and serve it up chilled. Fresh pineapple juice will ferment quickly, so drink it immediately.

Potting Up the Top

Every pineapple top is a houseplant ready to happen. Twist it off with a circular motion so that you leave no fruit on the stem, and then remove 10 to 15 of the small, bottom leaves from the stem. You'll see little brown or whitish roots already in place to grow. Put the stem in water about 1 inch deep, and leave it on a warm windowsill for a couple of weeks, after which time you should have roots. Then you can plant it in a pot, or in your garden if you live in a warm, frost-free part of the country. Being a

(continued on page 18)

Measuring Guidelines for Fruits

Fruit	Unit	Vol. or Pieces per Unit
Apples, fresh	1 lb.	3 medium
Apricots, fresh	1 lb.	8-12
canned, whole (medium)	1 lb.	8-12
halves (medium)	1 lb.	12-20
dried	11 oz.	2¼ cups
cooked, fruit and liquid		4⅓ cups
Bananas, fresh	1 lb.	3-4
dried	1 lb.	4½ cups
Blueberries, fresh	1 lb.	2 cups
frozen	10 oz.	1½ cups
canned	14 oz.	1½ cups
Cherries, fresh, red, pitted	1 lb.	2⅓ cups
frozen, sour, pitted	20 oz.	2 cups
canned, sour, pitted	1 lb.	1½ cups
sweet, unpitted	1 lb.	1¾ cups
Cranberries, fresh, uncooked	1 lb.	4 cups
sauce		4 cups
canned, sauce	1 lb.	1⅔ cups
juice	1 qt.	4 cups
Currants, dried	1 lb.	3¼ cups
Dates, dried, whole	1 lb.	60
pitted, cut	1 lb.	2½ cups
Figs, fresh	1 lb.	12 medium
canned	1 lb.	12-16
dried, whole	1 lb.	44
cut fine		2⅔ cups
Fruit juices, frozen	6 fl. oz.	¾ cup
canned	46 fl. oz.	5¾ cups
Fruits, frozen, mixed	12 oz.	1⅓ cups
canned, cocktail or salad	17 oz.	2 cups
Grapefruit, fresh	1 lb.	1 medium
sections		1 cup
frozen, sections	13½ oz.	1½ cups
canned, sections	1 lb.	2 cups
Grapes, fresh, seeded	1 lb.	2 cups
seedless	1 lb.	1½ cups
Lemons, fresh	3 lb.	12
frozen, juice	6 fl. oz.	¾ cup
canned, juice	8 fl. oz.	1 cup

Fruit	Unit	Vol. or Pieces per Unit
Oranges, fresh	6 lb.	12
diced or sectioned		12 cups
juice		4 cups
frozen, juice, reconstituted	6 fl. oz.	3 cups
canned, juice	46 fl. oz.	5¾ cups
mandarin, fruit and juice	11 oz.	1¼ cups
Peaches, fresh	1 lb.	4 medium
sliced		2 cups
frozen, slices and juice	10 oz.	1⅛ cups
canned, halves	1 lb.	6-10
slices	1 lb.	2 cups
dried	1 lb.	3 cups
cooked		6 cups
Pears, fresh	1 lb.	4 medium
sliced		2⅛ cups
canned, halves	1 lb.	6-10
Pineapple, fresh	2 lb.	1 medium
cubed		3 cups
frozen, chunks	13½ oz.	1½ cups
canned, chunks or tidbits	29 oz.	3¾ cups
crushed	29 oz.	3¾ cups
slices	20 oz.	10
juice	46 fl. oz.	5¾ cups
Plums, fresh	1 lb.	8-20
halved		2 cups
canned, whole	1 lb.	10-14
Prunes, canned	1 lb.	10-14
dried, whole	1 lb.	2½ cups
cooked		4-4½ cups
pitted	1 lb.	2¼ cups
cooked		4-4½ cups
Raisins, seeded, whole	1 lb.	3¼ cups
chopped		2½ cups
seedless, whole	1 lb.	2¾ cups
chopped		2 cups
Rhubarb, fresh, cut	1 lb.	4-8 stalks
cooked		2 cups
frozen, sliced	12 oz.	1½ cups
Strawberries, fresh, whole or sliced	1½ lb.	4 cups
frozen, whole	1 lb.	1⅓ cups
sliced or halved	10 oz.	1 cup

bromeliad, the pineapple appreciates water poured into its crown as well as on its roots.

Storing

To keep pineapple fresh longer, cut slices from the bottom as you need them, leaving the green top growth intact. Wrap the unused portion, with the top growth attached, in plastic wrap.

Watermelon

Freezing the Surplus

Got a surplus of watermelon? Scoop the pulp from the rind, removing the seeds as you go. Then run it through a food mill or blender, or mash it with a potato masher. Freeze the smooth pulp in ice cube trays, and you've got wonderful natural fruit pops.

Fruit Miscellany

Save the Rind

Don't discard the rind of lemons, grapefruit, or oranges. It makes excellent flavorings for cakes, frostings, and such. Wash it well and grate, being careful not to include the bitter white part under the rind. Put it in a tightly covered glass jar and store in the refrigerator.

Leftover apple, orange, or lemon rind can be put into your tea as it's steeping to add a wonderful flavor and aroma—just like the fancy gourmet tea blends.

Quick, Natural Desserts

For a quick dessert, an unsweetened can of fruit can be opened and frozen. When ready to serve, put the frozen fruit in a blender or food processor and spoon it into stemmed glasses. Top it with chopped nuts.

You can make another easy, light dessert by freezing a fresh fruit, like kiwi fruit or melon, and then shaving it into small chilled bowls.

Naturally Sweetened Frozen Fruits

To freeze peaches and other fruits without sugar, use orange juice instead of the traditional sugar syrup. Slice the fruit into thawed orange juice concentrate, making sure the slices are thoroughly coated to keep them from darkening. Two large cans of concentrate will easily do for a crate (about 20 pounds) of peaches.

Keep Fruit Looking Fresh

A coating of lemon, orange, or pineapple juice will keep cut fruits from browning.

Using Dried Fruit

There's really no need to rehydrate dried fruit before you add it to a recipe, because even the hardest dried raisins or prunes will become soft and moist when cooked in recipes that contain plenty of liquid, like custards, puddings, stuffings, and moist tea breads.

Fruited Gelatins

There are several fresh fruits that, when included in a gelatin dessert or salad, will prevent the gelatin from firming up. They are pineapple, figs, papaya, and kiwi fruit. Save them for other uses.

Cleaning Small Berries

Small berries, such as huckleberries, can be cleaned by gently rolling them back and forth with your hand across a dry terrycloth towel placed on the counter. They will come clean and, as a bonus, they will have lost their little stems, which are so tedious to remove by hand.

Beans and Grains

Soaking Beans Quickly

To speed up the soaking time for beans, pour boiling water, rather than cold, over them and let them soak for 1 hour instead of overnight.

Cooking Out the Gas in Beans

This little trick may not get all the gas out of your beans, but it'll cut it down: Throw away the water you've soaked the beans in; cook the beans in fresh water for 15 minutes, then discard that water and start again with fresh *boiling* water.

Or try adding about a teaspoon of fennel seed to the beans' soaking water. Then cook as usual. You'll find that much of the gas is gone from your beans.

Pot or Scotch Barley vs Pearled Barley

Use pot or Scotch barley rather than pearled barley, which has the outer nutritious husk removed. Pot or Scotch barley has only a single outer layer removed, not the whole husk.

Encouraging Popcorn to Pop

To get your corn to pop more easily, sprinkle it with warm water an hour before popping.

Rx for Reluctant Popcorn

If your popcorn won't pop, you can remedy the problem by putting the popcorn in an airtight jar or container, adding a little water, and refrigerating it overnight.

Nonsticky Pasta

To prevent pasta from becoming sticky after cooking, drain it in a warmed colander and serve it in a warmed dish. The secret is to keep it warm. As the pasta cools, the starch in it gets sticky.

Or sprinkle grated Parmesan cheese over the drained spaghetti and toss. It not only keeps the noodles separated, it flavors them as well.

Don't Salt the Pasta

If you're watching your salt, don't add it to the cooking water when you're cooking pasta. It doesn't keep the pasta from sticking together; it's mainly used for flavor. The pasta may cook at a higher temperature with salt in the water, but the difference is hardly noticeable.

Reheating Pasta

To reheat pasta, just place it in rapidly boiling water for a few minutes and then drain.

Easier Pasta-Maker Cleanup

Don't wash your pasta maker or pasta-making attachment after you're through with it. Rather, remove the larger pieces of dough by hand and

Cooking Beans

Dried Beans (1 cup)	Approximate Cooking Time Regular	Pressure-cook
Adzuki	45–50 min.	15–20 min.
Black (Turtle)	45–60 min.	10 min.
Black-eyed pea	1 hr.	10 min.
Chick-pea (Garbanzo)	2 hr.	15–20 min.
Fava	45–60 min.	not recommended
Kidney	1½ hr.	10 min.
Lentil	30 min.	6–8 min.
Lima	45–60 min.	not recommended
Baby lima	45–50 min.	not recommended
Mung	1½ hr.	8–10 min.
Pea, split	35–40 min.	not recommended
Pinto	1½ hr.	10 min.
Soybean	3 hr.	15 min.
White (Great Northern, Marrow, Navy, Pea)	45–60 min.	4–5 min.

then let the small pieces dry overnight. Dried pasta dough flakes right off with no special cleaning.

Storing Beans and Grains

To protect dried grains and beans from insects during storage, spread a thin layer on a baking sheet and heat for 30 minutes in an oven set from 140° to 160°F. Or place them in a freezer that maintains a temperature of 0°F for three to four days.

Put a dried hot pepper in each jar or plastic bag of dried beans or grains to keep away weevils and other insects.

Hulling Soybeans

To hull soybean sprouts or other large-seeded sprouts, swish them in a pot of water. The hulls will float to the top and can be poured off. Add more water, swish, and pour off again.

Measuring Guidelines for Grains

Grain	Unit	Vol.
Cereals (see also Cooking Grains)		
bulgur	1 lb.	2¾ cups
cooked		8 cups
cornmeal		
white	1 lb.	3½ cups
yellow	1 lb.	3 cups
cooked		16⅔ cups
grits	1lb.	3 cups
cooked		10 cups
oats, rolled	1 lb.	6¼ cups
cooked		8 cups
rice, brown	1 lb.	2 cups
parboiled	14 oz.	2 cups
soy grits, stirred, low-fat	1 lb.	3 cups
Pasta		
macaroni, 1″ pieces	1 lb.	3¾ cups
cooked		9 cups
macaroni, shells	1 lb.	4–5 cups
cooked		9 cups
noodles, 1″ pieces	1 lb.	6–8 cups
cooked		8 cups
spaghetti, 2″ pieces	1 lb.	4–5 cups
cooked		9 cups

No-Fail Cooked Rice

To cook a perfect batch of basic long-grain brown rice, bring 5 cups of water to a boil in a 5-quart pot. Add a tablespoon of butter. When it melts, slowly add 2 cups of brown rice, bring water to a boil again, reduce heat, and simmer, tightly covered, for 45 minutes. Turn heat off, fluff rice with a fork, re-cover pot, and let stand for another 10 minutes.

Reheating Cooked Rice

To reheat refrigerated or thawed frozen rice, add 2 tablespoons of liquid for each cup of rice and simmer in a covered pot for 5 minutes.

Or put it in a vegetable steamer that has a tight-fitting lid. You'll have fluffy hot rice in less than 5 minutes, with no burned pot bottoms.

Cooking Grains			
Grain (1 cup)	Cooking Water (cups)	Cooking Time	Cooked Volume (cups)
Barley	3	55 min.[1]	3
Buckwheat	2 or 5[2]	15 min.	2½ or 4
Bulgur	2	15-20 min.	2½
Cornmeal	4	25 min.	3
Millet	3	45 min.	3½
Oats	3	30-40 min.	3½
Rice, brown	2	35-45 min.	3
Rice, wild	3	1 hr. or more	4
Rye berries	4	1 hr. or more	2⅔
Triticale	4	1 hr.	2½
Wheat berries	3	2 hr.	2⅔

1. If whole grain (pot or Scotch) barley is used, it must be soaked overnight in 4 cups water and then drained before cooking.

2. Buckwheat is traditionally cooked by first stirring a raw egg into the dry grain to keep the grains separate, and then adding 2 cups of liquid for a dry, fluffy cooked grain. Or it can be cooked without the egg, in 5 cups of liquid, to yield a creamy consistency for eating as cereal.

Peanuts and Raisins in Rice

Jazz up your cooked rice by adding a few raw peanuts or some raisins to the cooking water. The peanuts will cook and the raisins will plump up beautifully, giving you a most unusual and flavorful rice.

Herbs

The Best Time to Gather

An herb's aromatic oils are strongest in the morning, after a night's rest. So gather the leaves as early in the day as possible, after the dew has dried, but before the sun gets hot.

Longer Refrigerator Storage

Fresh herbs with long stems, such as dill, parsley, and basil, will keep in a tall cup of water in the refrigerator for three to four weeks. Cover the herbs loosely with an upside-down plastic bag and change the water every four days.

When You Dry Herbs . . .

When drying herbs, hang them upside down in clean brown paper bags. The bags keep out light and catch any seeds or leaves that may fall off the stems. Cut a few holes in each bag to increase air circulation.

Freezing

Before placing herbs in the freezer, strip the leaves from their stems and lay them in a single layer on a baking sheet. Once they're frozen, pack them in heavy plastic bags or freezer containers. Since the leaves don't have a chance to mat together as they freeze, it's easy to open the plastic bag or container and take a pinch of frozen herbs as you need them.

To keep dried spices and herbs longer, store them in the freezer rather than in the cupboard.

Better Frozen Basil

To best preserve the flavor and color of frozen basil, blanch it by holding it with tongs and swishing in boiling water for about 30 seconds. Dry it thoroughly before freezing.

Cold-Dried Parsley

You've heard of freeze-dried parsley, but have you heard about *cold-dried* parsley? Rinse off fresh parsley, pat it dry, and put it in a small brown paper bag in the refrigerator. In about a month, the parsley will have dried, but it will still be very green and aromatic—much more so than plain dried parsley. You can add it to dishes as you need it; just place some of the parsley between the palms of your hands and rub them together to crush the leaves. Don't substitute a plastic bag for the paper one—the parsley will rot instead of dry.

Spices Can Lose Their Spice

Since spices lose their punch after a while, it's a good idea to write the date that you first used the spice on the can. Discard spices after a year.

Homemade Herb Butter

Herb butter is a wonderful way to preserve the flavor of fresh herbs.

Blend fresh chopped herbs into a stick of softened butter, shape the mixture into a long roll, wrap it in foil, and keep it in the refrigerator for up to two weeks or in the freezer for as long as three months. Slice as needed as a salt-free flavor enhancer for rice, vegetables, or fish.

Herb Vinegars

When you've frozen and dried all the herbs you can possibly use until next summer but still have some left, use them (particularly chives, basil, tarragon, oregano, and sweet marjoram) to make your own herb vinegars. Bring vinegar almost to a boil and pour it over a few sprigs of an herb that you have placed into a clean, hot jar. Cool, cover, and store in a cool, dark place. Use within a year.

Salt Substitutes

Keep a pepper mill filled with whole mustard seed near your range. A few grinds of mustard as you're cooking adds some zing to dishes, without an overpowering mustard flavor. Other spice seeds work as well, and you can even blend a few to your own taste. They make excellent salt substitutes.

Bringing Garden Parsley Indoors

Don't pot up parsley from your garden and bring it into the house right away. The shock of transplanting *and* indoor temperatures might be just enough to do it in. Instead, pot it up and keep it outdoors for two weeks first, and bring it in before it's so cold that your home heating is on regularly.

Parsley after Garlic

Garnish spicy foods, especially those that contain garlic, with fresh sprigs of parsley, and encourage all your guests to finish with a piece. You'll be much more pleasant company for one another since parsley is a natural breath deodorizer.

Fish

Skinning Made Easier

It's easier to skin a frozen fish than a fresh one, so you might find it convenient to gut your fresh catch and freeze it, then skin each fish as needed, right from the freezer.

Thawing Frozen Fish

When preparing frozen fish fillets, thaw them for no more than 30 minutes at room temperature. Cook the fish in the firm and frosted state, before it drips much of its essential juices. Thawing completely removes the moistness, flavor, and nutrients with the juice. If you want to completely thaw the fish, do so in the refrigerator because it will retain much more of its moistness than the same fish thawed at room temperature.

Preparing for Freezing

Taste tests in the Rodale Test Kitchen have found that dipping fish fillets in lemon juice before freezing gives the fish a firmer texture and a fresher flavor.

Fish Salad from Leftovers

Make a chilled fresh fish salad using broiled or baked fish left over from last night's dinner. Follow the directions for your favorite tuna fish salad, substituting the cooked and chilled fresh fish. Or toss the fish with blanched and chilled fresh vegetables and a dressing of oil, lemon or lime juice, and fresh herbs.

Milder Bluefish

To eliminate the strong flavor of bluefish, soak the fillets in milk for 1 hour and cut out the dark underside of the fish before cooking.

Low-Calorie Fish Dressing

A quick dressing for poached fish can be made by combining plain yogurt with some Dijon-style mustard, lemon juice, and fresh dill.

Care for Fresh Fish

Don't leave fresh fish soaking in water because the flesh will become flabby and the flavor poor. Wash it quickly, drain it, and pat it dry carefully with paper towels.

Saving the Essence of Shrimp

Don't throw away the shells as you peel shrimp. Instead, wash them thoroughly and put them in a small pot over low heat with some butter. As the butter melts, it will pick up the flavor of the shrimp shells. Then strain the butter, discard the shells (which have served their purpose), and use the butter to season broiled fish, pasta, or rice.

How Much Seafood Should You Buy per Person?

Type	Quantity per Person
Clams, in the shell	6–8
Crab meat	¼–⅓ lb.
Fish, whole	¾ lb.
fillets or steaks	⅓–½ lb.
sticks	4–5
Lobster, live	1 small–medium
meat	¼–⅓ lb.
Oysters, in the shell	6
shucked	¼ pt.
Scallops	¼–⅓ lb.
Shrimp, unpeeled	⅓–½ lb.
peeled	¼–⅓ lb.

Poultry

Storing Poultry Safely

To prevent bacterial growth in poultry while in the refrigerator or during thawing, never store anything in the cavity of the bird, including giblets.

Long-Term Freezing

To freeze chicken parts for longer storage, wrap each piece of chicken individually in a plastic bag and then overwrap all the packages in a moisture-proof material, like freezer wrap or a freezer plastic bag.

Cooking Frozen Chicken

No need to thaw frozen chicken parts before you cook them. Just bake them 15 to 20 minutes longer than you would if they were fresh or thawed.

Broiling in Flavor

To add flavor to broiled chicken parts, brush them beforehand with honey, a lemon-honey mixture, maple syrup, soy sauce, frozen fruit juice concentrate, or mayonnaise combined with lemon juice and Parmesan cheese.

The No-Mess Way to Stuff Poultry

To stuff a turkey, goose, duck, or chicken without making a mess on the countertop or in the roasting pan, place a canning jar funnel in the opening of the bird. Then tip the fowl up and scoop in the dressing as though you were filling a jar with fruit when canning.

How Much Stuffing?

Generally ½ cup of stuffing is needed for each pound of the turkey's weight.

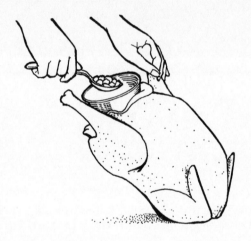

Measuring Guidelines for Poultry	
Bird	Single Serving
Under 12 lb.	1 lb.
12-20 lb.	¾ lb.
Over 20 lb.	½ lb.
Boneless	⅓-½ lb.
Prestuffed	1½ lb.

An Alternative to Trussing String

If you've run out of twine to truss your chicken or turkey, use waxed dental floss. It doesn't burn, and you can tie knots in it without it tearing. It's also cheaper than trussing string.

Defeathering Chickens

When butchering chicken, try using a strawberry huller to pick out the pin feathers.

Meats

Wrapping for Storage

Commercially wrapped poultry or meat can be kept in the refrigerator for one or two days, but for longer keeping, the store wrap should be removed and the meat rewrapped loosely.

Meat Tenderizers

Want to tenderize a tough piece of meat? Choose a recipe that has fruit in it, particularly pineapple, crab apples, bananas, figs, papayas, or kiwi fruits—all of which contain tenderizing enzymes. Moist cooking is best; never dry cook (i.e., roast) tough cuts.

You can also tenderize meat by marinating it in lemon juice for several hours in the refrigerator before cooking.

A Low Oven for Roasting

You'll find that if you roast meats at 300° to 325°F instead of the normal 350° to 375°F, they will shrink less, be more tender, and be easier to carve. It's worth the extra cooking time.

If You Must Interrupt Roasting

Don't tightly cover or wrap a roast you've taken out of the oven because dinner is delayed and you want to stop the cooking temporarily. You may be keeping the meat warm this way, but you'll also be steaming it. Cover it loosely. When you want to continue roasting, roast at the same or a slightly higher temperature—never at a lower one.

Resting the Roast

Turn off the oven to "rest" a roast 10 to 15 minutes before serving it so that the meat juices can be absorbed by the meat. The roast will then lose less of its juices when you slice it.

Cleaner Broiling

Put a thin layer of water in the broiling pan before broiling meat, fish, or poultry. This makes the pan easier to clean later, and the fat doesn't smoke as much.

Measuring Guidelines for Meats

Meat	Unit	Vol., Servings or No. per Unit
Fresh or frozen		
boned or ground	1 lb.	3–4 servings
with minimum amount bone (steaks, roasts, chops, etc.)	1 lb.	2–3 servings
with large amount bone (shoulder cuts, short ribs, neck, etc.)	1 lb.	1–2 servings
diced		1 cup
Cured and/or smoked		
bacon	1 lb.	24 slices
frankfurters	1 lb.	4–12 links
ham	1 lb.	
cooked, ground		2½–3 servings
diced		1½–2 cups
luncheon meat, sliced	12 oz.	8 slices
Canned		
corned beef	12 oz.	4 servings
ham, smoked	1½ lb.	6–8 servings
diced		3¾–4½ cups
luncheon meat	12 oz.	4 servings
sausage, Vienna	4 oz.	8–10 links
Dried		
chipped beef	4 oz.	1⅔ servings

If you want to reheat meat but don't want it to dry out, place a few lettuce leaves on a piece of foil, and put your meat on top of the lettuce. Close the foil and heat the meat in a 350°F oven. The lettuce will gently moisturize the meat.

Sautéing

Make sure meat for sautéing is at room temperature and patted dry before adding it to the pan. Otherwise the moisture will cause splattering.

Hurry-Up Hamburgers

When you're in a hurry you can cut the cooking time for hamburgers by making several holes in the center of each patty.

Ground Meat Substitutes

Weaning yourself from red meat? Try ground turkey instead of ground beef. Many butchers now sell it, and in addition to being more healthful than beef, it's usually also cheaper.

Cooked bulgur can be substituted for all or part of the ground beef in your favorite chili, stuffed pepper, or tomato and meat sauce recipes.

Better Than Bread Crumbs

Instead of using bread crumbs as a filler for meatloaf, burgers, or fish or vegetable patties, use a whole grain flaked cereal such as bran, rice, or corn. You'll find it more flavorful, and it's more nutritious, too.

Food Preservation

Glass vs Plastic

Most refrigerated foods keep longer in glass jars than in plastic containers because plastic is a bit more porous than glass.

Canning

Checking Canning Lids for a Good Seal

When canning, check your jars 24 hours after processing; any leaky jars or jars with lids that don't have a depression in the center should be refrigerated and the contents used promptly.

Checking Out Jars for Canning

If you want to use recycled mayonnaise jars and other food jars for pressure canning, test them first. Fill the jars with water and put them in a pressure canner. Bring it up to pressure, keep it there for a few minutes, and then bring it down rapidly. The jars that break should obviously be thrown away, but the others have passed the test and can be used as canning jars. Just remember to use new canning lids and rings, rather than the screw-on caps that came with the jars.

Protecting Canning Jars from Mold

If you have a damp storage area, wipe the outsides of your filled canning jars with white vinegar to keep mold away.

Freezing

Quick-Cooling Blanched Vegetables

Plunging blanched vegetables into chilled water is the quickest way to cool them for freezing, but did you know that all that water can wash away water-soluble vitamins and minerals? There is an alternative method, but you have to have plenty of ice cubes ready. Pour a thin layer of the vegetables into a flat pan resting in another pan filled with ice cubes. Then cover with a plastic bag filled with more ice cubes until the vegetables are cooled.

Thawing Foods

To thaw meat for dinner without having to leave it on the counter all day (where it often thaws too quickly) or in the refrigerator (where it often thaws too slowly), place the frozen meat in a small, Styrofoam picnic chest. By the time you get home in the evening, the meat is thawed, but the insulation of the chest has kept it cool.

Finding Your Frozen Treasures

To make it easier to find foods packed into a freezer, when filling the freezer place fruits on one side, meats in the middle, and vegetables on the other side. You might even want to draw a map showing what types of food are where as a reminder.

Approximate Yield
of Frozen Fruits from Fresh

Fruit	Fresh, as Purchased or Picked	Frozen
Apples	1 bu. (48 lb.)	32–40 pt.
	1 box (44 lb.)	29–35 pt.
	1¼–1½ lb.	1 pt.
Apricots	1 bu. (48 lb.)	60–72 pt.
	1 crate (22 lb.)	28–33 pt.
	⅔–⅘ lb.	1 pt.
Berries*	1 crate (24 qt.)	32–36 pt.
	1⅓–1½ pt.	1 pt.
Cantaloupes	1 doz. (28 lb.)	22 pt.
	1–1¼ lb.	1 pt.
Cherries, sweet or sour	1 bu. (56 lb.)	36–44 pt.
	1¼–1½ lb.	1 pt.
Cranberries	1 box (25 lb.)	50 pt.
	1 pk. (8 lb.)	16 pt.
	½ lb.	1 pt.
Currants	2 qt. (3 lb.)	4 pt.
	¾ lb.	1 pt.
Peaches	1 bu. (48 lb.)	32–48 pt.
	1 lug box (20 lb.)	13–20 pt.
	1–1½ lb.	1 pt.
Pears	1 bu. (50 lb.)	40–50 pt.
	1 western box (46 lb.)	37–46 pt.
	1–1¼ lb.	1 pt.
Pineapples	5 lb.	4 pt.
Plums and Prunes	1 bu. (56 lb.)	38–56 pt.
	1 crate (20 lb.)	13–20 pt.
	1–1½ lb.	1 pt.
Raspberries	1 crate (24 lb.)	24 pt.
	1 pt.	1 pt.
Rhubarb	15 lb.	15–22 pt.
	⅔–1 lb.	1 pt.
Strawberries	1 crate (24 qt.)	38 pt.
	⅔ qt.	1 pt.

*These include blackberries, blueberries, boysenberries, dewberries, elderberries, gooseberries, huckleberries, loganberries, and youngberries.

Saving on Freezer Containers

Freeze leftover soups, stews, and casseroles in containers that you'll be cooking the food in later. But to avoid having all your pans and casserole dishes tied up in the freezer, remove the food when frozen by dipping the pan in hot water for a few minutes, and then put the food in a labeled freezer bag. When you're ready to cook it, the food fits right back into the pan.

Making Ice

After you finish a quart or half-gallon cardboard carton of milk, rinse it well, fill it with water, and freeze it. When summer comes and you need

Approximate Yield of Frozen Vegetables from Fresh		
Vegetable	Fresh, as Purchased or Picked	Frozen
Asparagus	1 crate (12 2-lb. bunches) 1–1½ lb.	15–22 pt. 1 pt.
Beans, lima (in pods)	1 bu. (32 lb.) 2–2½ lb.	12–16 pt. 1 pt.
Beans, snap (green and wax)	1 bu. (30 lb.) ⅔–1 lb.	30–45 pt. 1 pt.
Beet greens	15 lb. 1–1½ lb.	10–15 pt. 1 pt.
Beets (without tops)	1 bu. (52 lb.) 1¼–1½ lb.	35–42 pt. 1 pt.
Broccoli	1 crate (25 lb.) 1 lb.	24 pt. 1 pt.
Brussels sprouts	4 qt. boxes 1 lb.	6 pt. 1 pt.
Carrots (without tops)	1 bu. (50 lb.) 1¼–1½ lb.	32–40 pt. 1 pt.
Cauliflower	2 med. heads 1⅓ lb.	3 pt. 1 pt.
Chard	1 bu. (12 lb.) 1–1½ lb.	8–12 pt. 1 pt.

ice to cool blanched vegetables for freezing you can use these solid chunks of ice. Also, these frozen containers help keep the freezer full for maximum efficiency. They can also be used in picnic chests and punch bowls.

Blanch before Freezing

Vegetables are safe to freeze without blanching, but they may not taste as good or be as nutritious. Vegetables are blanched to destroy enzymes that, if not killed, can affect color, flavor, or nutritive value, especially vitamins A and C. After a taste test of blanched and unblanched frozen vegetables in the Rodale Test Kitchen, all tasters preferred the blanched vegetables.

Vegetable	Fresh, as Purchased or Picked	Frozen
Collards	1 bu. (12 lb.)	8–12 pt.
	1–1½ lb.	1 pt.
Corn, sweet (in husks)	1 bu. (35 lb.)	14–17 pt.
	2–2½ lb.	1 pt.
Eggplant	1 lb.	1 pt.
Kale	1 bu. (18 lb.)	12–18 pt.
	1–1½ lb.	1 pt.
Mustard greens	1 bu. (12 lb.)	8–12 pt.
	1–1½ lb.	1 pt.
Peas	1 bu. (30 lb.)	12–15 pt.
	2–2½ lb.	1 pt.
Peppers, green	⅔ lb. (3 peppers)	1 pt.
Pumpkin	3 lb.	2 pt.
Spinach	1 bu. (18 lb.)	12–18 pt.
	1–1½ lb.	1 pt.
Squash, summer	1 bu. (40 lb.)	32–40 pt.
	1–1¼ lb.	1 pt.
Squash, winter	3 lb.	2 pt.
Sweet potatoes	⅔ lb.	1 pt.

Cold Storage
(For individual vegetables, see also Vegetables, in this chapter.)

A Mini-Root Cellar from Your Window Well

Basement window wells can make effective, quick, and easy mini-cold-storage areas. Preferably choose wells that are in the shade, such as on the north side of your house, to prevent temperature swings caused by the sun. Cover the outside of the well with a scrap piece of plywood that you've insulated on the inside. Insulate the inside of the well, too, with wood shavings, straw, or insulation scraps. Open the basement window to keep temperatures inside the well between 32° and 40°F.

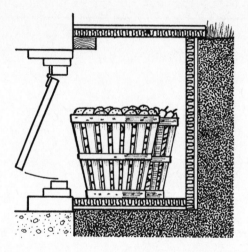

Cellar Steps for Storage

If you have an outside entrance to your cellar, you can use the steps there for cold storage. You'll need to have a door separating the steps from the cellar itself to keep out basement heat. Temperatures in the stairwell will go down as you go up the steps, so you'll have to experiment a bit to see which crops should go where. If the air is too dry, set pans of water at the warmest level for extra humidity.

Freezer Chest Root Cellar

If you have no root cellar, you can make yourself one out of an old freezer chest. Sink a freezer into the ground, right up to its lid. Slope the ground around the freezer for water runoff, and you'll have a handy root cellar for storing fresh vegetables.

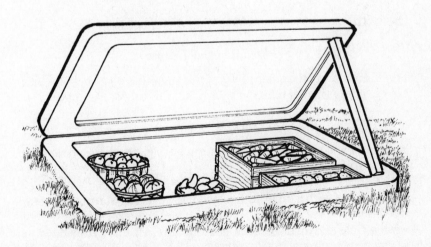

Styrofoam Chest Root Cellar

To extend the storage life of a few root crops, set up your own mini-root cellar in a Styrofoam chest. Carefully brush excess dirt off the vegetables, but don't wash or scrub them. Then put your turnips, potatoes, carrots, or other root crops in the chest in an unheated place, such as a garage or porch in the winter. If temperatures inside the chest can be kept just above freezing, the vegetables should keep for many weeks.

Wintering Over Root Vegetables

To make digging up wintered-over root vegetables in the garden easier, put a good layer of leaves over the vegetables, cover it with a strip of plastic, and then add another heavy layer of leaves. The plastic keeps the bottom layer of mulch dry so that you won't have a frozen layer of leaves to shovel through when you want some vegetables in winter.

Maintaining Humidity for Root Cellaring

Most root crops and leafy vegetables keep best when the humidity is 90 to 95%. If your storage area is very moist, keep the vegetables loose and uncovered in bins. If too-low humidity is your problem, pack the vegetables, especially carrots, beets, and parsnips, in damp sawdust, sand, or moss to cut down evaporation. You can also try storing them in perforated plastic bags, although this last can be a bit tricky, since you'll have to watch for surface molds.

Salads

Cooked Romaine Lettuce

Don't throw away the outer leaves of romaine lettuce just because they are not pretty enough to put in your salad. Cook them like spinach.

Salad Dressings

To keep oil and vinegar dressing from separating, add ½ teaspoon of egg white and shake vigorously.

If you have to keep a salad with mayonnaise dressing at room temperature before serving, keep the mayonnaise and the salad separated until serving time. Mayonnaise is an acid mixture whether refrigerated or warm, but when combined with the salad ingredients its acidity is lowered, and it becomes a medium for bacterial growth.

Hints for Keeping Lettuce Longer

Organic Gardening readers must eat a lot of lettuce—or at least store a lot of it—because we've gotten dozens of hints for keeping lettuce fresh for more than a week in the refrigerator. Here are some of the most popular ones:

- Wet several thicknesses of newspaper and wrap them around a head of lettuce. Then place it all in an open plastic bag and store it in the refrigerator. The lettuce will keep well for up to two weeks so long as you don't seal the bag but allow air to circulate. A clean kitchen towel works as well as the newspapers.

- Remove any badly bruised outer leaves and close the lettuce in a clean plastic bag with a wire twist. The natural moisture in the lettuce will keep it fresh, as long as the bag has no holes in it and is sealed tight.

- To keep your lettuce crisp for a day or two, slice off the stem end and then run tap water into the head through this end. Remove any wilted outside leaves and submerge the head in a bowl of water for 30 minutes or more. Then drain out most of the water, put the lettuce in a plastic bag, and seal it with a wire twist. Refrigerate for at least half a day, and the lettuce will be clean and crisp.

A Make-Do Gelatin Mold

Have you ever wanted to make a molded gelatin salad and found that you have no mold? Just use a clean, empty can, such as a soup or coffee can. To unmold once the gelatin has set, dip the can in warm water very briefly, and invert it over your serving plate. Then puncture the bottom of the can with a can opener to release the pressure. The salad should slide out easily.

Soups and Sauces

Add Cold Water to Stocks

If the stock or soup you're making needs more water, add cold, not boiling water. Boiling water can toughen the simmering meat.

How Much Water?

A good rule of thumb for how much water to add when making soup is to pour in enough water to cover the meat and/or vegetables in the stockpot by 2 inches. When preparing chicken stock use a quart of water for each pound of chicken.

Desalting the Soup

If you have oversalted your soup or stew, put a cut piece of apple or potato in it for a while as it simmers, then remove and discard it. The apple or potato will have absorbed some of the salt, and you will have saved the supper.

Adding Color to Your Stock

Your stock will pick up a nice, golden brown color if you simmer onion skins along with the rest of the stock vegetables. Just pull off and discard the outer skin and chop the rest of the onion along with the inner skin. You save yourself the trouble of peeling, too. Of course, you have to strain the stock before adding the soup ingredients.

Onion skins will do the same thing for gravy; just be sure to strain it before serving.

Defatting Soup or Gravy

An easy way to skim the fat from soup or gravy is to make the food a day ahead and refrigerate it. The fat will rise to the top as it cools, and you can remove it easily with a spoon or spatula. If you are in a rush, cool your soup or gravy quickly in the freezer.

Another way to take the grease off soup or gravy is to swish a lettuce leaf gently and slowly over the surface. The lettuce will absorb the grease.

Natural Sweetening for Tomato Sauce

If the tomato sauce you're using isn't sweet enough, add some grated carrots rather than sugar. It works wonders.

Stocking Up on Stock

Keep a plastic pitcher in the freezer. After potatoes are finished boiling or vegetables are finished steaming, add their cooking water to the pitcher. Then, when you want to make soup, you've got your vegetable broth all ready in the freezer.

Sprouts, Nuts, and Seeds

Freezing Sprouts

Bean and seed sprouts can be frozen, but they lose their crispness. You won't notice they're limp if you use them for cooking. They're good in soups and breads.

Drying Sprouts

You can dry sprouts in a very low oven and then grind them in a blender or food processor. They're great as thickeners for soups and gravies, as casserole toppings, and as additions to breads.

Make-Do Sprouters

The filter (some call it the strainer) from an old coffee percolator makes a dandy seed sprouter. So does cheesecloth stretched and secured with a rubber band over the opening of a glass jar.

Hulling Black Walnuts

Black walnuts from backyard trees are difficult and messy to hull by hand. Instead, hull them by running over them with your car. Make a trough from scrap lumber the width of a tire and as long as you like. Put the walnuts in the trough to prevent the nuts from shooting out from under the tire as you roll over them before they are cracked. This works best if your driveway is a solid surface, like concrete.

Wear thick rubber gloves when removing the hulls from black walnuts. The dark, acrid fluid can irritate wounds and will most certainly stain bare hands.

Cracking Nuts without a Nutcracker

A small bench vise will crack all kinds of nuts.

Home-Roasted Almonds

Save yourself some money and buy raw almonds rather than roasted ones. You can easily roast the raw nuts at home by putting a layer on the tray of your toaster oven or on a baking sheet in your regular oven and baking them at 325°F for an hour or so. Check them frequently so that they don't overbrown. Let them cool, and you'll find them to be crunchy and flavorful, without the oily saltiness you can expect from most of the roasted kinds.

Chopping Nuts

Have no fancy gadgets to chop nuts? Simply put them in a plastic bag (a cloth bag is even better) and roll over them with a rolling pin.

Homemade Cashew Butter

Cashew butter can be made by blending in a blender or food processor 1 cup of roasted or raw cashews with 1 tablespoon of vegetable oil.

Hulling Sunflower Seeds

Plunging sunflower seeds in boiling water for a few minutes will make hulling them easier.

Vegetables

Asparagus

Cooking the Stalks

An easy way to cook long stalks of asparagus without having to cut them into little pieces and without having to use a very large pot is to steam them in a tall coffeepot. Put about 1 inch of water in the bottom, cover, and steam as usual for 5 minutes.

Broccoli and Cabbage

Salvaging the Stems

All those tough green stems you find on broccoli are really tender hearts masquerading in stringy coverings. Peel off the outer skin and slice the tender white heart into ¼-inch thick circles. Sauté up a feast.

Salvaging the Tough Leaves

The tougher, larger leaves on the outer part of a cabbage don't have to be thrown away if they are in good shape. Blanch them and stuff them with a mixture of ground beef, raw rice, and tomato sauce, plus your favorite seasonings. Top them with sauerkraut or more tomato sauce and bake them in the oven, or freeze them for later baking.

Freeze, Don't Blanch, the Leaves

Instead of blanching cabbage leaves before you stuff them, freeze them overnight. This little trick results in leaves just as limp and easy to roll as if they were blanched.

Carrots

Save Those Carrot (and Potato) Peels

There's no reason to peel carrots (and potatoes); just scrub them with a good stiff brush that you save just for vegetable cleaning. The peel and skins are high in fiber and contain a number of nutrients. Unpeeled potatoes are wonderful as french fries and can also be boiled and cut up for potato salad.

Cool Storage

Have more carrots than you'll be able to use in a few weeks and not enough room in your refrigerator? Wrap the unwashed carrots in wads of newspapers and then layer them in a large plastic bag. Tie it closed and put the bag in a cool, but not freezing, place—about 40°F is just right. An unheated basement or garage is usually ideal. The carrots will keep for a few months, and so will other root crops, like turnips and parsnips. (See also Food Preservation, in this chapter.)

Celery

Perking Up Droopy Stalks

If you have some rubbery, droopy celery that you think is beyond hope, give it one more chance. Let it stand in cold water for a few minutes, shake it to remove excess water, then place it in an airtight plastic bag and leave it in the refrigerator for three or four days. Unless it was really far gone, you'll find it recrisped and usable once again.

Drying

Make your own dried celery leaves by cutting the good, fresh leaves from the stalk you're using. Wash them, pat them dry, and spread them on a baking sheet. If you've got a gas stove, put them in the oven with only the pilot light on, and in a little over 24 hours they'll be almost brittle dry

(continued on page 46)

Measuring Guidelines for Vegetables and Legumes

Vegetable/Legume	Unit	Vol. or Pieces per Unit
Asparagus, spears, fresh	1 lb.	16–20
cooked		2 cups
canned	14½–16 oz.	12–18
frozen spears, cuts, and tips	10 oz.	2 cups
Beans, green, fresh	1 lb.	3 cups
cooked		1¾ cups
frozen	9 oz.	1½ cups
canned	15½ oz.	1¾ cups
Beans, kidney, canned	16–17 oz.	2 cups
dried	1 lb.	2½ cups
cooked		5½ cups
Beans, lima, shelled, fresh	1 lb.	2 cups
cooked		1⅔–2 cups
frozen	10 oz.	1¾ cups
canned	16 oz.	2 cups
dried	1 lb.	2½ cups
cooked		5½ cups
Beans, navy, dried	1 lb.	2⅓ cups
cooked		5½ cups
Beans, soybeans, dried	1 lb.	2 cups
Beets, without tops, fresh	1 lb.	2 cups
cooked		2 cups
canned	16–17 oz.	2 cups
Broccoli, fresh, cooked	1 lb.	2 cups
frozen spears, chopped	10 oz.	1½ cups
Brussels sprouts, fresh	1 lb.	4 cups
cooked		2½ cups
frozen	10 oz.	18–24 sprouts
Cabbage, fresh, shredded	1 lb.	3½–4½ cups
cooked		2 cups
Carrots, without tops, fresh, shredded	1 lb.	2½ cups
diced		2 cups
cooked		2–2½ cups
frozen	1 lb.	2½ cups
canned	16 oz.	2 cups
Cauliflower, fresh	1 lb.	1½ cups
cooked		1½ cups
frozen	10 oz.	2 cups
cooked		1½ cups

Vegetable/Legume	Unit	Vol. or Pieces per Unit
Celery, fresh	1 lb.	2 bunches
cooked		2–2½ cups
Corn, fresh ears	12	
cooked, cut		5–6 cups
frozen, cut	10 oz.	1¾ cups
cooked		1½–2 cups
canned, cream style	16–17 oz.	2 cups
whole kernel	12 oz.	1½ cups
Eggplant, fresh, diced	1 lb.	2½ cups
cooked		2½ cups
Greens, fresh, cooked	1 lb.	3 cups
frozen	10 oz.	1½–2 cups
Lentils, dried	1 lb.	2¼ cups
cooked		5 cups
Lettuce, head	1 lb. (about)	6¼ cups
leaf	1 lb.	6¼ cups
romaine	1 lb.	6 cups
endive	1 lb. (about)	4¼ cups
Mixed vegetables, frozen	10 oz.	2 cups
canned	16–17 oz.	2 cups
Mushrooms, fresh, sliced	1 lb.	2–3 cups
canned	4 oz.	⅔ cup
Okra, fresh, cooked	1 lb.	2¼ cups
frozen	10 oz.	1¼ cups
canned	15½ oz.	1¾ cups
Onions, fresh	1 lb.	3 large
chopped		2–2½ cups
frozen, chopped	12 oz.	3 cups
canned	16–17 oz.	2 cups
Parsnips, fresh	1 lb.	4 medium
cooked		2 cups
Peas, black-eyed, fresh, cooked	1 lb.	2⅓ cups
frozen	10 oz.	1½ cups
canned	16–17 oz.	2 cups
Peas, green, fresh, in pod	1 lb.	
shelled		1 cup
cooked		1 cup

(continued)

Measuring Guidelines for Vegetables and Legumes—Continued

Vegetable/Legume	Unit	Vol. or Pieces per Unit
Peas, green—*continued*		
frozen	10 oz.	2 cups
canned	16 oz.	2 cups
dried, split	1 lb.	2¼ cups
cooked		5 cups
Peppers, green bell, fresh	1 lb.	5-7
Potatoes, white, fresh	1 lb.	3 medium
cooked, diced or sliced		2¼ cups
mashed		1¾ cups
Pumpkin, fresh, cooked, mashed	1 lb.	1 cup
canned	16-17 oz.	2 cups
Radishes, fresh, sliced	6 oz.	1¼ cups
Rutabaga, fresh, cubed	1 lb.	2½ cups
cooked		2 cups
Sauerkraut, canned	15-16 oz.	3 cups
Spinach, fresh	1 lb.	3 cups
cooked		1 cup
frozen	10 oz.	1½ cups
canned	15 oz.	2 cups
Squash, summer, fresh, cooked, mashed	1 lb.	1¾-2 cups
frozen, sliced	10 oz.	1½ cups
Sweet potatoes, fresh	1 lb.	3 medium
canned	16-17 oz.	1¾-2 cups
Tomatoes, fresh	1 lb.	3-4 small
cooked		1½ cups
canned, whole	16 oz.	2 cups
sauce	8 oz.	1 cup
Turnips, fresh	1 lb.	3 medium
cooked		2 cups

and ready to store in plastic bags or glass jars. If your stove doesn't have a pilot light, set it at the lowest possible temperature, and check the celery leaves frequently. They should be dry in about 12 hours. Dried celery leaves can be crumbled into soups, casseroles, salads, and breads.

Chilies

Chili Oil Relief

The oil in chili peppers is so pungent it can actually burn your skin. Washing irritated areas in vinegar water will bring much more relief than will just soap and water.

Hot Chilies for Hot Weather

Take a tip from those who know in sunny (and hot) Mexico. Eating chilies and other hot, spicy foods in hot weather will cool you off by stimulating your circulation and causing you to perspire.

Chili Paste

An easy way to prepare fresh hot chilies is to blend them with a little water in a food processor or blender. The paste that results can be added to a dish a little at a time to achieve the heat you want. (Chilies vary in heat so taste them cautiously before using.)

Corn

De-Silking

To remove silk from corn, just run a damp paper napkin or towel lengthwise down the ear. The silk will cling to the paper, making removal quick and easy.

Or try a nylon hair brush. It's fast, efficient, and doesn't damage the kernels.

Garlic

Peeling Made Easier

Peeling garlic cloves each time you need them can be a nuisance. Instead, peel several at a time, put them in a glass jar, and cover them with olive oil. The cloves will stay fresh for months as long as they are covered with the oil. And the garlic-flavored oil is wonderful for salad dressings or for sautéed vegetables.

To remove garlic skins easily, smash each clove with the side of a knife blade first; the peel will come off in a snap. If you're using a garlic press for one clove at a time, don't even bother peeling it; the press will squeeze the garlic right through the skin.

Garlic cloves will peel easier if you first separate the heads and then pour boiling water over the individual cloves. Let them stand for 5 minutes, then drain and cover with cold water until cool.

Mincing

Mince garlic along with fresh herbs. The herbs add bulk to make mincing easier and also catch the garlic oil that usually ends up lost on your cutting surface.

Ginger Root

Storing

To keep the cut ends of ginger root moist, store the ginger with the cut end buried in sand.

You can also peel and slice the ginger root, place it in a jar, and cover it with sherry or a mild vinegar, like rice vinegar. As long as it's covered by the liquid, it will keep for several months. If you slice the ginger fine enough, you can spoon out just as much as you need and add it right to your recipe.

Onions

Peel Extras

To save time when you're cutting onions, peel one or two extra and refrigerate them in a plastic bag. They will keep for three or four days refrigerated, whether whole, sliced, or chopped.

Parsley Deodorizer

When chopping onions, garlic, and other strong vegetables, save parsley for chopping last, since it helps remove any strong odors from your chopping board and hands.

Don't Bother Sautéing

Sautéing onions until limp is a step that is used to add butter or oil to onions and make them less pungent. Save time and cut out fat by using fewer or sweeter onions and just add them directly to the remaining ingredients, or steam the onions slightly first.

Storing Onions, Garlic, Potatoes

If you only need to slice half an onion, slice the top or sprout end. The root half will last longer in the refrigerator.

Net shopping bags (also called French shopping bags) are great for storing onions, garlic, and potatoes. Conveniently expandable, they maintain air circulation around these vegetables, which is important for their good keeping. For the best storage, hang them in a cool, dry spot, such as the top of your basement stairs.

The Great Onion Cry-Off

The editors of *Organic Gardening* invited their readers to tell them how to cut an onion painlessly (for the cutter, that is; no one can speak for the onion). Talk about a responsive readership! Four hundred forty-nine solutions arrived in the mail. Once they got rid of the duplicates and the really bizarre suggestions (like putting an onion slice behind your ear while you're cutting the rest), the editors narrowed down the number to the 20 most popular ideas and tested them out. Seventy-five pounds of onions later, they had the winners. While no one method worked for everyone every time, these were the techniques that met with the most success:

- Wear swimmers' goggles or a scuba mask. Both shield the eyes from the irritating mist that's released from the tissues of the onions as you cut them. One caveat though: Testers had a problem with their goggles fogging up.

- Chill the onions. Testers who kept onions in the freezer for 15 minutes or in the refrigerator for an hour before cutting said it made a difference. Cold slows down the movement of highly volatile molecules so that not as much of the onion's tear gas billows into the cook's face.

- Cut the onion under running water. You've got to have nimble fingers and keen eyesight for this one. No one seems quite sure why this works, but there's speculation that the water could dissolve and wash away the fumes.

Although they will look a bit bizarre, worn-out pantyhose will work just as well as net bags, particularly for onions and garlic. Drop one onion or garlic bulb into a toe of the pantyhose and tie a knot. Add another onion or garlic bulb and tie another knot. Keep going until both stockings are full. When you want an onion just cut off the bottom one, leaving the knot in place.

Rx for Sprouted Onions

If some of your stored onions start to sprout, plant them as onion sets in your garden, provided it's springtime. If it's not, plant them in a flower pot instead, to grow in a sunny window; use the green tops that emerge as you would green onions.

Potatoes

Fried Skins

Wash the potatoes before you peel them, removing any scarred or spoiled spots, eyes, sprouts, and the like. Then peel the potatoes and save the skins for frying. Frying them in a little oil for about a minute will give you the same munchy tidbits that bars and restaurants charge high prices for. Season them with melted cheese, soy sauce, nutritional yeast, or an herb mixture, and serve crisp and hot.

Storage

Don't store potatoes near apples because apples give off ethylene gas, which causes potatoes to spoil.

Store potatoes and whole ginger root together and they will keep each other fresh.

Quick Home Fries

If you don't have time in the morning to wait for home-fried potatoes to cook, cut raw potatoes into very small pieces, about the size of small dice, and sauté them with your eggs.

Quicker Baked Potatoes

To speed up cooking time for baked potatoes, press a clean aluminum nail through them to facilitate heat transfer during the cooking process.

Cooking Potatoes (and Cauliflower and Cabbage) with Lemon

When cooking white potatoes, add about 1 teaspoon of lemon juice to each pound of potatoes; the lemon juice keeps them white and adds a nice flavor. The same goes for cooking cauliflower and cabbage.

Better Mashed Potatoes

Isn't it silly to throw away the potato cooking water that contains so many nutrients, and then add just milk to the potatoes for mashing? A much better idea is to save the potato water and mix it according to the directions on the box with dry milk for mashing. This way, you get the benefits of the potato water *and* the milk, and save some money to boot.

Easy Boiling

Boil potatoes in a french fry basket that fits inside the pot. When finished, they'll lift out easily and drain automatically.

Squashes

Zucchini Milk from a Bumper Crop

When you have an overabundance of zucchini, peel it, cut it into chunks, and liquefy it in a blender. This zucchini milk can be frozen in convenient-size containers and used as a substitute for milk in breads, puddings, biscuits, meat loaves, and the like. Three medium zucchini (1¼ pounds) yield 2 cups of zucchini milk.

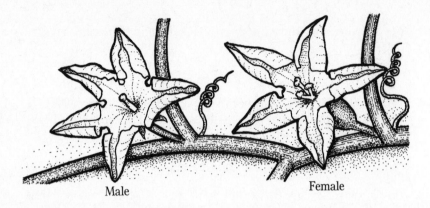

Male   Female

Blossoms for Good Eating

Squash and pumpkin blossoms make for wonderful eating. If you check the squash and pumpkin plants carefully, you'll notice that there are both male and female blossoms on each plant. The female ones have a thick ovary on the back that will become a squash, while the male ones have a thin stem right up to the flower. The plant makes many more male flowers, and these are the ones that you want to pick. Wash them gently, then dip them in a mixture of flour and egg, or in a pancake batter, and fry them lightly like a pancake. Serve with honey or syrup for breakfast, or with butter or lemon as a side dish for dinner. Since the blossoms only last one day, gather them in the morning, when they are fully opened.

Tomatoes

Easy Peeling

Plunge fresh tomatoes briefly into boiling water, then into cold water. The skins will crack and be easy to remove. You can crack the skins of peaches and plums the same way.

To make garden tomatoes peel more easily, rub the dull side of a knife over the tomato first.

Better Slicing

To insure that tomato slices stay firm and intact, slice them lengthwise, rather than crosswise. If you do this you won't be cutting through the ovary walls of the tomato, releasing pulp and juice.

Easier Tomato Sauce

There is no good reason to peel tomatoes for spaghetti sauce. Whirl them in a blender or food processor before cooking them, and the little bits of skin that result will cook down so that you don't notice them at all in the final sauce.

Restoring the Tomato's Vitamin C Content

Before drinking tomato juice or eating tomato products, squeeze a little lemon juice on top and you will add some of the vitamin C that was processed out.

Canning

When canning tomatoes or juice, the pulp and water sometimes separate. This is due to a "breakdown" in the tomato enzyme that happens when tomatoes or juice are prepared and allowed to stand too long before being canned. Separation is not harmful, it just looks unappealing. To prevent this, prepare enough tomatoes for one canner load at a time, and put them up as quickly as possible.

Broiling and Baking Stuffed Tomatoes

When broiling or baking stuffed tomatoes, place them in muffin tins to keep them from falling over or rolling around.

Ripening Green Tomatoes

To speed up the ripening process of mature green tomatoes brought in from the garden before the first frost, store them with apples in a confined space, such as a plastic bag or a picnic chest. Tomatoes release ethylene gas as they ripen and so do apples, and the extra "charge" from the apples will speed the tomatoes along.

Freezing Whole

Here's a quick way to freeze whole tomatoes; it's an especially good trick in the middle of hot August when you're inundated with a bumper crop: Freeze whole tomatoes on baking sheets, and, when frozen, store them in plastic bags. The skins will conveniently crack during freezing, making it easy to remove them once the tomatoes have thawed.

Freezing for Winter Salads

Hard, pink winter tomatoes are hardly worth eating. Anticipate the winter doldrums in fall by picking the nicest, most tasty tomatoes from your garden and slicing them for sandwiches. Freeze them in a single layer on a baking sheet, and, when frozen solid, remove them to plastic bags, seal, and store in your freezer. Then, a few minutes before you serve a winter salad, take a few slices from the freezer and run them under water, or leave them on the kitchen counter for a few minutes, just until they're thawed a bit but are not yet soft. Chop them and use them to garnish your salad. The slightly frozen tomatoes will taste a whole lot better than the pink tennis balls you can buy in the store.

Other Vegetables

Vegetable Snacks

Kids and adults alike will reach for the natural munchies if they are right at hand. Cut carrots, celery, and peppers into snack-size lengths and store them upright in a glass jar. Twist the lid on tightly, and they'll keep crisp in the refrigerator for several days. What's more, since the glass is clear, you can quickly see what munchies the refrigerator has to offer.

Save That Vegetable Water

Don't throw away the vegetable cooking water; freeze it instead in ice cube trays. Then pop the frozen cubes into soups, gravies, and sauces as you need them.

Eat the Radish Leaves

Save the leaves of fresh radishes to add extra zing to your cooking. Clean and chop them, then add them to your stir-fried vegetables. They're not nearly as hot as the roots, just mildly peppery.

Don't Salt Eggplant

Salting and pressing eggplant may get rid of some of the bitter juices, but it also removes some of the water, which makes the eggplant more able to soak up cooking oil. It's fine to use eggplant unsalted and unpressed in any of your recipes.

For Longer-Keeping Mushrooms

If your mushrooms come in a plastic container, unwrap them and refrigerate them in a plastic bag instead. Be sure you punch or cut holes in the bag so that the mushrooms can breathe. They'll keep longer when stored this way.

Quick-Cooling Soup

Put frozen peas in children's hot soup to cool the soup quickly and easily.

Stuffing

There's no need to parboil peppers before you stuff them. Stuffing them raw is easier because they are cold and firm; they're also more nutritious this way. To make raw stuffed peppers more tender, bake them 5 to 10 minutes longer than your recipe calls for.

Spicing Up Steamed Vegetables

To add zest to your favorite steamed vegetable, toss it with a little vinaigrette or Italian dressing.

Vegetable Leftover Garnishes

If you have leftover cooked vegetables, add them to a container of oil, vinegar, and seasoning, making sure they are covered with liquid. Refrigerate and remove as needed for salads and garnishes. More vegetables can be added, but start from scratch weekly.

Frozen Vegetables for Casseroles

Frozen vegetables can be taken from the freezer and added directly to a casserole that will be cooked; they're already precooked.

Kitchen Miscellany

(See also The Kitchen in the chapter, Bathrooms, Kitchens, and Other Places You Hate to Clean.)

A Quick Fire Extinguisher

If you cook with electricity, keep a box of baking soda near the stove. Should an electrical fire start, baking soda will extinguish it immediately.

Free Paper Plates

The foam trays that supermarkets wrap packaged foods in can be cleaned and used for picnic plates instead of paper ones. They are strong and easy to handle. Just make sure you don't reuse any trays that contained raw meat.

Drying Recycled Plastic Bags

Hang a mini-clothesline in your kitchen closet and keep clothespins handy so that you can hang rinsed plastic bags up to dry and reuse.

Wooden spoons standing upright in a crock on the kitchen counter make a handy place to dry plastic bags and rubber gloves. Place one over each spoon.

Cheesecloth Substitute

A piece of nylon stocking is a good substitute for cheesecloth. Use it to strain soup or other foods. (Make sure it's clean, of course!)

Make-Do Colander

If you're in a bind, you can make a quick, disposable colander by punching holes in an aluminum pie plate and bending it a bit to the shape you need. This is especially useful for picnics and camping.

Stubborn Jar Lid?

Don't struggle with a jar that has a stubborn lid. Hold it upside down under hot tap water and rotate the jar slowly. Heat traveling through the water and into the metal lid will loosen it just enough that it can be twisted off with little effort when the jar is turned upright.

Or try placing a wide rubber band around the rim where your hold it, and then open it. You'll find that the rubber band helps your hand get a good grip and should make opening the top much easier.

You can also get a better grip on a tight-fitting jar lid by putting on a rubber glove before you try to unscrew it.

Useful Kitchen Measurements

1 pinch = ⅛ tsp.	½ cup solid butter = ¼ lb.
60 drops = 1 tsp.	1 cup solid butter = ½ lb.
3 tsp. = 1 tbsp.	2 cups solid butter = 1 lb.
2 tbsp. = 1 fluid oz.	1 sq. baking chocolate = 1 oz.
4 tbsp. = ¼ cup	1 pkg. unflavored gelatin = 1 tbsp.
8 tbsp. = ½ cup	1 cup shelled walnuts = ¼ lb.
16 tbsp. = 1 cup	1 cup shelled pecans = ⅓ lb.
2 cups = 1 pt.	1 pkg. dry yeast = 1 oz.
4 cups = 1 qt.	juice of 1 lemon = approx. 3 tbsp.
16 oz. = 1 lb.	juice of 1 orange = 5–6 tbsp.
4 tbsp. flour = 1 oz.	1 tbsp. cornstarch = ½ oz.
4 cups flour = 1 lb.	1 tbsp. potato starch = ½ oz.
2 cups granulated sugar = 1 lb.	1 #1 (8-oz.) can = 1 cup
5 lg. eggs = 1 cup	1 #2 (20-oz.) can = 2½ cups
8–10 egg whites = 1 cup	1 #2½ (28-oz.) can = 3½ cups
13–14 egg yolks = 1 cup	1 #3 (32-oz.) can = 4 cups
2 tbsp. butter = 1 oz.	

A Kitchen Ruler

Keep a ruler handy in the kitchen so that when a recipe requires, for instance, a 9-inch pie plate, or dough rolled into a 12 × 8-inch rectangle, you can check your dimensions quickly.

Three Cutting Boards for Kitchen Safety

Keep three cutting boards: one for poultry and meats, one for onions and garlic, and one for everything else. Or keep two, with one of them two-sided so that you can use one side of the board only for onions and garlic and the other side for raw meats and poultry. Raw meats and poultry can contaminate foods that will not be cooked before serving, and onion and garlic oils can penetrate porous wood, leaving lingering flavors.

Handy Substitutes

If you don't have:	Use:
1 tsp. baking powder	¼ tsp. baking soda plus ½ cup buttermilk (to replace ½ cup liquid called for in recipe)
1 cup buttermilk	1 tbsp. lemon juice or vinegar plus sweet milk to make 1 cup
1 cup catsup or chili sauce	1 cup tomato sauce plus ¼ cup honey and 2 tbsp. vinegar (for use in cooked mixtures)
1 oz. unsweetened chocolate	3 tbsp. cocoa plus 1 tbsp. butter or margarine, or 3 tbsp. carob plus 2 tbsp. water
1 cake compressed yeast	1 pkg. or 2 tsp. active dry yeast
1 tbsp. cornstarch (for thickening)	2 tbsp. flour or 4 tsp. quick-cooking tapioca
1 tsp. dry mustard	1 tbsp. prepared mustard
1 tbsp. chopped fresh herbs	1 tsp. dried herbs
1 small fresh onion	1 tbsp. instant minced onion, rehydrated
1 clove garlic	⅛ tsp. garlic powder
1 cup tomato juice	½ cup tomato sauce plus ½ cup water
1 whole egg	2 egg yolks (in custards)
1 cup whole milk	½ cup evaporated milk plus ½ cup water OR 1 cup reconstituted nonfat dry milk plus 2 tsp. butter or margarine

Kitchen Scale Accuracy

To check the accuracy of your kitchen scale, place nine pennies on it. They should weigh 1 ounce.

Protecting Recipes

Keep a piece of plastic wrap in every cookbook you use. Cover the page you're working from with the plastic so that any spills can be wiped off without soiling the book itself.

Watch for a sale of photo albums, the kind that have sticky, plastic-covered leaves inside. They are great for keeping recipes that you've cut out of newspapers or magazines but haven't tried yet. Once you give them a try and like them, you can transfer them to a more permanent home.

Candles from Jelly Wax

Save the wax from the top of homemade jellies. Wash it, and store it in a metal can until you have enough to make candles. The candles will smell just like the jellies that were under the wax seal.

Uses for Paper Bags

Brown paper bags aren't just good for holding garbage and lining little boxes. Drain fried foods and cool cookies on them.

A Drinkable Cold Pack

A frozen can of fruit juice doubles as a cold pack during the morning to keep your lunch cool, and a good drink by the time lunchtime comes around and it has thawed.

Deodorizing Cooking Oil

To remove food flavors (except fish) from cooking oil, slice and cook a raw potato in it.

A Handy Weight for Pressing Foods

If a recipe calls for weighting down foods (like salted eggplant or sauerkraut) and you don't have anything to do the job, put a new plastic bag inside another one (to reduce chances of leaks), fill it with water, and twist it closed. You've got an instant weight that fits containers of all sizes.

Homemade Nonstick Spray

To make your own nonstick spray, combine equal parts of vegetable oil and liquid lecithin in a pump bottle. Liquid lecithin can be found in natural foods stores.

Wise Shopping

When shopping, pick up perishables last to avoid the thawing or warming of frozen or refrigerated foods.

During the hottest days of summer, take a cooler containing ice packs along to the supermarket and pack in it any refrigerated or frozen items for the trip home.

Keep your shopping list attached to your refrigerator. This way, when someone uses the last bit of a food or grocery item, he or she can note that it needs replenishing.

Homemade Vinegar

When your fresh cider naturally turns to vinegar and you want to stop the vinegar from getting stronger, strain the "mother" (the layer floating on top) out through three layers of cheesecloth and discard. Then refrigerate the remaining vinegar.

A Handy Oil Dispenser

Put your cooking oil in a clean, well-rinsed dish detergent bottle. You'll find that the squirt top makes pouring oil cleaner and easier than having to deal with a screw-on cap.

Jellying without Sugar

Unlike commercial and apple pectin, low-methoxyl pectin will jell any fruit for jams without sugar. It uses calcium salts instead, so you can use as little or as much sweetening as you want. The food mail order house, Walnut Acres, Penns Creek, PA 17862, sells the pectin and calcium salts with instructions for use.

Keeping Wheat Germ

To preserve the vitamins in wheat germ, refrigerate or freeze it. It can be stored in the freezer for one year and in the refrigerator for six months.

2 Bathrooms, Kitchens, and Other Places You Hate to Clean

The Bath

Sink, Tub, and Tile

Bleach Cleaner

Use bleach in a clean squirt bottle on shower stall glass, on the tile surrounding bathtubs, and on shower curtains to clean off and control mildew. Just squirt and scrub clean. Use this in a well-ventilated area and try not to get the bleach on your skin. For stubborn stains, leave the bleach on the soiled area for several minutes before rubbing.

Vinegar Soak

If bathtub and sink fixtures are dull with soap film, soak a cloth in vinegar and wrap it around the faucet or handle. Leave the cloth on for a minute, then remove it and polish your fixtures to a shine.

Unstick Tub Decals

Use hot vinegar to remove those stubborn, sticky no-slip decals from the bathtub. Vinegar also removes stick-on hooks from painted walls or the refrigerator, and price tags and labels from china and glass. To remove stick-on hooks, saturate a cloth or sponge with vinegar and try to squeeze the liquid behind the hook so that it comes in contact with the adhesive.

Toilet

Baking Soda Scrub

Instead of using commercial toilet bowl cleaners, try baking soda and vinegar. Just sprinkle baking soda into the bowl, then drizzle with vinegar and scour with a toilet brush. This combination not only cleans but deodorizes as well.

Bleach Soak

If you're leaving the house for a few days, pour about ¼ cup of bleach into your toilet. It'll work to clean the bowl while you're away.

The Kitchen

Appliances

Baking Soda Scouring Mix

A combination of liquid dishwashing detergent (not automatic dishwasher detergent) and baking soda works well as a nonabrasive cleaner for appliances, Corning Ware, and sinks. Just use a squirt of the liquid and a sprinkle of the soda, rub, and rinse.

Alcohol Cleanser

Clean appliances and stainless fixtures without leaving streaks by using a cloth moistened with rubbing alcohol. Alcohol also works well on ceramic tile, Formica, windows, and mirrors and is much cheaper than commercial cleaners. However, it should not be used on wood or painted surfaces.

Keep Your Dishwasher Stain-Free

Most discoloration inside a dishwasher is around the edges of the door and body, which are untouched by dishwashing action. So remember to periodically clean these areas, and don't keep the dishwasher door closed when the inside is damp or wet.

Ammonia Oven Cleaner

After a spill in the oven, soak a cloth in ammonia and leave it on the burnt area for an hour or so. You will then be able to scrape off the spot easily without harming the enamel.

Salt Cleans Up Oven Spills

Ordinary table salt will also clean up messy oven spills. Let the oven cool, then wet the spill. Sprinkle on the salt, let it work for a few minutes, then scrape it away and wash the area clean.

A Sweeter Refrigerator

Keep charcoal briquets in the refrigerator to sweeten the air. To refresh them, just heat the briquets gently in a heavy pot; you'll find that the odors they have absorbed will vanish into thin air. If you do this periodically, the briquets should last almost forever.

Countertops and Sink

Baking Soda Takes Out Stains

To remove stains from Formica countertops, make a paste of baking soda and water, apply it to the stain, leave it on for a minute or two, then wipe it off.

Unclogging Drains

To clear a clogged drain, try this simple technique before using a chemical product: Pour ½ cup of salt down the drain, followed by boiling water. Continue to flush with very hot tap water until the clog breaks.

Preventing Clogged Drains

Here are some preventive measures that will leave your drains worry-free:

- Grease and food particles should be wiped away with leftover soiled napkins or paper towels before dishes are rinsed.

- Fatty liquids left over from cooking should be allowed to cool so that solidified fat can be lifted off and discarded rather than rinsed down the drain.

- All drains where hair is washed should be protected by a screen.

- If the hose from your washing machine empties into a tub, you can prevent dirt and lint from washing down the drain by tying a nylon stocking to the end of the hose. You don't need the entire length of stocking, just about 12 inches, including the foot. Tie the cut end to the hose and let the rest hang down. Remember to change it periodically.

Net Drain Basket

If you don't have a drain basket for your kitchen sink, stuff a piece of nylon net into the drain. In addition to catching food particles and other debris, it's easy to clean out and cheaper than buying a new drain basket. Just be sure to wash it in hot, sudsy water at the end of each day because it will collect dirt and bacteria.

Dishes, Glassware, and Utensils

Bleach Makes Glasses Sparkle

Adding a capful of liquid bleach to the dishwater makes glasses sparkle and silverware shine. It even gets rid of that greasy feeling on plasticware. Bleach will dry out your hands, though, so you may want to wear rubber gloves when doing the dishes.

Unsticking Glasses

To loosen two glasses stuck one inside the other, fill the inner glass with cold water and submerge the outer glass in hot water. Expansion and contraction from the temperature difference will often free them.

Floors

Margarine De-Tars Vinyl

To get tar off a vinyl floor, first carefully scrape up the excess with the dull side of a knife, then rub vigorously with margarine or butter. Rub again with your fingernail or anything that won't scratch the floor, such as a wooden spoon or Popsicle stick. Finally, wipe up the tar with a dry cloth.

Dishwasher Detergent Makes a Good General Scrub

For scrubbing floors, walls, glass, porcelain, and the outside surfaces of refrigerators and stoves, try automatic dishwasher detergent. The detergent is spot-resistant and contains water-softening agents, so everything gets clean and shiny without rinsing. Dissolve ¼ cup of detergent in 1 gallon of *very* hot water, and wipe the surface with a dry cloth after scrubbing.

Ceramic Tile Cleaner

A mixture of water and vinegar makes a good ceramic tile floor cleaner. It removes most dirt without scrubbing and doesn't leave a film. Use ¼ cup of vinegar to 1 gallon of water.

Baking Soda Scrub

To remove black heel marks from the kitchen floor, rub them with a paste of baking soda and water. Just sprinkle baking soda on the mark and rub with a damp sponge. Don't use too much water or the baking soda will lose its abrasive quality.

Pots, Pans, and Kitchen Tools

Mesh-Bag Scrubbers

The plastic mesh bags that onions come in are great for scrubbing vegetables like carrots and potatoes. You can even use one in place of a scouring pad on pots and pans. They're also good for cleaning dishes, sinks, and tubs because they don't scratch.

A Toothbrush for Cleaning Graters

Keep an old toothbrush by the kitchen sink for cleaning vegetable and cheese graters. It gets into all the nooks and crannies that a sponge can't reach.

Cleaning Kettles

To get rid of that buildup of calcium or lime in your kettle, simply pour in about ¼ cup of vinegar and add about a quart of water. Bring the water to a boil and allow it to boil for 10 to 15 minutes. Empty the pot, wash and rinse it thoroughly, and the white deposits will be gone.

Cutting Board Deodorizer

To eliminate odors from cutting boards, rub them with a paste of baking soda and water, then rinse well. For really bad odors, you may want to leave the paste on for a short time before rinsing.

Smooth Away Cutting Board Scratches

To smooth away scratches on a wood cutting board, use a medium- to fine-grade sandpaper on the splintered areas and rinse the board in cold water. Don't soak it or it will warp and split. To make the wood more stain-resistant and prevent it from drying out gradually from normal use,

Cleaning Pots and Pans

There are many ways to clean stains and baked-on foods from your pots and pans. Here's a rundown on everything from soaking to scrubbing:

For Baked-On Foods

- Pour a few inches of water into the pot or skillet and bring it to a boil. Boil for a few minutes, and the food will scour out much more easily.

- Rinse the pot with cold water, then sprinkle the burnt area with table salt. Allow the salt to remain on the burn for about 10 minutes before scrubbing out the pot. You may have to repeat the application.

- Fill the pot halfway with hot water, then add ½ cup of vinegar and 2 tablespoons of baking soda. Bring the mixture to a boil, cover, and simmer for 30 minutes. Finally, wash the pot.

- Make a paste of baking soda and water and leave it on the burnt area overnight before scrubbing the pot.

- Cook tomato juice or tomato sauce in the pot, then wash out.

- For a cast-iron pan, wipe up grease and any loose pieces of food with a paper towel. Fill the pan with water and detergent and set it on the stove to simmer. This will loosen most of the burnt-on food, but the temper of the pan will be destroyed. To reseason the pan, heat some oil in it for a few minutes before cooking in it again.

coat the board with salad or mineral oil. Allow the oil to remain on the wood briefly, then wipe it off.

Sweetening the Air with Herbs and Spices

Place spare sprigs of fresh herbs directly on the oven rack toward the end of the baking or roasting time. The aroma will stimulate your family's taste buds and welcome arriving guests to the anticipated feast.

To freshen the room air, sprinkle some sweet spice such as ginger or nutmeg on the floor. Then vacuum it from the floor first, before vacuuming the entire room.

For Stains

- In a SilverStone pot or pan: Combine 3 tablespoons of automatic dishwasher detergent with 1 cup of water, or 3 tablespoons of oxygen bleach made especially for delicate fabrics and 1 teaspoon of liquid dishwashing detergent with 1 cup of water. Pour the mixture into the pot and simmer until the stains disappear. Then wash the pot well, dry it, and coat it with a thin layer of vegetable oil.

- In an aluminum pot or pan: Gently boil rhubarb in the pot until the stains disappear. Fill the pot as full as you can with water; otherwise, the lower portion will look cleaner than the top.

- In an aluminum or enamel pot or pan: Fill the pot with water and boil a lemon in it until the stains disappear. Use half a lemon for a small to medium-size pot and a whole lemon cut into halves for a large pot. For any grey metal marks remaining, apply lemon juice directly to the marks and rub with baking soda.

- In a stainless pot or pan: Rub "rainbow" marks with a cut lemon or with a cloth soaked in lemon juice until the stains disappear.

- In a copper-bottomed pot or pan: Mix table salt and vinegar to a gritty paste, apply, and work in with a fine (00) steel wool pad. You can also use catsup, believe it or not, (regular, not salt-free). Apply it evenly to the pot's bottom, let it stand for 30 minutes, then wipe it off.

After cooking, boil cinnamon and cloves in water on the back of the stove to freshen the air.

Lemon Air Freshener

To freshen the air in your kitchen, especially after cooking fish or cabbage, place a whole, unpeeled lemon in a 300°F oven for about 15 minutes, leaving the door slightly open. Turn off the oven and let the lemon cool before removing it. You can also boil lemon rind in water for a citrus scent.

Sponge Salvager

A soured sponge can be salvaged: Saturate it with lemon juice, then rinse it out thoroughly several times. It will be as good as new. This also works for little rag-mop-type dish and bottle washers and brushes used for cleaning dishes and vegetables.

Steel Wool Pad Savers

Don't throw out that half-used steel wool pad. You can save it from rusting by putting it in a solution of water and baking soda. The soda acts as a rust inhibitor. Change the soda-water solution every so often to keep it fresh, and keep the solution covered to prevent evaporation.

Another way to save a used steel wool pad is to freeze it in a plastic bag. It thaws quickly, and there's no rust.

Carpeting and Furniture

Carpeting

Preventing Static Shock

To prevent static shock in carpeting, mix 1 part liquid fabric softener with 5 parts water in a spray bottle. Mist the carpet lightly. Once dry, your carpet won't give anyone a nasty shock.

Carpet Precleaning Treatment

If your rug needs to be cleaned, first sweep it. This will make the nap stand up and will loosen embedded dirt. After sweeping, vacuum. The rug should show a noticeable improvement, and you may decide not to clean it after all.

Removing Pet Stains and Odors

When a pet wets the rug, vinegar will kill the odor and prevent staining, so long as you get to the spot right away. First absorb as much moisture as you can with dry paper towels. Then mix 2 cups of white vinegar in a gallon of cold water. Apply the vinegar mixture to the spot with a clean cloth or paper towel and gently blot the stain. There is a chance, however, that the vinegar may bleach some dark, sensitive colors, so try this on an inconspicuous area first.

Or try sprinkling cornmeal lightly over the rug. Leave it on for 1 to 2 hours, or longer if the odor is really bad, then vacuum.

Keep Rugs Vacuumed

Regular vacuuming will keep your carpet looking fresh and new. Professional rug cleaners suggest light vacuuming a couple of times per week and a more thorough cleaning at least once each week. Too much vacuuming doesn't ruin the carpet; soil and stains are the culprits. A powerfully suctioned vacuum cleaner will dig up loose particles that have worked their way down into the carpet pile. If the dirt stays there, it could cause matting and discoloration, so choose a vacuum cleaner with strong suction. One with a brush and beater bar is ideal for carpets in heavily trafficked areas.

Furniture
(See also Cabinets and Furniture in the chapter, The Well-Maintained Home.)

Removing Marks, Scratches, and Spots . . .

To remove white spots or water marks, dip a cloth or a cork into vegetable oil, then into cigar or cigarette ashes. Rub with the grain, across the spot. Keep rubbing and dipping until the spot disappears. If this doesn't work, try vegetable oil and table salt or vegetable oil and pumice.

Rub broken pieces of pecans or Brazil nuts into scratches to darken them. Alternately, try rubbing the scratches with a little raw linseed oil, or use commercial crayonlike stick shellac of the proper hue.

. . . And Burns

To remove burns from furniture, try rubbing down the burns with 0000 steel wool and wiping the surface clean with alcohol.

. . . And Dents

To remove dents, steam them out. (Note: Don't attempt this if the finish is shellac or if the wood is a veneered layer.) Use a small amount of paint remover to take off the finish covering the dent. Dampen a lint-free cloth, place it over the dent, and hold a hot clothes iron against the cloth. Check every 30 seconds or so to see if the dent has swelled out. When the dent has disappeared as much as it's going to, let the spot dry. Restain if necessary, and seal with oil or varnish.

Removing Water Rings

To remove water rings from wood, squeeze white toothpaste onto a damp cloth, rub with the grain of the wood, then polish.

Here's another method for removing water spots from wood: Mix equal parts of cigarette or cigar ashes and margarine or butter to make a paste, rub it on the spot with a circular motion, then wipe clean.

Furniture Covers That Slide Right On

Do you have trouble putting covers back on foam cushions? Wrap the cushion in a plastic dry cleaner's bag. The cover will then slip right on.

Tightening a Cane-Seated Chair

When the caning in a cane-seated chair loosens, it can be tightened easily if the caning isn't broken. With a sponge and hot water, give the chair seat a thorough soaking and rubbing, using a little detergent if the chair is dirty. As the caning dries, it will tighten up.

Homemade Polish

To make your own furniture polish, mix together ⅓ cup each of boiled linseed oil, turpentine, and vinegar. Apply to furniture with a soft cloth and wipe it dry. Then wipe with another soft cloth.

Uncovering Original Wood

To determine what the original wood looks like on a piece of furniture that is heavily varnished, scratch a hidden section of the piece with a coin.

Cover Up Wrought-Iron Scratches

To cover up scratches in black wrought-iron furniture, use a black crayon, then rub over the area with a dry cloth to blend it in.

Wax Chair Legs

Wax the bottoms of the legs of your chairs to prevent scratching your floor when they're moved about.

Removing Pet Hair

Remove cat or other pet fur from upholstered furniture and pillows with a damp sponge. Slightly moisten the sponge and drag it along the furniture surface. The fur will collect on the sponge. (See also the chapter, Clothing Care.)

Dust Your Drawers

You can vacuum dust from drawers without removing the contents by covering the vacuum cleaner nozzle with a section of old pantyhose or cheesecloth.

Remove Stuck-On Paper

To remove paper that is stuck to a wood table or chest, try putting a few drops of furniture oil on the paper, then loosen it by rubbing with a soft cloth. Peel off the paper with your fingers. Oil the entire surface to even the finish, and polish it a few days later.

Wood Categories

The division of wood into softwoods and hardwoods doesn't relate to physical hardness. Softwoods are woods from coniferous trees, such as pine, which are porous and moisture bearing. Hardwoods are woods from deciduous trees, such as oak, teak, and birch.

Glass, Metals, and Other Materials

Glass

Homemade Glass and Mirror Cleaners

Try this homemade glass cleaner: 1 pint of rubbing alcohol, 2 tablespoons of clear ammonia, and 2 tablespoons of liquid dishwashing detergent. Mix well for shiny, streak-free windows.

Here's another recipe for sparkling windows without streaks: Mix ½ cup of cornstarch into about 2 quarts of warm water. Apply with a sponge, then wipe dry with absorbent cloth or old towels. It's great for car windows and bathroom mirrors, too.

You can also clean mirrors and windows with newspaper moistened in 1 pint of cold water to which a few drops (about 1 teaspoon) of vinegar have been added. The paper should be squeezed almost dry. Follow this by rubbing briskly with a dry, soft paper towel for a fine luster.

Metals

Lemon Soak

You can clean badly tarnished unlacquered brass without scrubbing by giving it a good long soak overnight in a bath of lemon juice and salt. Use 1 tablespoon of salt to ½ cup of lemon juice. The grime and tarnish will then wipe off easily. This method also works on copper. For large or odd-shaped pieces, saturate a cloth in the lemon-salt solution and wrap it around the piece. Once brass or copper has been cleaned, you may want to consider shellacking it to prevent retarnishing.

Worcestershire Rub

Use Worcestershire sauce to clean and polish unlacquered brass. Pour the sauce on a damp cloth and rub, then wipe the brass with a clean damp cloth and dry it. It's the acid-salt combination in the Worcestershire sauce that eats away at the tarnish.

Lemon Copper Cleaner

To clean tarnished unlacquered copper, rub the copper with half a lemon dipped in salt. Then rinse and wash in hot soapy water, wash again in clean water, and dry well.

Pewter Care

The best way to clean pewter is to wash it with warm water and mild soap. Pewter should never be put in the dishwasher because it has a low melting point.

Toothpaste Fights Tarnish

To clean tarnish off silver without using a silver polish, coat the silver with toothpaste, then run it under warm water, work it into a foam, and rinse it off. For stubborn stains or for silverware with intricate grooves, use an old soft-bristled toothbrush.

Revive Old Polish

If your metal polish becomes hard, don't throw it away. Just add some hot water to it and stir until smooth.

Baking Soda Cleanser

You can remove tarnish from silver with baking soda. Sprinkle the soda on a damp cloth and rub it on the silverware until the tarnish is gone. Then rinse and dry well.

Other Materials

Jewelry Cleaners

Clean gold rings with toothpaste and a soft toothbrush instead of using expensive jewelry cleaner.

Another homemade jewelry cleaner is a mixture of sudsy ammonia and water. Let your jewelry soak in it for a few minutes, then polish with a soft cloth.

Brick Cleanup

Come spring, it's time to remove soot and creosote from the hearth and fireplace. Make an old-time cleaner by adding 1 quart of hot water to ½ cup of yellow laundry soap (such as Fels Naphtha). Heat the mixture until the soap has thoroughly dissolved. Allow the mixture to cool, then add ½ pound of powdered pumice and ½ cup of ammonia. Mix well, and you'll have a soft soap compound that can be brushed onto soiled areas. Leave it on for at least 30 minutes, and then scrub with a stiff brush and warm water. Rinse thoroughly.

You can also clean soot and smoke stains off your fireplace brick with a solution of 1 gallon of hot water and 1 cup of washing soda. Scrub the bricks with a brush and wipe clean with a paper towel. (Washing soda is available at hardware stores and some supermarkets.)

If interior brickwork becomes dingy or pale with time, you can restore the original color by painting on a thin coat of boiled linseed oil. Before applying the oil, wash the bricks and allow them to dry thoroughly.

To remove paint, plaster, or years of grime from old brick and stone walls, you can sandblast it yourself with rented equipment. But consider that sand eats away mortar, drastically wears surrounding wood, and etches window glass that hasn't been covered; the equipment must be trailed behind your vehicle; and sand ends up nearly everywhere.

General Cleaning

Removing Crayon Marks from Walls

To remove crayon marks from painted walls, scrub with toothpaste, then rinse and wipe. This works well on enamel paints as well as flat paints.

Another way to remove crayon marks from walls and furniture is to pour ammonia on a cloth and rub the marks. Rinse and dry immediately. Do not use ammonia on stained, finished pieces because it may dull or remove the finish. If in doubt, try it on an inconspicuous area first.

Grease Pickup

If you spill grease on a wood floor, immediately pour very cold water on the spot or put an ice cube on it. The grease will harden and can then be scraped off with a knife.

Iron Cleanup

To remove burnt-on starch from the bottom of your iron, sprinkle table salt on a sheet of wax paper and iron with a cold iron. Then polish the iron with silver polish until the stain is removed.

Another way to clean off an encrusted or scorched iron bottom (but not a Teflon-coated one), is to polish it with very fine waterproof sandpaper. Made to be used wet, the sandpaper does a fine job of cleaning and eliminating scratches. (You can also try very fine steel wool or a nonabrasive cleanser such as Bon Ami.)

To rid your steam iron of lime deposits, fill it with vinegar, turn on the heat for about 10 minutes, then unplug it and lay the iron on its side so that the vinegar flows out through the steam holes. Complete the process by rinsing the inside of the iron with water.

Dust Your Bulbs

Dust the light bulbs of your lamps frequently. Light bulbs are often overlooked when you're cleaning, but they shouldn't be because dust blocks out some of the light. Your dusty bulbs will shine brighter after a cleaning.

Remove Vase Discoloration

Lime and other substances in water discolor flower vases and other receptacles in which water stands for a period of time. One way to remove such stains is with tea leaves and vinegar. A couple of tea bags' worth of tea left in a vase of vinegar (⅔ strong tea, ⅓ vinegar) will loosen and dissolve the stains within a day or so. With a bottle brush and detergent, you can make the vase sparkle again.

Brush Out Radiators

If you find it difficult to clean your radiators, try using a long-handled auto snow brush. It's just the right width to fit between the slots and long enough to brush out dust from underneath.

Air Out Old Books

To get a musty odor out of old books, place the books outdoors in the sun and frequently fan out the pages so that the air can reach them. Brush off any mildew or mold. If the pages are damp, sprinkle cornstarch between them and brush it off after a few hours.

Hanging Curtains without a Snag

When putting new or freshly ironed curtains on a curtain rod, place a thimble or a finger from an old glove over the rod end. The curtain will then slip on easily without tearing. With flat rods, slip a small butter knife into the opening at the end before putting the curtain on.

Candle Smarts

Almost all candles made today are smokeless and dripless except for the few purposely made to drip. Refrigeration may sometimes make a candle burn a little slower, but room conditions where the candle is burning are more important than any other factor in affecting the tendency to drip and to burn rapidly. If there is a draft, even the most expensive dripless candles will drip, have erratic flames, and burn two to three times faster than the same kind of candle in a draft-free spot in the same room. Never position a candle by an open window, air conditioning duct, or vent.

Another factor is the length of the wick. Always cut off the excess; otherwise, the burning wick will fall over and melt the side of the candle. This will ruin the well in the center (which helps to contain melted wax) and cause the candle to drip.

Recycling Electric Blankets

To remove wires from an electric blanket that no longer works, cut the stitches around the plug-in and bottom binding. Open the bottom edge enough to see the vertical tacking between the top and bottom sections. Start at one side and pull the wire out until it gets too tight to pull. Cut the wire off and repeat the pulling and cutting across the blanket. Then reattach the bottom binding, and you've got a still-serviceable blanket.

Keep Piano Keys White

An organ or piano should not be closed so that the keys are hidden. Keys should be exposed to air and light and should be played frequently. Air circulation guards against warping, light bleaches keys (especially ivory) and keeps them white, and frequent use prevents discoloration and develops a beneficial patina on ivory.

Woodstove Shine

To shine your black woodstove, rub a piece of crumpled-up wax paper over the stove when it is warm.

Household Pests

Ants

Vinegar Repellent

To stop ant invasions in your kitchen, wash or spray countertops, cabinets, and floors with equal parts of vinegar and water.

Baby Powder Barricade

To keep ants out of a room, sprinkle baby powder where they enter, such as on a windowsill or under doors. The ants won't walk through the powder.

Check Firewood for Ants

Carpenter ants nest in wood and can cause structural damage. They are fond of moist or partially decayed wood and often get a free ride into the house when firewood is carried in. To avoid having your firewood infested with ants, store it elevated to break contact with the ground and to promote air circulation, and cover it to keep it dry. Inspect the wood before bringing it into the house, and bring in only a small amount at a time.

Peppermint Guardians

Try planting peppermint around all the entrances to your house. It may deter ants from entering. Every once in a while, go out and crush some of the leaves; releasing the mint oils makes the plants more effective.

Cockroaches

Homemade Roach Powder

Powdered boric acid is a very effective cockroach killer. It's the main ingredient, along with sugar and powdered nondairy coffee creamer, in a popular commercial roach powder. It is inexpensive and relatively safe, but it should be kept away from children and pets. Sprinkle the white powder in all the dark, warm places that cockroaches love: under sinks and ranges, behind refrigerators, in cabinets and closets, and so on. The roaches will walk through the powder, then clean themselves, much the way a cat preens. Once they ingest the powder, they die. When the powder gets vacuumed up or swept away, apply more.

Another roach powder can be made from a mixture of 36% borax, 16% flour, 10% confectioners' sugar, and 38% cornmeal.

Cucumber Chasers

The cucumber is an effective cockroach chaser. Place cucumber skins wherever you have a cockroach problem. The vegetable's repellent quality comes from a naturally occurring compound in the plant called trans-2-nonenal.

Bay Leaves Drive Away Roaches

Place bay leaves in the pantry, in cupboards, and on shelves to drive away cockroaches. The various chemical compounds present in bay leaves have been found to be cockroach repellents.

Get Yourself a Cockroach Eater

If you've got cockroaches that just won't go away, there is a sure cure— but it's definitely not for the faint-hearted. Buy yourself a gecko lizard. House geckos are 4 to 5 inches long and not too pretty, but they love to munch on roaches. They'll do a fine job, if you can stand to hear them devouring their late-night snacks! Geckos prefer warm climates, so if you live in the North, you'll have to provide your pet with temperatures in the 70s and a warm resting place. And geckos don't mix well with other pets—your cat or dog may try to eat it!

Other Nasties

Flea Control

Your cat or dog can bring fleas into your home. Fleas lay eggs in your pet's coat, and the eggs drop off as the animal moves about the house. Within a few days the eggs hatch to the larval stage and live in rugs, bedding, and furniture cushions. At this stage they can be easily vacuumed away. Be particularly fastidious about dust, because it is one of the larvae's favorite habitats. After you vacuum, sprinkle diatomaceous earth in all the affected areas to destroy any remaining larvae. (Diatomaceous earth can be purchased in organic gardening supply stores.) (See also Cats, and Dogs, in the chapter, Pets and Backyard Livestock.)

Camphor Keeps Mice Away

If you have mice, buy camphor gum. It comes in 2-inch squares, looks like paraffin, and has a very strong camphor odor that mice do not like. Place the squares where the mice invade, but keep your children and pets away from it. You can find camphor gum in hardware and garden supply stores.

Wasp Wetter

To catch wasps that get inside the house, quickly spray them several times with a water mister. The weight of the water on their wings keeps them from flying and makes them easier to catch.

Bats in Your Belfry?

When their natural habitat is disturbed, bats often take up residence in buildings. Fortunately, there's no real trick to eviction. Just wait until they leave on their own at dusk to go out and feed. From outside, watch where they exit; then, go to your attic while they're out and seal off entrances with hardware cloth, caulk, weatherstripping, or fiberglass insulation. Be sure to wear protective clothing; you can pick up rabies from bat feces. And never swing at or chase a bat; it may turn on you and bite.

Keep Your House Free of Pests

One sure way to get rid of cockroaches, flies, ants, and other household pests is to take away their food supply and shelter. The kitchen is where most of these pests are found, so it is the first place to start your clean-up campaign:

- Clean under refrigerators, behind stoves, and other hard-to-reach areas that attract pests.

- Vacuum and/or mop up all food and liquids from the floor.

- Empty your trash container frequently, or keep garbage tightly covered.

- Don't forget to scrub greasy exhaust fan blades.

- Be sure all of your food is stored properly, and keep your storage areas dry.

- Repair small cracks or holes in walls or floors to eliminate an entryway for bugs.

As for the rest of the house, remember that cockroaches and other insects can live in tiny spaces. They're found behind baseboards and window and door frames, between cabinets and walls, and behind loose kickplates, molding, and trim.

Controlling Fleas

A good common-sense approach to controlling fleas in your house is offered by the Environmental Protection Agency publication, "Common Sense Pest Control for the Home and Garden." It suggests doing "spring" cleaning in late summer because it is during this time and in early fall that fleas become a serious problem. Since fleas love to hide in rugs and dust, it is important to vacuum and wash all floors, rugs, and other surfaces to which your pets have access. Throw away the vacuum cleaner bag immediately. This thorough cleaning should eliminate the adult fleas as well as the developing larvae. Give your pets a good brushing and bath at this time, too.

3 Clothing Care

General Care

Cleaning and Drying

Be Kind to Wet Wool

Wool is very weak when wet. Do not pull, wring, or rub wet wool garments.

Airing Rids Mothball Odor

To eliminate mothball odor from clothes, give the garments a good airing, followed by a 10- to 15-minute tumble in a warm clothes dryer.

Turn Garments Inside Out

Turn your garments inside out before machine washing and drying to reduce wear on edges and creases. You should also do this if you frequently hang your clothes outside to dry because turning them inside out prevents the sun from fading colors.

Cool Rinse

When machine washing, use cool rinse water to retain fabric finishes and to save energy.

Dry and Remove

Remove your clothes from the dryer promptly. Excess heat can break down fabric fibers.

Getting the Most from Your Dry Cleaner

To get the most out of the money you spend at the dry cleaner, be sure to point out stains and explain exactly what it was that caused the spot. This helps your cleaner determine the best method for stain removal.

If you have clothing with unusual features, such as a skirt with buttons down the side instead of the back or front, make sure your dry cleaner is aware of it. Once the garment has been pressed incorrectly, you may find the creases hard to remove at home with an iron, and the clothing will have to be re-pressed professionally.

Squeeze-Clean Knits

When hand-washing knits, gently *squeeze,* rather than wring, the water out of the clothes. You can also lay the garment on a colorfast towel, roll it in the towel, and gently squeeze. Wringing will outstretch the fabric.

Rinse and Rinse Again

Rinse hand-washed clothes until the water is clear. Soap residue attracts oil and dirt.

Wash with Gloves

Wear rubber gloves when hand-washing pantyhose and especially delicate knits. A tiny split in your fingernail can catch on delicate fabrics and cause pulls and runs.

Drying Heavy Blankets

You can dry heavy blankets on the line quickly and without stretching by using this technique: Hang the blanket across the line with the binding down. Then pull the opposite corners down. Water will drip from the lower corners, yet air will still circulate inside the fold.

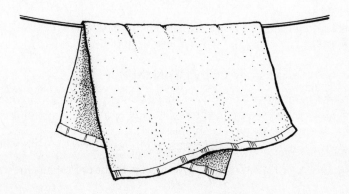

Hot Rocks for Drying Boots

To dry out boots, heat a can or panful of clean round pebbles in the oven, pour them inside the boot, and rattle them around until the pebbles cool. The heat will be absorbed into the boot and dry out the moisture. Some synthetic boot linings may melt from too much heat, so test for heat sensitivity first by holding a hot pebble in one spot for a few seconds.

If you're camping and your boots get wet inside, pull two rocks from the campfire and put them on the ground. Then slip the boots upside down on stakes so they're over, but not touching, the rocks. You'll have dry boots by morning.

Pillowcase Lingerie Bag

Don't waste money on a mesh lingerie bag. Machine wash delicate items in a pillowcase. You can close the case with a rubber band, or you can sew on a snap or Velcro fastener.

Sponge Off Pet Hair

Remove pet hair from your clothes in a jiffy this way: Dampen a sponge with warm water, wring out the sponge, and lightly wipe it over your clothes. It will pick the hair right up. If it doesn't pick up most of the hair, try wetting the sponge with a solution of several drops of glycerin to 1 cup of water.

Brushing Off Sweater Pills

To remove those stubborn "pills" from sweaters, use a round, natural-bristle brush and simply brush over the surface of the sweater. The pills will be removed without pulling the sweater fibers.

Ironing
(For cleaning irons, see also General Cleaning in the chapter, Bathrooms, Kitchens, and Other Places You Hate to Clean.)

Steam Out Wrinkled Wool

To get wrinkles out of wool clothes, hang them up in a steamy bathroom (such as while you shower) or press them under a towel or pressing cloth with a steam iron. Steam accentuates wool's natural resiliency. *Never* use dry heat—it makes wool brittle and easy to scorch.

Iron Them Clean

Never iron dirty clothes. Heat can permanently set stains.

Foil Your Ironing Board

Place aluminum foil, shiny-side up, between the ironing board and cover pad. It reflects heat and cuts down on ironing time.

Use Your Iron Instead of Basting

When sewing, it's often quicker to iron than to baste something down. Measure, pin, and press your hems in place before sewing; press under facing edges before hemming them; turn under the seam allowance on patch pockets and press before sewing them to your garments.

Chilling Clothes Retains Moisture

Keep sprinkled clothes in a plastic bag in the freezer or refrigerator until you're ready to iron. This doesn't harm the fabric, and it makes ironing quicker and easier by keeping the moisture in the clothes. Frozen clothes will be a bit stiff and should be allowed to thaw for a few minutes.

Storage

Hanging Wool

Hang your wool jackets on wooden or rounded plastic hangers instead of metal ones. Wood hangers won't stretch the jacket shoulders. Wool sweaters, however, should be folded rather than hung up.

In the Bag

Never store garments completely covered by polyethylene bags (such as the bags from the dry cleaner). Polyethylene emits a gas that can change the color of dyes on some clothes. Use these bags only as capes over the shoulders of garments to prevent dust from settling. Paper is a good wrap to prevent dust accumulation, as is cloth.

Vinyl and nylon garment bags sweat in warm, humid weather and in extreme climates could leave clothes soggy, leading to mildew. Cotton garment bags breathe, but they also pick up moisture and must be kept in a dry place, and they do not offer moth protection.

Protecting Clothes from Insects

Thoroughly clean your winter wardrobe before packing clothes away for the warm months. Food stains, perspiration, and body oils attract insects, such as the clothes moth and carpet beetle, whose larvae will have a summer-long feast.

When washing clothes at home before storage, don't use fabric softeners or starches — they attract silverfish.

No matter how thoroughly you clean your clothes, you won't keep the bugs away if your storage area is humid or dirty. Clothing should be stored in airtight storage containers (cardboard boxes are good for storage as long as they are clean and can be securely sealed).

Use mothballs and crystals in *sealed* storage spaces to prevent dissipation of the mothball vapors. Mothballs should ideally be hung above areas to be treated because the vapors are heavier than air and will drop. Crystals should never directly touch clothing, nor should they be used with leather or furs.

Aromatic herbs and spices, such as southernwood, wormwood, rue, tansy, mint, and lavender, repel moths. Dry and crumble them, then sew them into cheesecloth, muslin, or linen bags. Suspend the bags in closets and garment bags, and tuck them into dresser drawers. Occasionally squeeze the bags to crush the contents, and shake them a bit to release more scent.

Keep Leather Breathing

Leather needs to breathe, so store leather garments in a well-ventilated area. It is recommended that you do not cover leather garments. If you must cover them to protect them from dust, use a cloth bag. Cotton pillowcases make handy bags, as do sheets sewn up on three sides.

Give Woolens a Rest

Give your wool clothes a chance to air out and "rest" between wearings. Wool will return to its original shape if it isn't worn day after day.

De-Shine Worsteds

Have your worsted garments become flat and shiny with age? Try steaming them to raise the nap. If this doesn't work, dip a cloth into pure white vinegar and rub it lightly and briskly over the worn area. The shine will be gone, and the odor will disappear when the vinegar dries. Vinegar is a very weak bleach. Don't try this on dark or vivid colors without testing an inconspicuous area first.

Eliminating Static Cling

Do you have a problem with static cling? Try hand lotion. Take just enough to rub into your hands and smooth it in until it has disappeared. Then rub your palms over your pantyhose or slip, and the static cling will disappear. In a pinch, sprinkle your undergarments with water.

Irregulars vs Seconds

The terms "irregular" and "seconds" do not mean the same thing. Irregulars have only minor defects, but seconds may have serious flaws.

Wax Pantyhose Toes

To prevent nylon pantyhose from developing holes in the toes, rub the toe section with paraffin after each washing.

Stain Removal

Blood

Cornstarch Paste Remover

You can remove bloodstains quickly by covering them with a cornstarch paste, then rinsing from the back of the stain with lukewarm soapy water.

Bubble Away Blood from Leather

To take fresh bloodstains out of leather, dab a small amount of hydrogen peroxide on the spot and let it bubble. Then wipe it off.

Cold-Water Soak

Pour a bit of hydrogen peroxide on bloodstains before soaking the garment in cold water for several hours or overnight. Then launder as usual. (Test an inconspicuous area of the garment first, as the hydrogen peroxide may bleach the fabric.)

Stain Removal Methods

Stain	Methods*	Stain	Methods*
Blood	• Soak in cold water for 30 minutes. • Spread on paste of cornstarch, cornmeal, or talcum powder to dry. Brush away. • Dab hydrogen peroxide on fabrics that will take bleaching. • Persistent stains can be dabbed with diluted ammonia. (Do not use on acetates.)		rinse thoroughly as soon as stain disappears.
		Deodorants & antiperspirants	• Wash or sponge with warm water and liquid laundry detergent. • To restore color, sponge with ammonia (diluted for silk or wool); sponge or rinse with water.
Chewing gum	• Rub with ice cube until gum flakes off. • Loosen by soaking in white vinegar or rubbing with egg white before laundering.	Egg	• Sponge on cold water. (Never use hot water —it will set stain.)
Coffee, tea (black)	• Stretch stained portion of fabric over bowl, pour boiling water on stain from height of 1–3 feet. • Try applying a few drops of white vinegar to stain.	Fruits, berries	• Sponge first with cold water before stain can set. • Pour salt or hot water on stain; soak in milk before laundering. • Stretch over bowl, pour on boiling water from height of 1–3 feet. • For nonwashables, dab with few drops of eucalyptus oil. Leave on for several hours. Sponge with liquid laundry detergent and water. (Never use soap.) • Sponge old stains with white vinegar.
Cosmetics (eye shadow, foundation, mascara, blusher)	• If fabric is washable, apply liquid laundry detergent to stain and rub until thick suds form. Rinse. Repeat. • If yellow stain persists, dab on mixture of equal parts of mild hydrogen peroxide solution and water. Watch carefully and	Grass, flowers, foliage	• Sponge on diluted alcohol for washables and nonwashables.

*Use only one at a time.

Stain	Methods*	Stain	Methods*
	• If stain remains, use mild solution of hydrogen peroxide.		with water. Add few drops of ammonia. • Use mild solution of hydrogen peroxide.
Gravy	• Soak washables in cold water to dissolve starch. • Sponge cool water on nonwashables. Then apply absorbent cloth.	Lipstick	• Rub with cold cream or shortening. Wash with club soda.
Grease (cooking oil, salad dressing)	• For nonwashables, make paste of baking soda, cornmeal, or cornstarch to absorb. • For washables, pour on boiling water before washing. • Dab with water and ammonia.	Mustard	• Work glycerin into stain. Flush with detergent solution. *Do not use soap.*
		Nail polish	• Sponge back of fabric with banana oil; if necessary, sponge on rubbing alcohol combined with drop of ammonia.
Ice cream, milk	• Soak washables in cool water, dab on liquid laundry detergent, rinse. Then bleach if necessary. • Treat with few dabs of ammonia mixed with detergent.	Paint	• Remove while fresh. Sponge with soap and water. Use turpentine afterward. For latex, sponge on rubbing alcohol. • For old paint, dab on banana oil.
Ink	• Dab on rubbing alcohol liberally and allow to soak before blotting with cheesecloth. • Work in concentrated ammonia, then apply vinegar to neutralize ammonia. • Apply lukewarm glycerin, then flush	Perspiration	• Wash with warm water and detergent. • Use ammonia on fresh stains, vinegar on old stains. • Hold over ammonia fumes to restore color.
		Scorches	• Rinse in cold water immediately.

(continued)

Stain Removal Methods—Continued

Stain	Methods*	Stain	Methods*
Scorches—continued	• Boil in 1 cup of soap and 2 quarts of milk. • Wet with soapsuds. Place in sunlight. • For nonwashables, sponge with hydrogen peroxide.		boiling water from height of 1–3 feet. • Pour on salt or hot water; soak in milk. • Apply cold water, sponge with glycerin and detergent, then apply few drops of ammonia and detergent. (If stain turns pink, apply white vinegar.) • Squirt with soda water.
Tomato-based sauces	• Soak in cool water for 30 minutes. Work undiluted liquid laundry detergent into stain.		
Wine	• For washables, stretch over bowl, pour on		

Food and Drink

Club Soda Rub

To remove alcohol or food stains, immediately place a towel under the spot, apply club soda, and rub gently toward the spot's center. Repeat several times until most or all of the stain disappears.

Removing Chocolate Stains

To remove chocolate, cocoa, and carob stains, scrape off as much of the food as possible with a dull knife. Then wash the garment in warm soapy water. Sponge stubborn stains with hydrogen peroxide *or* a mixture of 1 teaspoon of sodium perborate to 1 pint of hydrogen peroxide. (Use only on colorfast fabrics—this solution is a mild bleaching agent.) Allow the mixture to remain on the fabric for up to 30 minutes, then wash.

Boil Away Fruit Stains

To take fruit and wine stains out of clothing and tablecloths, use boiling water. While a kettle of water is coming to a boil, lay the stained cloth over a bowl in the sink, with the stain facing you. Pour all the boiling water onto the stain, holding the kettle at least 12 inches above the stain. Then launder as usual. If the stain is not fresh, allow the cloth to soak in the water that was poured on it until the stain disappears. Don't use boiling water on shrinkable fabric that should only be washed in cold water.

Tenderizer for Baby Formula Stains

Remove baby formula stains by rubbing on a paste of unseasoned meat tenderizer mixed with water. Roll up the clothes and wait a few hours before washing.

Dishwasher Detergent Paste for Stubborn Stains

To remove stubborn food stains from washable fabrics, try making a paste of water and automatic dishwasher detergent. Apply it to the stain, let it work for 5 to 10 minutes, then rinse thoroughly and wash as usual. You may want to test this on an inconspicuous section of fabric to make sure it won't adversely affect the color.

Ink and Paint

Removing Dried-On Paint

Even dried-on paint can often be removed with lacquer thinner. Rub it on, let it penetrate, rewet the fabric, and rub again. Then launder with work clothes or wash separately by hand.

Removing Fresh Ink

A fresh ink spill can be taken out by blotting the excess and soaking the material in milk for 30 minutes. Then wash as usual.

Another way to remove fresh ink is to pour liquid laundry detergent on the stain and rub vigorously, then rinse.

You can also try rubbing milk on the spot. Be sure you place the garment on a nonstaining surface such as glass with a paper towel or old cloth underneath because the milk will loosen the ink, which will then run and stain the surrounding area. Leave the milk on for a few minutes before laundering as usual. It may take several applications to remove the stain. If the stain is really stubborn, pour liquid laundry detergent directly on the milk-soaked stain and rub it vigorously.

Hair Spray Removes Ball-Point Ink

To remove ball-point pen ink, saturate the stain with hair spray, then blot the spot with a damp cloth. Do not rub. Repeat the application of hair spray and the blotting until the ink has lifted out, then launder.

Oil and Grease

Shortening Gets Out Grease

To remove machine grease from clothing, rub solid shortening into grease spots, then wash as usual.

Cornstarch for Grease

To get freshly spilled oil or grease out of clothing, cover the spot with cornstarch and put a paper towel under the stained area to absorb the grease that goes through the fabric. Let the cornstarch absorb the grease, then brush off the garment and launder. Depending on the fabric and the size of the stain, you may have to repeat applications of cornstarch before laundering.

Getting That Spot Out

Here are some things to keep in mind for successful home stain removal:

- Test the spot remover on hidden areas of the fabric.

- Work from the wrong side of the fabric using a blotter underneath.

- Don't rub. Use light brushing strokes to avoid leaving a ring.

- Use a weak solution several times rather than a few applications of a strong solution.

- Do not iron stains. Heat can set stains permanently.

- If you're not certain what the stain is, some experts suggest dabbing on eucalyptus oil and leaving it overnight to "float" out the spot before proceeding with other methods.

Shampoo Out Collar Rings

Shampoo rubbed into soiled shirt collars and cuffs before laundering helps remove "ring around the collar" because shampoo is made to dissolve body oils.

Other Stains

Cream of Tartar on Collars

Get perspiration stains off shirt collars by wetting the collar with warm or hot water and rubbing in cream of tartar. Then launder as usual.

Fast Action Beats Stains

Try to remove stains from your clothes as quickly as possible. Fresh stains can usually be removed easily because they haven't been absorbed into the fabric.

Brush Off Mud

Don't try to wipe mud off your clothes. Let the mud dry, then brush it off. Any remaining dirt can be sponged away with soapy water from the back of the stain or can be removed by laundering.

Bleach Out Rust

To remove rust from white clothing, soak the clothes in lemon juice, then bleach them in the sun. Do not try this method if the manufacturer warns against bleaching.

Rhubarb Removes Rust

If you have a supply of rhubarb on hand, it just may do the trick in removing rust stains from clothing. Cut five or six stalks into ½-inch lengths and bring them to a boil in about 1 cup of water. Boil the rhubarb until it is soft, then drain off the hot "juice" and pour it on the rust stain. After this treatment, wash the garment as usual.

Alcohol for Grass Stains

Remove grass stains by dabbing them with diluted rubbing alcohol, then liquid laundry detergent. Launder as usual.

Sewing and Mending

Buttons and Buttonholes

Easy Button Removal

When removing buttons from clothing, slide a comb under the button and cut the thread between button and comb with a razor blade. With this method, there's less chance of accidentally cutting the material. If you don't have razor blades in the house, try using a sharp fillet or boning knife instead.

Sew with Dental Floss

Sew on frequently popped buttons with dental floss—it's stronger than regular thread and will withstand abuse on children's clothing and on work clothes.

Scissors Stopper

Has your scissors ever slipped when you were cutting open a newly sewn buttonhole so that you cut through the stitching at the end? Next time, put a pin across each end of the buttonhole inside the stitching before you cut, to stop the blades of the scissors before they go too far.

Sew in Extra Buttons

Borrow a trick from the better clothing manufacturers, and sew an extra button or two in an inconspicuous spot inside your just-made garment. If you lose one, a replacement will be right at hand, and even though laundering may have faded the buttons a bit, the new one will match.

Patterns

Lay Out Beforehand to Prevent Waste

Most pattern companies give fairly generous yardage recommendations to make it easy to lay out the pattern, but this can mean from ¼ to ½ yard of waste. Buy your pattern first and experiment with various layouts at home on a folded sheet before you buy the fabric. With fabric costing as much as $20 to $25 a yard, even a quarter of a yard saved can add up to several dollars.

Careful Storage Saves Patterns

When you find a pattern you really like, you'll probably want to use it again, so be careful how you put it away. First, lightly press each pattern piece with a warm iron, then repair any tears with clear tape. Fold each piece with the name and number on top, and clip the pieces for each garment together. Write down any adjustments you made to the pattern and the amount of material you actually used. Slip this note into the envelope with the pattern so that you'll be all ready the next time you use the pattern.

Sew-by-Number

Most pattern pieces are numbered in the order in which the garment is assembled. That is, pieces numbered 1 and 2 will be sewn together first, piece number 3 will be added, and so on. To save time looking through a stack of cut fabric pieces for an elusive pocket flap or other small piece, stack the pieces in numerical order, with the highest number on the bottom of the pile. This will make it easy to pick up each piece in sequence and add it to your garment.

Press Your Patterns and Fabric

Before you lay out a pattern, press the pattern pieces. A badly wrinkled pattern can make a difference in the fit of your finished garment. Press the fabric well, too, especially the center crease. If this crease doesn't press out completely, refold the fabric to avoid the creased area.

Pattern Size Book

Keep a small notebook of pattern sizes for yourself and anyone else you sew for, and take it with you when you go shopping. You can jot down the name of the store where you saw just the right fabric on a day you were too busy to stop in, and you can make note of details you see on ready-made clothing that you'd like to try at home. You can also pin in sample swatches from clothes you've made so that you can match accessories.

Marking and Cutting Fabric

Slash Seam Allowances

Tired of making tailor's tacks to mark all those large and small dots along the seam allowances? Instead, cut ¼-inch slashes straight in from the cutting edge opposite the dots — one centered slash for a small dot and two, one on each side, for a larger one. You'll find these slashes easy to match up when you are pinning the garment pieces together. For transferring dots on the pattern other than those along the seam allowance, tracing paper and the pressure from a dried-up ball-point pen work on most fabrics.

Perfectly Straight Edge

For squaring off yard goods such as drapery or upholstery material, where a straight edge is important, use a carpenter's square. Line up two edges of the fabric at a time and get the yard goods perfectly square.

Fusible Interfacing Saves Time

Fusible interfacing is a great time saver because it bonds to the fabric when ironed on, eliminating the need for basting. With this method you can save money as well: When the interfacing is to be cut from a pattern piece that has a seam allowance, trace the piece onto the interfacing on the seam line rather than the cutting line. Since the seam allowance should be trimmed off fusible interfacing before it is applied to the fabric, this saves more than 1 inch on every piece.

Wrong-Side Interfacing

Some patterns direct you to apply interfacing to the facing of a garment instead of to the garment itself. Unless you are using a very delicate or sheer fabric, or the facing is to be turned to the outside of the garment, don't do it. Interfacings are meant to add body and shape and should be applied to the *wrong* side of the garment, not to the facings.

Mark Your Darts

The tip of a dart marking is sometimes difficult to see when the fabric is folded ready for sewing. If, when you are tracing the dart, you mark a short line (½ inch is sufficient) across the tip, you will find it easy to see exactly where the dart ends when you are ready to stitch it.

Trace on the Wrong Side to Make Pockets

Welt or buttonhole pockets needn't be intimidating. For easier placement, trace the markings from the pattern to the wrong side of the fabric, then sew along the marked lines with contrasting thread and the largest stitch your machine can sew. The welt or binding can then be basted exactly on this line and machine-stitched in place. (Remember to reset the stitch size before you apply the welt or binding.)

Mark Your Machine for Seam Allowances

Many sewing machines are marked ⅝ inch from the needle to make sewing the correct seam allowance easier, but if yours isn't, mark it yourself. Place a short piece of adhesive tape or masking tape on your machine to the right of the needle. On this tape, mark a thin, straight line with permanent ink exactly ⅝ inch from the needle at a right angle to the front of the machine. You might also mark the other widths, such as ¼ inch, ½ inch, and ¾ inch, on the tape, since you may occasionally come across a seam allowance in these sizes. Use a different color for each line to avoid confusion.

Grade Seams for Turning

On parts of a garment that are to be turned after sewing, such as collars, cuffs, and pocket flaps, be sure to "grade" the seams after sewing. That is, trim each seam allowance to a different width to avoid a ridge when the piece is turned and pressed.

Mark the Wrong Side of Fabrics

If your new fabric has a barely perceptible right and wrong side, mark large lines or circles over the entire wrong side with tailor's chalk. Then there will be no more wondering if you've just assembled two left sleeves!

Mark the Underlining

When underlining a skirt or dress, transfer the dart or pleat markings to the underlining only. Once you have basted or pinned the outer fabric and the underlining together, baste the darts or pleats through both layers on the fold lines. This will keep the layers aligned properly while you sew the darts or pleats in place.

Sewing

Close Up Thread Holes

To close up the thread holes you made in your fabric when you ripped out a seam, dampen the holes with vinegar and rub briskly with an old toothbrush. Cover with a cloth and iron at the medium heat setting.

Press Every Seam Open

Press every seam open before you cross it with another seam. This is one of the most important rules in sewing if you want professional-looking results.

See Thread Better

Do you have trouble threading a needle? Try holding the needle and thread against a contrasting background—a dark-colored surface if you're threading a light-colored thread, and a light-colored surface if you're threading a dark-colored thread. It really helps your depth perception.

Delinting Your Sewing Machine

When sewing velours, corduroys, and other lint-producing materials, keep a small watercolor paintbrush sprayed with a wax-free dusting spray near your sewing machine. It's handy for quickly dusting off the sewing area and is great for cleaning hard-to-get-at places around and behind the bobbin.

The small nylon brush that comes with electric razors is just right for cleaning the lint from around the bobbin and under the feed dog in the sewing machine. Its slim shape enables it to get into the tiny crevices.

One-Way Thread

If you have trouble with thread twisting and knotting as you sew, try threading the needle before you cut the thread from the spool. This ensures stitching in the proper direction of the thread and prevents twisting and knotting.

Paper-Clip Hems

When hemming a garment, you can avoid pricking your fingers by holding the hem in place with paper clips instead of pins.

Lump-Free Hems

To prevent lumps and large pleats along the hemline when you are hemming an A-line skirt or dress, run a gathering stitch along the bottom edge of the garment. Pin up the hem at each seam, then gently pull the gathering thread until the edge of the garment fits the hemline. Adjust the gathers and sew the edge in place.

Smooth Waistband

To make a firm, smooth waistband with less bulk on a skirt or slacks, place the waistband pattern along an edge of your fabric, with one seam line on the selvage. Fold the waistband on the marked fold line as usual, and sew the wider side to your garment, right side to right side. The selvage edge will be ready to hand sew to the inside, right on the line of stitches, with no turn-under or seam binding necessary.

Make Gathers with Buttonhole Thread

If you have a long piece of fabric to be gathered, wind the bobbin of your sewing machine with buttonhole thread. Loosen the tension and set the machine for a long stitch. Sew just next to the seam line, in the seam allowance, the length of the piece to be gathered. Put a pin at one end of the row of stitching and wrap one end of the buttonhole thread around it. Pull the other end of the thread until the piece is the desired length. Buttonhole thread will not tear easily under stress as ordinary thread will.

Pressing Darts

When you are pressing darts to one side, place the tip of the dart near the narrow end of the ironing board with the bulk of the fabric hanging over the end of the board. This helps shape the garment and allows you to press the dart very flat and smooth without wrinkling the fabric near it.

Skirt Raising

If you have an A-line skirt that is just a little too long and a little too tight, don't despair—raise it. Remove the waistband and zipper and put the skirt on. Pull it up until it fits correctly at the hips. If you're lucky, you won't even have to alter the hemline. Tie a string around your waist and mark the skirt all the way around at the string. Take the skirt off and trim the top ⅝ inch above the marks. Reset the zipper (you'll have to open the seam a little) and sew the waistband back on. If the waistband fits as is, ease the skirt to fit; if it is a little tight, lengthen it by adding a piece of fabric that will be lapped under when the waistband is fastened.

Avoid Zipper Gaps

When you are putting an open-at-one-end zipper in slacks, a skirt, or a dress, cut the zipper tape to exactly ⅝ inch above the bars at the top of the zipper. Line up the ends of the tape with the top edge of the seam and you will avoid a gap above the zipper when you sew on the facing or waistband.

Oil Helps Vinyl Slide Smoothly

Artificial leathers and vinyl tend to stick to the pressure foot when you are top-stitching them. To make them glide along smoothly, moisten a cotton ball with baby oil and run it over the seam line on the right side, before stitching. Remember to thoroughly wipe the finished vinyl and the pressure foot to remove any traces of oil before sewing another fabric. Real and artificial suede will move more smoothly through the machine if the bottom of the pressure foot is covered with a piece of vinyl tape. Cut out the open areas after the tape is in place. Do not use baby oil on suede or any fabric other than vinyl.

Keep Appliqués in Place

To hold appliqué pieces while you sew around them, bond them in place with double-faced fusible interfacing. This is especially helpful when you're applying several small pieces. Felt appliqué can be held without stitching by coating the back of it with a thin layer of white glue, then pressing it in place with a hot iron.

Test Your Fabric

If you are uncertain of the fiber content of your fabric, test launder it and press a premeasured piece before you sew with it. To be on the safe side, do this even when you know the content, as the particular weave can make a difference in the reaction of a fabric to soap, detergent, water, or heat. Remeasure the piece after pressing to check for shrinkage, and compare the color with an unlaundered piece to be sure it's colorfast.

Front-to-Back Sewing

When you want to make an A-line skirt and the only fabric you really like is an uneven plaid, don't give up. Frequently it's almost impossible to tell the right side of the fabric from the wrong side. If this is the case with the fabric you have chosen, simply cut one front piece and one back piece of the skirt from a single thickness of the fabric, turn the fabric over, match the plaid, and cut the other two pieces.

Needlecrafts

Storing Embroidery Floss

A 60-drawer organizer like the ones used to store nuts and bolts makes a great cabinet for embroidery floss. Mark the front of each drawer with the color number of the floss for easy selection.

Keep Needlepoint Yarn Short

When doing needlepoint, don't use pieces of yarn more than 18 inches long. Yarn cut longer seems to thin down from all the stretching it gets while you're working with it, making it difficult to give the finished piece a smooth look.

Double-Knit Sweater Flbows

To strengthen the elbows of home-knit sweaters, thread a darning needle with a piece of matching yarn and weave along the knitted pattern to create a "double-knit" elbow patch. You will find that the knitted yarn has both a vertical and horizontal direction. Weave your matching yarn over and under the vertical yarn of the knitted pattern, and for extra protection, weave over and under the horizontal yarn as well.

Mending

Patch-In Knee Pads

When patching the knees of your gardening jeans, leave the top of each patch open like a pocket so that you can slip in pieces of foam rubber for knee pads. They will make kneeling more comfortable.

Prolonging the Life of Leather Goods

To prolong the life of leather gloves and house slippers, which always seem to outlast their stitching, resew them with dental floss. First rub the floss over a lump of beeswax to prevent fraying, and repeat every two or three stitches. Properly tightened and tied off, the new stitching should outlast the leather.

Reviving Frayed Shoelaces

Make frayed shoelaces usable again. Cut off the frayed end, then fold the end of the lace in half lengthwise. Put one or two staples through it, then stiffen the end with household cement or waterproof glue worked into the fabric. When dry, remove the staples; the new tip will thread readily and should last the life of the lace. Round and very narrow laces don't need to be stapled before being glued.

Another way to recycle shoelaces with missing tips is to dip each end in clear nail polish to stiffen it, or dip the end in glue, twist it to a point, and allow it to dry.

4 The Well-Maintained Home

Doors and Windows

Doors

Protect Outdoor Locks from Freezing

To keep precipitation from freezing up the padlocks on outbuildings, cut out a piece of inner tube (measuring roughly 6 inches square) and nail it over the lock as a flap.

Doors That Stick

To free a door that rubs on a high spot in the floor, securely tape a piece of rough sandpaper on the spot. Just through normal use, the door gradually will be sanded so that, after a few days, it will clear the obstruction. Then remove the sandpaper.

Doors That Won't Stay Open

Chances are you have a door in your home that refuses to stay ajar when you want it to. To remedy this problem, cut the brush end with an inch of handle off an old toothbrush, and drill two pilot holes in it to receive nails or screws. Remove the door and screw or nail the piece of brush to its underside. Or, to keep a door all the way open, attach the brush to the floor where the door reaches the end of its swing.

Doors That Exclude Noise

Modern hollow-core doors are as light in weight as they are transparent to sound. If you wish to cut down on the noise entering a room, install a solid door and see that it seats tightly; gaps can let in appreciable noise. You can use the hollow-core door on a closet or as a drafting or sewing table.

Saw twice to make 3 cabinet doors

Recycled Doors

Old frame-and-panel doors, available at auctions, dumps, and shops recycling building materials, are cheap and adaptable to several uses. Consider them for new closets or, sawed horizontally through the rails, for cabinet doors and frame-and-panel wainscoting.

Rx for Musty Closets

Air circulation discourages condensation. Replace a mildew-prone closet's solid doors with louvered doors to get rid of the problem.

Windows

Glazing Pointers

If you use a caulking gun to make your home more weathertight, you may have found that as you apply the material it has a nasty tendency to pile up, leaving an uneven and ugly finish. You can smooth and spread these clumps by rubbing over them with an ice cube. The caulking won't stick to the ice, and the result is a smooth finish.

When glazing a skylight or attached greenhouse with silicone sealant, wear clean cotton gloves to avoid leaving fingerprints. The silicone won't adhere to fingerprints.

To remove old putty that adheres to windowpanes, first remove the window from the casement and cut through the putty with a utility knife, keeping the blade parallel with and directly against the frame to avoid damaging it. Place strips of paper towel along the pane's edges and pour a small amount of lacquer thinner onto the towel. Once the putty has been soaked by the solvent, it will easily come off the glass.

When replacing windowpanes, you'll find that a butter knife does a good job of applying putty. Slowly and firmly draw the blade along the pane edge. The result is a clean, straight putty job with a pleasantly curved bevel.

Glazing windows can be a frustrating chore if the putty doesn't cooperate. Use a clean, smooth putty knife, and make sure that the putty is at least room temperature. A dirty, rough knife tugs at the putty, and cold putty won't spread properly.

Weatherstripping Materials Rated

Weatherstripping can cut your fuel bills by as much as 15 percent, but only if you use the right materials on properly hung windows and doors. Metal tension strips are the best possible choice for weatherstripping the sides of ordinary doors; standard door sweeps are best for sealing door bottoms; and metal or plastic tension strips are the best choice for standard, double-hung windows.

Glass with Maximum Gain

You'll get the greatest solar gain with a single pane of low-iron glass and the least with tinted glass.

Glazing Longevity

Which glazing material lasts the longest? Barring accidents, glass easily lasts half a century or more, compared with 25 years for acrylics, 10 to 15 years for polycarbonates, 8 to 12 years for fiberglass-reinforced polyester, 7 to 10 years for weatherable polyester, and just 8 months to a year for polyethylene.

Sunspace Framing

Aluminum loses heat 2,000 times faster than wood. When purchasing framing for a sunspace (or when buying new windows for your house), stick to wood (either treated with a preservative or clad on the exterior with aluminum for durability) or aluminum that has a built-in thermal break.

Flattering Flashing

Flashing around skylights and elsewhere on a home can be an eyesore, but you can have it blend in better with your house if you paint it. It must be treated before paint will adhere to it, though. First, prepare the surface by etching it with regular supermarket vinegar. Lightly wash the vinegar over the surface of the flashing, then wipe it off. Next, apply a coat of primer. Then spray-paint the flashing whatever color you like.

Old Glass

You *can* cut old glass even though it has a reputation for being extremely brittle. In fact, it is no more brittle than new glass, but it is apt to be thin and to have impurities and irregular inner tensions. Make sure the surface of the glass is clean before cutting, and use very little pressure with the wheel cutter.

Old Windows

To salvage old, weatherbeaten window frames and sashes, seal the wood with linseed oil before painting. Mix ½ cup of boiled linseed oil with ½ cup of paint thinner, and brush on liberally after scraping off loose paint. Allow the oil to dry at least 24 hours before applying a second coat. (Especially battered wood may benefit from a third application.) Give the oil at least three days to be absorbed before sanding lightly. Then apply an alkyd primer, and finish with either alkyd or latex paint.

Old Hardware

With time, old door and window hardware becomes caked with successive layers of paint and grime. To clean these items, remove them and place them in an enamel pan. Cover with water and add about 4 tablespoons of baking soda per quart of liquid. Place the pan over low heat and allow the mixture to simmer for 15 to 20 minutes; the paint should come off with the persuasion of a stiff brush. Return stubborn pieces to the pan for another 30 minutes or so of simmering.

When Brass Hardware Is Too Brassy

Traditional brass hardware is enjoying a comeback, but you may not care for the shiny, brand-new look of brass that's been protected with lacquer. If you want the brass to tarnish naturally, remove the finish with lacquer thinner. Air will then come in contact with the metal and oxidize it.

Window Security

For a simple lock on a sash window, drill a hole through the top edge of the bottom sash and at least halfway into the top of the bottom of the upper sash. Then insert a 3½-inch nail. This device will prevent the window from being opened from the outside, and it is invisible to would-be intruders. To ensure that the nail won't jiggle out, drill the hole at a slight downward angle. The nail should not be so tight that you can't remove it in a hurry, as in the event of a fire in the home. For greater security, drill two holes for two nail locks, one on either side of the window. Be careful to miss any seals that the sash may contain.

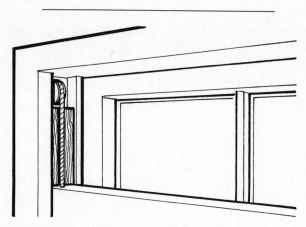

Another way of securing a double-hung sash window is to fashion a piece of wood that stands behind the sash cord. It should be tall enough to allow the lower sash to be raised about 6 inches—permitting fresh air to enter but not would-be thieves. Paint or stain the piece to blend in with the surrounding wood trim. The device can easily be removed if you want to raise the window all the way. (See also Doors and Windows in the chapter, Safe and Sound.)

Floors

Silence That Squeak

Squeaky floorboards that are otherwise in good shape can be silenced with a number of lubricants—powders, such as talcum or graphite, or liquid furniture wax. Just squirt a bit of the lubricant into the joint through a nozzle.

Thin Floorboards Go Down Easier . . .

If you're putting down tongue-and-groove wood flooring, the job will go easier with boards that are 6 inches or less in width. Almost inevitably, some of the boards will be bent, and it's much easier to force a narrow board into line.

. . . But Wide Floorboards Look Nice

You *can* lay boards a foot or two wide. But you'll have to drive counter-sunk screws and plug them—a time-consuming job. Expect wide boards to contract and show gaps in cool, dry weather; discount this as part of their rustic charm.

Refinishing

You don't necessarily need to rent massive power sanders to refinish an old varnished floor. If you aren't after a brand-new, down-to-bare-wood finish, try removing the varnish with water-soluble paint stripper, working gradually, in 4-foot squares. A scrub brush will help work the finish loose. Then sprinkle on a commercial compound known generically as oil-dry, used by garages to soak up the oil from floors. Brush off the oil-dry with a push broom, then clean the floor with paint thinner. It is now ready for an oil finish and waxing. The resulting flooring will have the rich patina that comes with age and will fit in better with older, traditionally furnished homes.

Tung Oil

For a floor finish that has a deep, waxy luster, use a tung oil product designed for floors rather than polyurethane. Oil intended for use on floors is not straight oil, but several ingredients blended for optimum drying and durability. Although oiled floors can be waxed and buffed periodically to keep up their appearance, a good tung oil finish can go waxless, with periodic applications of the product.

Removing Glued Carpet

Indoor-outdoor carpet is often glued down on floors or porches for a quick, cheap covering. But there's nothing quick about trying to remove the carpet once it's worn or stained. In well-ventilated areas, you can pour methylene chloride under the carpet, then scrape the carpet up with a wide-bladed putty knife or wallpaper scraper. Facilitate lifting the carpet by first cutting it with a utility knife. This method is messy and the fumes noxious. As an alternative, place dry ice on the carpet to make the glue brittle and vulnerable to the putty knife.

Unsticking Chewing Gum

Dry ice may also work for you on chewing gum—to help free it from floors and carpets. The gum becomes brittle and will break free. (For removing other stains from fabrics, see also Stain Removal in the chapter, Clothing Care.)

Removing Tiles and Linoleum

And the quick freezing of dry ice can remove stubborn floor tile or linoleum adhesive that defies scraping. You can make it brittle by placing big blocks of dry ice over it. After a few minutes, work at the chilled adhesive with a thin-bladed scraper.

Checking for Basement Dampness

Before you decide to convert a basement area to a room or work space, test the walls and floor for dampness. Tape a 12-inch square of plastic from a dry cleaning bag to the walls and floor at several places. (Be sure to tape all around the perimeter so that the plastic cannot vent.) If, after several days, moisture collects between the plastic and the surface, you have a dampness problem that will have to be solved before you start your project. Ideally, make this test in the spring, when the soil around the house is at its dampest.

Preventing Wood Rot

Guard against wood rot in your home by inspecting wooden framing members on a periodic basis. Look for wood that appears to be bleached out or that has brown crumbling patches on its surface. Poke any suspicious-looking wood with a screwdriver or ice pick. If the wood is spongy or splinters easily, then fungus probably has been at work. To help prevent further decay, scrub any small patches of dry rot with a wire brush, then rub table salt into the wood.

Basement Labels

Label the parts of the electrical and plumbing systems that lurk in your basement. Identify each fuse or circuit breaker, hot and cold water shutoffs, heating system controls, gas and water meters, and drain cleanout access covers. Use adhesive stickers or tags on strings. For those items that don't lend themselves to labeling, sketch a rough map and post it on the back of the basement door.

Cabinets and Furniture

Cabinets

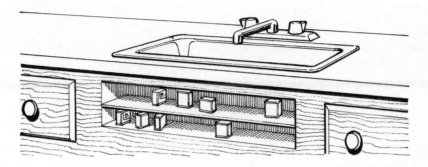

Built-In Spice Shelves

Kitchen cabinets often include one or two false drawer panels just below the sink because there isn't enough space for a drawer. But in many cases you can remove these panels and build in shallow shelves just deep enough to hold spice containers.

Make the Cabinets, but Buy the Doors

The trickiest part of making kitchen cabinets is the doors. Make your own cabinets, but save yourself time and the expense of special-purpose tools by purchasing ready-made doors from a woodworking firm (see the Yellow Pages for the companies that specialize in kitchens).

Countertops

Marble makes a great top for a counter, kitchen island, or baking center and can be bought fairly inexpensively at auctions and salvage businesses. But chances are that the pieces you find won't be the right size for your needs. To pay someone to cut the stone could undo the savings of salvaging the piece. You can do the job yourself if you have a router. Clamp the piece to the worktable, put on safety glasses, and trim the marble with a ¼-inch straight carbide bit. The work won't be as smooth as it would be if done by a professional, and you'll destroy the bit, but you can cut radiused corners and even make cutouts to suit your needs.

Everyone's familiar with slate roofs and blackboards, but slate countertops deserve a broader reputation. One-inch slabs of slate make a nearly indestructible work surface. Quarries may be able to polish the top, radius corners, and even make cutouts for a sink and cutting board.

To refinish an old soapstone countertop, use an orbital sander to get down to clean stone, fill holes with black epoxy paste, and bring out the color by rubbing in a very small amount of oil finish meant for wood.

Butcherblock

When oiling butcherblock, use a nontoxic product, such as vegetable oil or walnut oil, rather than a standard furniture oil.

For an inexpensive countertop that looks like butcherblock, edge-glue maple boards and hold under pressure with pipe or bar clamps until dry.

Adding Cedar to Your Closet

You can turn an ordinary closet into a cedar closet with little trouble. Thin, tongue-and-groove aromatic cedar boards are easy to nail up, and you need only cover part of a closet's interior to benefit from cedar's insect repellency.

Furniture

Filling Holes

When repairing holes and gaps in wood, you don't need costly plastic fillers. Use powdered wood putty and, instead of water, mix in latex or water-based paints or stains that you already have on the shelf. By experimenting, you can mix a wide range of wood tones. Always write down which mix worked with which wood.

You can make filler for woodworking by mixing sawdust from the wood with just enough Elmer's wood glue to make a workable putty. Once dried, the filler can be sanded and will take stain if little glue has been used.

Cleaning and Protecting Wood

Wash wood furniture with a solution of water and mild soap, such as Ivory or Murphy's Oil Soap. Dampen a cloth with the solution, wring it almost dry, and wipe the furniture section by section, drying with a clean, dry cloth as you go so that no section stays wet.

Before you set to work on an old piece of furniture with chemical finish removers, try an old standby — vegetable oil soap. This simple, nontoxic solvent may be all the help an antique needs.

Protect your wood furniture with a coat of oil *or* wax, but not both. You can put oil over oil, or wax over varnishes and shellacs. The only exceptions to this rule are self-sealing oils, like tung oil or one-step sealer stains, which harden to create a waxable coating.

To make a good-quality cabinetmaker's wax, melt 1 pound of yellow beeswax over hot water (*not* over direct heat; it could catch on fire), then cool slightly and add 1 pint of turpentine and 1 pint of boiled linseed oil. Let the mixture cool completely. Apply the wax with 0000 steel wool, and polish the wood with a soft cloth.

The Home's Exterior

Down in the Basement

Keeping It Dry

Clogged or improperly installed foundation drains can result in frost heaving and other foundation trouble. If you're having a problem with poor drainage, however, hold off tearing up your lawn until you've checked your gutters and downspouts. Clogged gutters or gutters that don't slope properly toward the downspouts may be the source of your problem.

Keeping It Warm

Have you isolated your basement from your living space by insulating the ceiling? If not, a foot of exposed, uninsulated concrete foundation around your home can account for as much as 22% of your total heat loss—and up to 28% if you live in a one-story home. (See also Heating in the chapter, Home Energy.)

Up on the Roof

Longevity of Materials

Need a new roof? When shopping for a replacement you generally get what you pay for. The ratio of cost and lifespan of three roofing materials, asphalt, cedar and slate, is 1:2:4.

Slate

A slate roof is expensive, but it will last about a century—probably longer, if the slate was quarried in Vermont or New York, and possibly less if it is Pennsylvania slate.

Since roofing slate often outlasts the building it covers, salvaged slate is occasionally available. To determine how much life is left in used slate, knock on it: Don't expect much wear from slate that sounds like wood or cardboard; good slate will have a ring to it when knocked, something like a heavy sheet of plate glass.

Roofing slates are usually punched with nail holes at the quarry, but you can make new holes in any of a few ways: Tap on the underside with the sharp head of a traditional slater's hammer; drive a nail through the underside; or drill holes with a ⅛-inch masonry bit.

Safety

When working on a roof with a pitch that threatens to send you sliding over an eave, tie one end of a lifeline around your waist and the other to a chimney or an immovable object on the other side of the house.

Walls, Etc.

Dampness from Within

Stained, blistered, or peeling paint on the house exterior is a telltale sign of condensation in the wall cavity. To deal with this problem, tighten up the inside of the house by sealing cracks and painting the walls with a vapor barrier paint, and reduce indoor humidity with proper ventilation.

Exposure Affects Weathering

Exterior walls may weather differently, depending upon what side of the house they're on because of the exposure to the elements each gets. Damage from the sun alone may mean you'll have to paint a south-facing wall twice as often as a north-facing one.

Mildew in Summer

In humid, warm weather, outside walls may become covered with mildew. Remove it by scrubbing with equal parts of ammonia and water. While household bleach also works against mildew, and can be sprayed on walls through a garden chemical sprayer that attaches to a garden hose, this solution may bleach paint and harm plantings below.

Fixing Loose Anchor Bolts in Concrete

When anchor bolts come loose from concrete, you can heat sulfur flowers until molten and pour the liquid around the leveled bolt. The sulfur will cool to become harder than concrete, and it enters every pore of loosened concrete.

A Stronger Concrete Wall

Here is an unconventional way of reinforcing a concrete wall with steel. Rather than buy steel rod or wire for the purpose, collect old bedsprings, wire them together as needed, place them in the ditch dug for the footer or wall, and dump in stones and concrete. The complex network of metal should make the structure a good deal stronger, at no cost.

Window Boxes

There are a couple of advantages to affixing window boxes to your house with pinned door hinges. You can tip up the boxes when painting the house; and by pulling the pins, you can remove the boxes to work with the flowers, make repairs, or bring perennials indoors for the winter.

Laying Decking

When laying wooden decking or porch flooring, try to install it barkside to the weather. You can tell the barkside (or outward-facing side) by looking at the curve of the annual rings on the end grain: These concentric rings should appear as a hill, rather than a valley. Boards laid this way will be less inclined to cup or split.

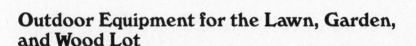

Outdoor Equipment for the Lawn, Garden, and Wood Lot

Chainsaws and Wet Wood

To keep a chainsaw from binding when cutting wet wood, wipe the entire bar with bar or chain oil as needed (when the saw is off!).

A Homemade Chainsaw Protector

Make a chainsaw protector from a section of ⅝- to ¾-inch rubber hose twice the length of your chainsaw bar. Slit the entire length of the hose

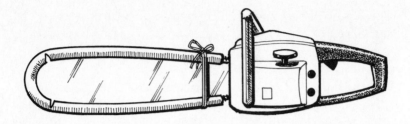

and slide it over the chain. Mark the hose where it will cover the top and bottom of the curved tip, then remove the hose and make two V-shaped notches about halfway through the hose. These notches will let the saw protector wrap around the bar tip without buckling. Put the hose back on your saw and tie it near the base of the bar with a short piece of string or twine. Now your chainsaw is ready for the bumpiest forest road.

A Handy Chainsaw Oil Container

A plastic mustard squeeze-bottle is the perfect container for chainsaw oil. It's convenient to carry along, eliminates the need for a funnel, and prevents drips and spills.

Chainsaw Oil

Chainsaw owners: Take note of the special oil sold for lubricating motor-cycle chains. It sprays on as a liquid, dries to a film, and contains molybdenum disulfide and other lubricants. The spray is especially good for saws without automatic oilers.

Spare Parts Kit for Chainsaws

Assemble a spare parts kit to keep your chainsaw at work. A chain loop (or even two), a spare bar of the right length and type, a clutch assembly,

Hold onto That Manual

Operator's manuals are valuable: They tell how to safely use an appliance or tool, where to get it repaired, and often how to make adjustments or repairs yourself. They also enhance the value of an item if you eventually should decide to sell it. But these manuals tend to disappear, in the shop or in the bottoms of drawers. Place them in a folder and tuck the folder in the home files. In the workshop, manuals can be hung on a nail near the tool they pertain to.

and a spark plug will cover most of the failures apt to occur in the middle of a job. These are parts that you will use eventually anyway, so this insurance costs nothing extra.

When to Sharpen Your Chainsaw

A dull chainsaw chain slows your progress greatly. It's time to sharpen a chain when you notice that the saw is producing fine sawdust instead of chips.

Tightening the Chain

Once installed, a new chainsaw chain will stretch out after a half-dozen log cuts or so, to the point that it should be tightened again. Do this to minimize wear and, more important, to keep the chain on the bar.

Protecting Your Axe Handle

To protect an axe handle from overswings that could crack it, wrap it near the head with strips of inner tube. The rubber acts as a resilient bumper.

When Splitting Logs

To keep logs upright when splitting them, set them within two old tires, stacked one upon the other. This also serves to keep splits from flying across the yard, and if you swing short the head will hit rubber rather than blade-damaging dirt and stones.

For an Even Pour

When pouring a liquid (such as gasoline or oil) from an unvented oblong can, hold the container as shown to get the most even flow. This works best because it allows air to easily enter the can and displace the fluid.

Wintering Your Mower

At the end of the grass-cutting season, drain both gasoline and oil from your lawn mower. Oil should be drained so that corrosive contaminants won't have all winter to damage internal parts. Evaporating gas will leave a hard, gummy scum in the carburetor and fuel lines and cause starting problems come spring. After draining the gas, run the engine to use up the dregs, then remove the spark plug and squirt a couple of shots of oil into the cylinder. Pull the starter cord a few times to distribute the oil inside the cylinder, and reinstall the plug. Finally, drain the oil out of the crankcase.

When Mowing a Wet Lawn

A lawn that's damp with dew or a recent rain is apt to clog the blades of a hand lawn mower. Before beginning to mow, coat the blades with vegetable oil. An easy way to do this is to fill a plant sprayer with oil and spray the blades as needed. (You can also use the oil to keep snow from sticking to a snow shovel and making it unnecessarily heavy.)

How to Hang a Swing without Leaving the Ground

To throw a line over a tree limb for anything from a child's swing to a radio aerial, use a fishing rod with a 4-ounce sinker tied to a leader of 30-pound test line. The leader will pull up the swing rope or aerial wire.

Long-Lived Fence Posts

Locust is the favorite wood for long-lived fence posts. But you can prolong the life of any wood with this simple trick. Pull a length of old inner tube over the bottom of the post, leaving enough extra so that the tube will fold over the ground and form a seal as the post is placed into its hole.

Repairing a Broken Bucket

To mend a cracked plastic bucket that leaks, all you need is an old table knife and a lighted candle. Heat the knife in the flame, then press the hot blade against the crack and rub slowly. The hot knife will melt the plastic and seal the crack.

Give Batteries a Second Chance

If you suspect that your flashlight is dimming prematurely, take out the batteries and clean the terminals with a pencil eraser. This removes oxides that may have built up, allowing current to flow more freely.

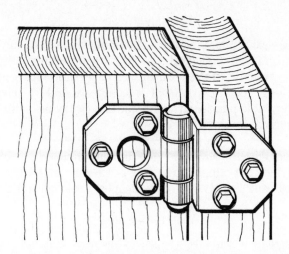

Heavy-Duty Hinges for Gates

For heavy-duty gate hinges, try car-door or truck-door hinges. They're readily available and can be anchored securely with lag bolts.

Painting and Stripping

Finishes May Be Hazardous to Your Health

Heat Guns

When removing old paint with a heat gun, remember to ventilate the room thoroughly, and use a respirator if available. A heat gun can cause volatilization of the lead in old paint, which may then be inhaled and absorbed into your bloodstream.

Indoors, Choose Latex

Don't use oil-based paint or paint stripper in a poorly ventilated room. Its ingredients may cause headaches and blurred vision, even brain damage and heart attacks. The room's air should be changed completely one to three times per hour. A breeze blowing through an open window isn't good enough; use two window fans, one to blow in fresh air and one to exhaust polluted air. Better yet, use latex paints indoors (they're water- based) and restrict oil-based paints and paint strippers to outdoor use. And even when using latex, good ventilation is still advisable.

Masks and Gloves

You should wear a paper mask when sanding or scraping any kind of paint, but paint containing lead is particularly hazardous. Suspect any paint made earlier than the 1960s. You can have paint chips analyzed for lead by a local health department or college laboratory. The cost of scraping away lead paint from your home may be tax deductible; check with the Internal Revenue Service.

Wear rubber gloves when working with paint remover. The chemicals not only irritate the skin, but also may permeate it and travel through your bloodstream. (See also Skin in the chapter, Look and Feel Your Best.)

Wood Preservative

Wood preservative is applied from a can like paint, but don't think of it as paint. By law, it is classified as a pesticide, and indeed it works by killing or repelling animal and plant life. Keep this in mind when using, storing, and disposing of it.

Protect Yourself with Vitamin C

When you have been exposed to chemical fumes from paint, finishes, or paint remover, consider increasing your intake of vitamin C, either in tablet form or through foods rich in this nutrient. Vitamin C acts as an antitoxicant, offering a measure of protection against certain chemicals.

Painting
(See also The Home's Exterior, in this chapter.)

Wet Wood Caution

If you can't wait for wood to dry thoroughly before painting, use water-based paint. Oil-based paint will float on damp wood and eventually peel; water-based paint will merge with the moisture in the wood and do a passable job of sticking.

Varnish Shouldn't Be Shaken

Never stir varnish. It has no color pigments that need blending, and stirring it will create air bubbles that can ruin an otherwise smooth finish.

Painting Metal

Before painting metal, prepare the surface by scraping it with a wire brush, cleaning it with a solvent such as lacquer thinner, washing it with detergent and water, and finally drying it.

If You Run Out of Paint in the Middle of a Job

Not sure you bought enough paint for a job? Then paint only as many walls as you can cover completely. If you have more paint mixed up, it is apt to be a slightly different shade, but when each wall is done entirely from one can or another, this difference is minimized. Because walls receive light of varying quality, we expect them to appear slightly different in hue anyway.

Perfume Your Paint

If you're bothered by the smell of oil-based paint, try adding 1 tablespoon of vanilla extract to a gallon of paint.

Stain Stamina

A coat of penetrating stain applied to a smooth wood surface may last only two to four years, but a second application, after the wood has weathered some, will last as long as ten.

Tobacco Stain

An inexpensive homemade stain can be brewed from a plug of dark chewing tobacco. Break up the plug and soak it in 1 pint of household ammonia. Cover the container and allow it to stand overnight, then strain it through a stocking. Use one to three coats to achieve the shade you're after, allowing at least 3 hours between coats. If the stain is applied indoors, provide ventilation to disperse the noxious ammonia fumes. Allow 48 hours drying time before sealing or varnishing.

Storing Leftover Paint

Most homeowners save leftover paint for eventual touch-up jobs. You can lengthen the storage life of these remnants by protecting the contents from freezing and the cans from rusting.

In time, a partly used can of paint or finish will develop a skin on top. When you're about to put away a can that won't be opened for a while, cut a disk of wax paper to the can's diameter, and simply drop it onto the surface of the paint before replacing the lid. The air in the can won't be able to react with the product, creating a skin.

Here's a simple way to have the skin form on the bottom of the can of paint (rather than on the top), where it won't do much harm. Hammer on the lid firmly and invert the can when you put it on the shelf (you may want to place the can over a foil pie plate until you're certain it's sealed). A skin will form, but it'll be on the bottom of the can and out of your way.

Brushes for Tight Spots

When painting inside corners, trim the paint brush's bristles to a V to save strokes and spread paint more evenly.

Absorbent Rags Are Best

Clean, soft rags come in handy for many household projects, including the spreading of certain oil-based finishes. But not every scrap from the rag bag works equally well; polyester blends aren't as absorbent or as soft as cotton. A good, cheap source of first-rate rags is a diaper service. They may sell you their worn diapers by the pound.

Synthetic vs Natural-Bristle Brushes

The next time you shop for paint brushes, remember that synthetic bristles (of nylon or polyester) are the best choice for latex paint. The water in this paint will degrade the bristles in natural-bristle brushes, which are intended for oil paint.

A Homemade Paint Pad for Screens

Need to paint a screen for a window or door? Tack a small square of short-nap carpet to a block of wood and use it as a paint pad. Dip it in paint and then squeeze most of the paint out of the pad by wiping it with a putty knife—otherwise, the paint will be too heavy and will block the openings in the screen.

Cleanup

Temporary Storage between Paintings

A good deal of the time spent in painting is devoted to cleanup, even if you use latex paint. On a job with latex paint that will stretch over a few days, place the tray, brush, and roller—unwashed—into a plastic bag and store it in the freezer. At least an hour before you're ready to resume work, take out the bag and allow its contents to warm up.

Help for Abused Brushes

Water-soluble paint remover is ideal for cleaning paint brushes, especially if they're hardened with old paint or varnish. Let them soak for a couple of days and then rinse them with water.

Making Cleanup Easier

You'll find it easier to get your hands clean after working in the garage or shop if you rub in a little waterless hand cleaner *before* you start the job. Rub it in well, getting it under and around the fingernails, and wipe off the excess. Don't rinse. The protective layer of cleaner prevents dirt from adhering to your skin.

Avoiding Paint-Lid Buildup

One of the messiest parts of a paint job is replacing the can's lid. When you pound it down securely, paint is apt to squirt out in any direction. To avoid the buildup of paint around the recessed rim, take this precaution as soon as you first open the can: Using a hammer and nail, punch holes at regular intervals all around the inside of the rim. The paint will drip through these holes and back into the can.

Preventing Clogged Nozzles

To keep spray paint can nozzles from clogging, remove the nozzles after use and store them in a small jar filled with paint thinner.

Stripping

Different Methods for Different Finishes

When you reach an impasse in removing finishes, switch to another stripping method. A heat gun works well on most paint, but if you come to a layer of old-fashioned milk paint, try ammonia; if you come to a layer of varnish, try a chemical paint stripper.

Stripping Hardware

You can strip the paint from old hardware with a simple homemade mixture of wood ashes and water. Place a pound or two of ashes in 3 or 4 gallons of water. Stir to release the caustic sodium and potassium hydroxides present in the ashes (although most of the ash is insoluble and will sink to the bottom). Add the items and soak them overnight. Then, wearing gloves, scrub the hardware with a toothbrush. If only the top layer of paint comes off, give the items a second treatment.

Stripping Shellac

If you go through lots of denatured alcohol when stripping old shellac from furniture and household trim, you may appreciate a cheaper source for the solvent than the hardware store. Gas stations selling gasohol may have straight alcohol for sale, at less than half the price.

Stripping Varnish

Before you tackle the job of removing multilayered varnish from old woodwork, try salvaging the finish by cleaning it with a strong household cleaner such as Fantastic. This works to remove the top layer of varnish and may restore the finish to an acceptable degree. Or you can make your own solution from equal parts of boiled linseed oil, turpentine, and white vinegar. Rub it in with fine steel wool. The last resort is a chemical remover, necessitating a toxicity mask (not a simple dust mask) or very good ventilation.

Making a Stripper Work Harder

Paint stripper tends to drip off furniture and woodwork before it has a chance to do its job fully. Try dribbling sawdust over the stripper to help the chemical adhere. If you don't have sawdust on hand, call on a local woodworking or millwork shop.

Plumbing

Pipe-Wrench Physics

You can double the leverage of a pipe wrench, with small chance of damaging it, by sliding over the handle a piece of pipe that's up to twice the handle's length. Do not do this with regular-duty adjustable wrenches, as they will not hold up under the added strain.

Dealing with Drips

Fix those leaky faucets. At a couple of drops a second, a leaky hot water faucet can drip over 1,000 gallons a year—equal to pouring a swimming pool's worth of hot water down the drain.

It's not difficult to replace the worn washer in a leaky faucet, but shopping for the proper size washer may be time consuming. When you do install a replacement, attach two or three extras to the shutoff valve below the sink, using a paper clip or piece of wire so that you always have the right size spare when you need it.

Septic-Tank Sludge

If the sludge on the bottom of your septic tank, together with the layer of material floating in the tank, is more than 12 to 15 inches thick, it's probably time to pump out the tank.

Unclogging Drain Lines

A hand-powered plumber's snake will clear drain lines that resist all attempts with a plunger. If used in conjunction with a running garden hose, it can even clear a blockage in the main drain to the street. First crank the snake and feed it into the pipe. Then withdraw the snake and flush the pipe by inserting a garden hose with the water turned on full blast. With a little bit of luck, this procedure may save you an expensive housecall by a plumber.

Emergency Repair

With an old inner tube and a couple of automotive hose clamps in the smaller sizes, you can keep a leaky pipe from flooding the basement. Cut a patch to cover the leaking section and secure it with the hose clamps for an instant (if temporary) seal.

Caulking with a Loaded Tub

If you find you're caulking around the bathtubs and sinks in your home every year or two, try this. Fill the bathtubs and sinks with water before applying the sealant, then leave them filled until the caulk has dried. This eliminates subsequent stretching of the caulk when the weight of water is added during daily use.

Bathroom Electrical Receptacles

In most locales, the electrical code requires that new bathroom receptacles be ground-fault interrupting—that is, the receptacle switches off if the current is leaking. These receptacles also make sense where electric tools will be used in damp places and where young children might place objects in the socket.

Protect Pipes from Freezing

Although special insulating jackets are sold to protect home plumbing in cold weather, you can keep pipes from freezing simply by wrapping them in fiberglass batts, 3½ inches thick and foil faced. Wearing gloves, cut the batts into strips, and wrap them around the pipe. Use duct tape —a strong, wide tape sold by hardware stores—to hold the insulation to the pipes.

A Soldering Tip

It's nearly impossible to solder a pipe joint if even the least amount of water is coming down the line. To absorb moisture before it can reach the joint, stuff a piece of bread up the pipe. Once the soldering job is done and the water is turned on, the bread will break up and be washed away.

Tools and Techniques

Tightening Up a Loose Screw

If a screw's hole is too large, whether because of wear or because you drilled it that way, you still can achieve a snug fit. Place one or two wooden matchsticks in the hole (minus the heads) so that the screw meets some resistance when it goes in.

Preventing Wood Splits When Nailing

You can keep a nail from splitting brittle or thin wood by drilling a pilot hole first, as you would for a screw; by lubricating the nail with soap or oil; or by blunting the nail's point (the wedged point of a sharp nail tends to part the woodgrain just as a log splitting wedge does, whereas a blunt point pushes fibers through to the other side, in effect punching a hole).

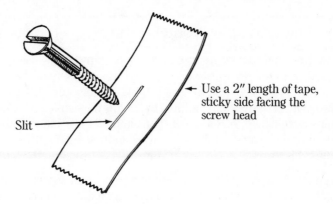

Use a 2″ length of tape, sticky side facing the screw head

Slit

Keep Screws from Slipping

To hold a screw to the end of a screwdriver when working in a hard-to-reach place, try this alternative to a magnetized blade. Cut a ½-inch slit in a piece of tape, as shown, and insert the screw shank up to the head. Then put the screwdriver into the head and fold the tape back to the blade. Once the screw is started, just pull the tape free.

Brass screws won't be drawn to a magnetic screwdriver, but small ones can be held in place by pressing a little beeswax into the slot of the head. Beeswax is available at hardware stores.

Rust-Free Nailing

In outdoor build-it projects, rust stains can spoil the appearance of a job. Bright nails offer little resistance to rust; nails plated with zinc are better. Least vulnerable to rust are nails dipped in molten zinc.

Lubrication for Nails and Screws

A block of paraffin comes in handy around the shop. Rub it on screws or nails to ease their entry into wood. You can also rub it on drawer guides for smoother operation; draw it over saw blades to keep them from binding; and apply it to the sole plates of electric tools to make them slide easily over the work.

Carpenters have found that beeswax will speed the entry of nails into hardwood or knots. But how can you arrange to have the wax on hand when you need it, especially when you're outdoors or up on a ladder? Simple: Drill a small hole into the base of the hammer handle and fill it with beeswax. Just dip nails into the hole before pounding them home.

Nail and Lumber Nomenclature

Don't be confused by the peculiar nomenclature that history has attached to the standard nail. "Penny" is a measure of the nail's length and is calculated by this formula: Simply subtract ½ from the length of the nail and multiply by 4. Only the shank is measured, not the thickness of the head. For example, if a job requires a 2½-inch nail, you should ask for an 8-penny nail (2½ minus ½ is 2, times 4 is 8).

Lumber is described by its nominal size, an industry convention that may confuse you on your first few trips to the lumberyard. For example, a 2 × 6-inch board in fact measures 1½ × 5½ inches; all narrower boards similarly are ½ inch less than their common name. On widths described as 8 inches or greater, the actual width is less by ¾ inch.

Folding Sandpaper

To make a sheet of sandpaper fold more easily to a useful size, first draw it over the edge of the workbench, back and forth. This gently and minutely fractures the thin layer of adhesive, which would otherwise be brittle.

Longer Life for Your Sandpaper

If used with an orbital sander or sanding block, fine-grit sandpaper may tear long before it is worn out. Try applying self-adhesive contact paper to the back of the sandpaper; the abrasive particles will wear out before the paper does. You can also buy adhesive-backed sandpaper.

To give extra life to worn sanding belts, remove them and reinstall them so that they'll revolve opposite to the manufacturer's recommendation. Unless you sand close to the edge of a board, the belt's glue joint probably will hold.

A Sanding Block

You can make a long-lasting sanding block by cutting a block of wood to fit snugly inside a sandpaper belt that's sold for belt sanders. The belt and its abrasive are highly durable. If the grit gets blocked up with paint or sawdust, rotate the belt aroud the block to expose fresh grit. As the belt rounds the corners of the block, most of the buildup will be dislodged.

Scrape, Don't Sand

For an ultra-smooth surface, don't sand—scrape. Draw a piece of Swedish steel, made for the purpose, over the work to shave off minute layers of wood. The result will be glassy smooth, without the tiny abrasions left by the particles in even the finest of sandpapers.

An Easier-to-Read Framing Square

Is your steel framing square getting hard to read? First, rub it down with 00 steel wool. Brush or spray on a coat of white oil-based paint, making sure to fill all of the indentations on the square. Then lightly wipe off the excess paint, leaving paint in the now easy-to-read measurements.

The Carry-Everywhere Ruler

You've got a fairly accurate ruler at the end of your arm. Measure and memorize the span of your outstretched hand, between the tips of pinky and thumb. (Note that your two hands may not be the same size.) Additionally, measure your fingers until you find a segment that comes close to an inch (try the distance from the thumb's second joint to its tip).

For Measurement Note-Taking

Have trouble keeping measurements in your head? Place a piece of masking tape on your folding rule or carpenter's rule, and you'll have a handy place to jot down those figures.

Dowel It

If nailing seems an unsightly way of doing a job, and you don't want to bother concealing nail holes with putty, try using an earlier form of the nail—the wooden dowel. Dowels can be cut from hardwood rods, carried by most hardware stores in several diameters. After drilling a test hole to check for snugness, drill through the piece to be attached and then into the second piece. Flatten the dowel on one side, either by filing or by hammering lightly, so that excess glue in the hole has a means of escape. Then place glue in the hole, spread more along the length of the dowel, and drive the dowel home, allowing some of it to remain outside the hole. When the glue has dried, either chisel or saw off the dowel close to the surface; it's best to protect the surface with a few layers of tape before you do this. Then sand down the remaining stub.

Clamping Cleanly

To prevent wood clamps from becoming part of the furniture when you're gluing joints, wrap a sheet of wax paper around each newly glued joint before clamping.

Removing Excess Glue from Joints

When a glued joint is clamped, excess wood glue is squeezed out. You can clean up immediately with warm water, but a thin finish-repelling coating may be left. Instead, try slicing off the partially hardened bead of surplus glue with a sharp wood chisel, an hour or so after assembling the joint.

A Rubber Band Clamp

For inexpensive gluing clamps suited to smaller projects, try the rubber bands sold by hobby stores as model airplane motors. Look for bands that come in rolls, and purchase a 5- or 6-foot length. You can wrap the bands around an object of almost any shape. They'll exert a great deal of pressure without marring the finish.

Longer-Lasting Drill Bits

Drill bits last longer if lubricated before each use. Ordinary lard is cheaper and better (it stays on the bit) than cutting oil. Just keep a jar of lard on the workbench.

A Homemade Drill Stop

To drill holes of a limited depth, make a drill stop from a section of a bottle cork. Measure the protruding length of bit frequently to make sure the stop hasn't shifted.

Tools for Less

If you're considering the purchase of an expensive power tool or workbench, check the ads of mail-order companies in woodworking magazines. These firms are intensely competitive, and their prices are low.

Spare Caps for Glue Tubes

When the top of a glue or caulking tube splits or is lost, the result is a sticky mess. For a sturdy, easy-to-grip replacement, try a wire nut, used to splice wires. Wire nuts come in many sizes and never break.

Lubrication for Knots

The next time you have trouble untying a stubborn knot, try lubricating it with a dusting of talcum powder.

A More Powerful Wrench

If you need a little extra leverage when using a combination wrench, simply hook the box end of another wrench onto the open end of the one you're using.

Overcoming Rust

When you are confronted with a mechanical part that's rusted solid, tie a cloth around the affected part and saturate it with penetrating oil such as WD-40. Allow the cloth to remain in place overnight before attempting to loosen the part.

When Your Hammer Makes a Bad Bounce

Do you have a hammer that seems to deflect unnaturally? The face of the head may be too smooth. Simply sand the face with emery cloth to roughen the metal slightly.

Cutting Plastic

To cut plastic sheets, use a circular saw with a small-toothed blade that's installed backward. The cut will be cleaner than if the blade rotated normally.

Repairing Work Clothes

Ordinary thread won't stand up to the abuse suffered by work clothes. To sew up the rips in your overalls, pants, and shirts, use either carpet thread or shoe repairman's thread. These are made up of woven nylon threads, but unlike the nylon monofilament sold in sewing stores, they are flexible and easy to sew with, as well as strong. Use a big-eyed upholstery needle, available from either a shoe repair shop or carpet store.

Safety Shoes Are Recommended

As comfortable as sneakers may be, they offer little resistance to rusty nails around a carpentry job. If work boots are too hot and heavy for you, try a lightweight hiking boot with fabric sides and a sturdy lug sole.

The Convenience of a Carpenter's Belt

You don't have to be a union carpenter to benefit from a carpenter's belt. By keeping tools and nails right at hand, the belt yields both convenience and safety—you won't be climbing ladders and scaling roofs with things clutched in your hands.

Walls

Drywall

Water-Resistant Sheets

Drywall, also known as gypsum board, becomes weak and crumbly when wet. If you plan to drywall a bathroom, use the water-resistant variety, identified by its green paper covering.

How to Locate Cutouts

Before nailing up a sheet of paneling or drywall, place a small bead of caulking around light switches and outlets. Then put the sheet in place and tap around the areas to be cut out. The back of the sheet will bear marks where you should cut holes.

Taping Tips

To smooth drywall compound at the seams, allow it to dry. Then, instead of sanding, dampen a terrycloth towel or sponge and rub lightly. The surface will soften, filling in low spots and leveling high spots— all without creating dust. A very light sanding may be needed for a perfect finish.

Priming drywall before taping offers two advantages: The water is not sucked rapidly out of the taping compound, and the drywall's paper covering isn't scratched when joints and nail dimples are sanded. After sanding, dust with a damp rag and then prime these spots with a paint primer. The primer accentuates uneven areas, making it easier to smooth low spots with joint compound.

If you're impatient to paint a new wall and don't have time to wait for the joint compound to dry, speed up the drying with a heat gun (used to remove paint) or a hairdryer. You'll soon be able to get on with papering or painting.

Plaster

Keeping Plaster from Drying Too Quickly

To keep plaster from drying out too quickly as you patch cracks, add a little vinegar to it—about 2 tablespoons to a quart of plaster.

Easy Patching

Small cracks and holes in a plaster wall can be patched simply with joint compound. It's inexpensive when purchased in quantity and spares you the mess of mixing patching plaster.

Wallpaper, Etc.

Removing the Old

Wallpaper is typically removed by wetting it down or steaming it. But the water won't penetrate if the papered wall has been painted. Remedy this by scratching through the paint with very coarse sandpaper or a wire brush; slashing a grid of cuts into the surface with a utility knife; dragging an old handsaw blade sideways across the walls; or using a wallpaper scratcher made for the purpose and available at hardware stores.

Before scraping off old wallpaper, spray it with a solution of hot water and about a tenth as much clear (distilled) vinegar. Use a plant mister with a big, comfortable squeeze handle.

Hanging the New

As you put up wallpaper, spray Lysol or another brand of antibacterial agent on the damp, pasted side (but don't risk staining the paper with an oil-based disinfectant). This will guard against the chance that mildew will grow in the paste and discolor the paper. (Note that some pastes and papers come with a chemical agent to discourage mildew.)

An inexpensive and interesting alternative to wallpaper is fabric. Strips of fabric are glued up as you would paper. The seams won't be ruler-straight because cloth is so flexible, but this may add to the soft, textural look.

Paper a wall of a study or children's room with topographic maps. Place your own quadrangle in the middle of one wall, and work out from there.

Trim the borders from each sheet, and apply the sheets to the wall with a light, smooth coat of wallpaper paste.

How to Find a Stud

You can locate wall studs without a commercial stud finder. Just use a compass, noting when the needle jumps.

A Soundproofed Wall

To cut down on noise carrying through walls, increase the weight of the wall surfaces. You can do this by nailing ½-inch insulating board on one or both sides of a wall and then covering the board with gypsum board that's at least ½ inch thick—the thicker, the better.

The Workshop

Plywood

Sheathing

When sheathing a stud wall, keep in mind that plywood installed with its grain running parallel to the grain of the studs is weaker than plywood installed "horizontally," i.e., with the grain running perpendicular to the studs.

Storage

Plywood will warp if not stored properly. Lay pieces flat, if possible, and support them at least every 12 inches. They also may be stored perpendicular to the ground if no less than ½ inch thick.

Plywood Pluses and Minuses

Plywood is synthesized lumber, in effect, made up of glued wood veneers. Its advantages are stability (each ply runs at right angles to its neighbors), strength in certain applications, relatively low cost, and availability in large sizes. A main disadvantage is appearance—edges that show the plies and may have to be covered with solid-wood edging; and a grain that may show through paint if you select a lower grade. Also, the glue quickly wears saw blades and router bits.

Grades

In shopping for plywood, save money by picking a grade that is no better than your purpose calls for. Both face veneers of a sheet are graded by letters, marked on the wood. If you plan to use a clear finish on a face, spend a little extra for grade N, a hardwood veneer without imperfections; you also may want this grade if you're after a particularly smooth surface for paint. Next best is A, which may show repairs to the face veneer but is intended to take paint. Grades B, C, and D are successively rougher—and cheaper. An A-D sheet (one face grade A and the other D) will work as well as more expensive A-A plywood if only one face will be visible, as in the bottom shelf of a cabinet.

If you are using plywood where it will be exposed to the weather or to water, select a sheet made with exterior-grade glue. Plywood marked "EXT" is for exterior use; "INT" stands for "interior."

Cutting without Splinters

Sheets of plywood tend to splinter when you cut them with a hand-held circular saw because the teeth of the saw pass upward as the blade rotates. To combat splintering, retract the blade so that it extends only about one tooth's length below the bottom of the sheet. Adjusted this way, the teeth come up through the wood at a shallower angle and will be less apt to make splinters.

Clear vinyl tape prevents tearout when a power saw is cutting across the grain of the surface veneer of fine hardwood-veneered plywoods.

Doorskin

A handy material to have around the workshop is doorskin—cheap and fairly attractive sheets of luan mahogany plywood. Doorskin has many uses. It makes good splines, because it fits neatly into a ⅛-inch saw kerf. Use it to spline wood together when gluing up. Doorskin serves as cabinet backs and drawer bottoms, again fitting into a ⅛-inch kerf. A strip of doorskin placed behind a piece of wood to be crosscut prevents tearout as the sawblade exits the wood. It can also be used as a template for dowel alignment. Drill right through a piece of doorskin into one wood piece, then flip the doorskin piece and carefully drill through the same holes into the second piece of wood.

Wood

Consider Local Lumber

A money-saving alternative to buying kiln-dried lumber at the lumber-yard or home center is the local sawmill. You're apt to find interesting woods not carried elsewhere, such as poplar, sassafras, fruitwoods, and regional species. You may have to settle for rough-sawn wood if the mill lacks a planer; this means smoothing the boards yourself, either at a millwork shop or at home with a planer. Given the time and muscle, hand planes will also do the job.

Rough Wood Is Cheaper

You'll pay less for lumber that is planed on one side only, and often the rough side will be concealed anyway.

Have Large Orders Delivered

If you are about to place a large order at a home center or sawmill, check their policy on delivery. It may be free on orders above a certain amount, sparing you the bother and expense of picking up the materials.

Confounding Cuts

When you're faced with cutting a piece of wood in a difficult place—so that you're using your weaker hand, or holding the saw upside down—try using an inexpensive dovetail saw. This handy tool is lightweight, cuts with a short stroke, and works rapidly because of its many tiny teeth.

Green Lumber

If you buy green lumber from a local sawmill, paint the ends of each board as you sticker them to dry. This will slow the release of the wood's water to the atmosphere and discourage checking at the ends.

Safety

Keep It Neat

A cluttered, sawdust-filled shop encourages accidents. Keep the floor around machines clear of obstructions that could trip you at a vulnerable moment. Sweep up sawdust as necessary: It may make your shop floor slippery, just as sand does on a shuffleboard table.

Scare Tactic

Woodworker Jeff Hufsey of Florida offers this novel safety tip. "The most effective thing that I've done to ensure safe practices is to take an hour, go through the phone book, and compile a list of all of the surgeons in the area who specialize in reconstructive hand surgery. I called each office and checked which hospitals are used by which surgeon. I neatly typed the name, phone number, and hospital, laminated the page in plastic, and nailed the list prominently to my workbench. This experience was nearly traumatic, and I have only to glance over at the list to become super-careful."

Metal Workbench Caution

If you use a metal workbench, ground it to a water pipe to protect yourself in case of a short while you're working with electrical equipment. This is especially vital if the floor is damp concrete.

When Working Outside with Power Tools

You run an added risk of electrical shock when using power tools outdoors. Protect yourself by installing a GFI (ground fault interrupter) outlet box. When this device detects minute leakages of current, it breaks the circuit.

Note Your Temperament

Your mood can predispose you to a workshop accident. Some experienced woodworkers will not use their power tools if they feel under the weather, tired, or just plain blue. (In fact, injured woodworkers have reported that their accidents were preceded by the notion that something was about to go wrong.)

Storage and Organization

Little Things

Store nails, screws, bolts, and washers in plastic-lidded coffee cans. Rather than label them, just tape a representative item to the outside of each can.

Sharp Things

To protect files stored in a drawer, line the drawer bottom with a piece of scrap carpet. This keeps the files from banging into one another and damaging their tiny teeth each time the drawer is opened and closed.

When stored among other tools, sharp hatchets, saws, and drawknives are a hazard both to themselves and to you. Make a simple blade guard by cutting a piece of garden hose the length of the blade, then slitting the hose so that it will fit over the sharp edge. Carefully honed edges will last longer, and you'll be less likely to cut yourself while reaching for tools.

Hard-to-Find Things

On the wall of your workshop, keep a list of the tools you misplace most often. Then take the list to the hardware store, and buy a spare of each item. You'll save yourself much time and distress if you keep on hand a second tape measure, phillips-head screwdriver, hammer, combination square—any small item that tends to get lost.

Moisture-Sensitive Things

Sealable plastic food storage containers are ideal for storing sanding belts or sheets of sandpaper. They prevent moisture from shortening the life of these abrasive sheets.

To protect rust-sensitive tools, place them in a drawer with this simple device: Perforate the lid of a small glass jar, and fill the jar with silica gel, a desiccant that can be renewed in the oven.

Keep Instructions at Hand

Before beginning a workshop project, place your step-by-step assembly instructions on a clipboard. Hang the clipboard in a visible place and keep track of your progress as you go.

A Use for Sawdust

Here's a use for the sawdust littering your shop: Make fire starters by pouring melted wax over sawdust placed in the compartments of paper egg cartons. (Don't use plastic cartons; they give off poisonous fumes when burned.) Stir the hot wax into the sawdust and allow it to cool. Break the compartments apart for use. (To safely melt the wax, place either paraffin or recycled candles in the top of a double boiler.)

Workshop Miscellany

When Kids Visit the Workshop

If your son or daughter likes to work alongside you in the workshop, keep on hand a few scraps of foam insulation. Children can saw and nail into these soft blocks without frustration.

A Cheap Workbench . . .

Need a workbench with storage for your basement workshop or garage? Watch auctions and flea markets for a discarded sideboard from a dining room set. Many of these are rather hideous in design, but they may be solidly constructed. Nail a sheet of plywood to the top, and you have an efficient workbench with storage drawers and cabinets. Or place a plywood top on a metal sink cabinet that's been discarded during a kitchen remodeling.

. . . And a Cheap Drafting Table

For an inexpensive drafting table, set a hollow-core door on two sawhorses. Cover the middle section of the door with a piece of vinyl board cover (available from drafting supply stores). Resilient and smooth, the vinyl will provide a good surface to draw on.

Lighting

Contrary to popular opinion, shining an intense beam of light on a particular task in a dark room is hard on the eyes. For comfortable viewing, the work surface should be lit so that it is only about three times as bright as the surrounding area.

5 Home Energy

Appliances
(See also In the Kitchen, in this chapter.)

Buy Efficiency

Usually, energy-efficient appliances are more expensive to purchase. Studies show, however, that these appliances are your best buy in the long run. They are usually of superior quality, they last longer, and they require less service. Many manufacturers now note their appliances' EER (Energy Efficiency Rating) or essential annual energy use right on their products to enable you to comparison shop.

Take Advantage of Off-Peak Rates

In order to cut down on their capacity needs, some utility companies encourage consumers to use more electricity when demand is normally low—in the evening and nighttime—by offering special rates. It may pay you to adjust your tasks at home so that you operate your dishwasher, washing machine, and dryer during off-peak hours if your utility has such a discount. Be aware, however, that if you sign up for off-peak discounts, you may pay a higher-than-normal rate when you use electricity during peak times.

Color vs Black-and-White TV

Color TV sets use almost twice the amount of electricity as black-and-white sets.

You Pay Extra for the Instant-On Feature

Many television models today have an instant turn-on feature. It gives you an instant picture because it's actually operating 24 hours a day. If yours has one, disconnect it, or unplug the set when you're not using it. This device can use up to 50% of the total amount of energy your set uses in one year.

Iron Clothes While Damp

Whenever you can, iron clothes while they are damp instead of drying them completely. You use your dryer less, and the clothes iron more easily.

Clothesline Drying Saves Energy

Use a clothesline or rack instead of the dryer, especially for thick, bulky items, for big energy savings.

Cooling

Keeping Sun Out

Drawing the shades or curtains to keep out unwanted sun in the summer helps to combat heat, but the sun will still penetrate the glass. The best way to prevent heat buildup is not to let the sun get in in the first place. Window overhangs and awnings, and shade trees and trellises that shade windows are far better sunscreens than interior shades and curtains. They're most effective on the south and west exposures.

Lights Produce Unwanted Heat

In hot weather, keep extra lighting to a minimum—especially the use of incandescent bulbs. They produce heat as well as light and can raise your home's temperature.

Air Conditioner Efficiency

If you use an air conditioner, clean or replace the filter at least once a month. This reduces operating costs by helping the unit to work more efficiently.

Air conditioners operate more efficiently away from direct sunlight. Install your air conditioner on the shady side of the house or under an awning or overhead trellis.

Reducing Humidity in Hot Weather

High humidity makes you feel warmer; this may be welcome in winter, but it's not in summer. In hot weather, reduce humidity by covering pots on the stove to minimize steam. Open the window when you take a shower to let steam and moisture escape.

Get Heat to Go Up and Out

Remember that heat rises, so open attic and second-story windows in hot weather. Consider installing a whole-house fan to "pull" hot air out of the house before you spend the money for an air conditioner.

To use a whole-house fan correctly, open windows to create an inlet about twice the size of the fan area. The fan should be large enough to produce about 30 air changes per hour. Calculate your home's volume (length times width times height) and multiply by 30 to find out how much air, in cubic feet, your whole-house fan should be able to move. To convert to the more common measurement of cubic feet per minute (CFM), divide by 60.

Maintaining Good Cross-Ventilation

A natural ventilation system is the most energy-efficient way to provide air flow in your home. Cross-ventilation results when some combination of openings on opposite walls permits a free flow of air from one side of the room to the other.

When possible, the window on one wall should be lower than the one on the opposite wall (if you have double-hung windows, open one from the bottom and the other from the top), and the higher one should be opened the most to allow for faster flow of air.

Build Natural Ventilation into a New House

When building a home, position windows low in the wall. This lets cooler air, which is closer to the ground, enter the house more quickly. And consider shading devices for south and west windows, where the sun is most intense.

Storm Windows Are Not Just for Winter

Keep storm windows and doors in place during the summer months if you use air conditioning. Just as they provide an extra window "skin" to reduce heat loss in winter, they reduce heat gain in summer.

Reflect Attic Heat Away

To block the flow of radiant heat from the attic down into the rest of your house during the summer, install reflective foil in your attic. This step can reduce heat passing through the attic by 20%. The higher the reflectivity, the better the foil works, so use bare, not coated, aluminum foil. Staple the foil to the rafters, leaving enough space at the eaves and the peak for air to circulate behind the foil. Foil placed over the attic floor will work, but it gets dirty easily, and its reflectivity is reduced.

Low-Speed Fans Are Best

A fan placed on a low ceiling that moves air at a rate of only 200 cubic feet per minute—just 2¼ mph—can make torrid 87°F air feel like it's a comfortable 77°F. Higher speed fans are less efficient coolers; they increase velocity but do not appreciably increase comfort. And high-speed fans use more energy and make more noise than low-speed fans.

Keep Cool in the Kitchen

To stay comfortable in the summer, cook meals outside on a grill and bake indoors only at night, when naturally cool nighttime air is available to reduce the temperature in the kitchen before the next hot day begins.

Design for a Warm Climate

If you live in a warm climate and you're building or remodeling a house, arrange the rooms so that the primary living areas are protected from the sun's heat during the summer. Closets, garages, utility and storage rooms, and other seldom-used spaces can act as thermal buffers to summer heat. The best warm-climate locations for these spaces are the east and west sides of a house, which are bombarded by the morning and afternoon sun respectively. You may also want to add doors that will allow you to close off heat-producing areas, like the kitchen and sunspace, from the main living spaces.

Landscape for a Warm Climate

During the summer, the high sun will cause a short, wide tree to shade a larger ground area than a tall, narrow tree will. Keep that in mind when planning an energy-efficient landscape.

Courtyard Walls Have a Cooling Effect

Live in a warm climate? Planning some outdoor landscaping? Build a courtyard. During the day, the high walls of a courtyard protect the enclosed area from hot winds and dust, give shade, and allow cool air to pool and collect. At night, the trees, plants, and water in a courtyard cool the air by evaporation. The taller the walls surrounding the courtyard, the cooler the temperature maintained inside.

Heating

A Weathertight Home Is Better Than a Solar Home

Planning a new house for a cold climate? Consider energy efficiency before solar efficiency. A super-weathertight house will probably save you more energy dollars than a good solar one.

Thermostats

Install dual setback thermostats in your home to automatically turn down your furnace during sleeping hours or at times when certain rooms are not in use.

Heat-producing fixtures and appliances may cause your thermostat to keep your home uncomfortably cool. To solve this problem, place your lamps, TV, and similar items at least 3 feet from the thermostat.

Lower the thermostat several degrees when entertaining three or more guests. The combined body heat will keep everyone warm.

High Humidity for Winter Comfort

Keep the moisture level of your home relatively high during the winter, either with a humidifier or with lots of plants. Higher humidity makes the body feel warmer.

Reflecting Heat Back into a Room

If you have radiators in your home, place a metal reflector behind each one to bounce heat into the center of the room.

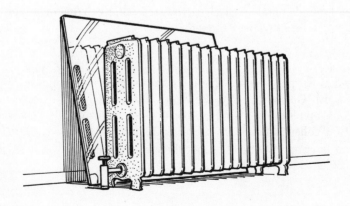

Best Returns for Conservation

You've finally decided to stop procrastinating and get to those energy conservation projects around the house. But which to do first? The following list will help you. These, according to most energy experts, are the ones that will give you your best return on investment, in the order in which they appear:

1. Upgrading your heating system. (Replace it with a new high-efficiency system, if what you have is really ready to bite the dust; or improve the efficiency of your present one by installing a setback thermostat, new flue damper, and such).

2. Upgrading your hot water system (with the same options as for the heating system).

3. Adding window insulation (movable insulation will be cheaper but not as convenient as new or additional storm windows).

4. Caulking around window and door frames and other openings to the outside.

5. Weatherstripping doors, windows, and other openings.

6. Insulating your attic or upper-story ceiling.

7. Insulating your exterior walls.

8. Insulating your crawl space or the ceiling of your unheated basement.

Vapor Barriers

Humidity indoors in winter is essential for comfort, but too much can cause condensation problems in your walls, if there is no vapor barrier there. Should you decide to insulate those walls, make sure the insulation has a vapor barrier that's facing the living space. If you're not insulating, an easy way to deal with the problem is to use vinyl wall covering or paint formulated especially as a vapor barrier.

Furnace Efficiency

Be certain your furnace is tuned up and replace filters frequently. These two simple precautions could save as much as 10% on your bill.

If you need a new furnace, look at the new pulse combustion or condensing ones. Furnaces 10 to 15 years old may be delivering only 50% of the energy in the fuel, while the latest, most efficient conventional firing units deliver about 80%, and the pulse units are claimed to deliver much more.

Small Heaters for Small Jobs

Use task heaters and space heaters whenever possible; they are less expensive and more efficient than your furnace for small jobs.

Don't Heat Closets

Keep closet doors closed. There's no need to heat (or air condition in summer) these spaces. Your storables, with few exceptions, couldn't care less what the temperature is.

Keep Yourself Warm

Whenever possible, heat your body, not your house. Use an electric blanket, an electric mattress pad, or a heavy quilt when you're in bed; wear sweaters and warm socks when working or relaxing around the house. You'll be much warmer for less money.

Double-Duty Ceiling Tiles

Soundproof ceiling tiles are a good idea. They not only help "quiet" a room, but they also act as insulation to hold in heat.

Double Doors for Convenience and Comfort

Double doors at the principal entryway make a convenient foyer for winter boots and, if you close the outside door behind you before opening the inside door, they also prevent blasts of cold air from entering your living space.

Keep a List of Problem Areas

Winter is the time when you notice all the heating problem areas in your house, such as loose-fitting windows and weak caulking. But it is also the time of the year when outdoor projects seem least attractive. If you can't take care of all the problems during cold weather, at least make a list of what needs to be done so that you'll remember it when the weather turns warmer and you can work comfortably outside.

Screens Shut Out Winter's Sun

Remove screens in winter; even fine-mesh screening can block up to 20% of the sunlight that could enter and help warm your home.

Reducing the Number of North Windows

If you don't need the natural window light, consider sealing off north-facing windows entirely in winter or cold-weather months. You can cover them with a rigid Styrofoam panel and then with a closed drape to hide the Styrofoam.

Taming a Snake to Keep Out Drafts

Drafts from under doors or windows can be blocked by laying a handmade "snake" across the crack. Make a tube out of material or use a kneesock or several socks sewn together. Stuff the sock with any bulky material, and then sew up the open end.

You can get really fancy and make a snake that is very effective for outside doors. Do this by sewing 1-inch pieces of Velcro tape at 12- to 18-inch intervals along one side of the snake. Then fasten the other half of the Velcro to the inside of the door with glue at the same 12- to 18-inch intervals. Finally, attach the snake to the door with the Velcro so that it hangs down over the crack. The Velcro will keep the snake at the base of the door no matter how many times it's opened.

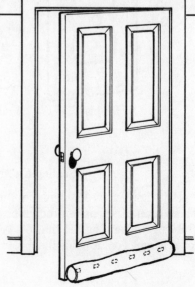

Insulating Your Screen Door

A wooden screen door can be turned into an inexpensive storm door by covering the screen with a piece of rigid plastic like Plexiglas. You can fasten it to the door with duct tape, or you can drill small holes in the plastic and use wood screws. Screw it in firmly but be careful not to screw it in too tightly; you could crack the Plexiglas. And take care not to drill the holes too close to the edges of the Plexiglas for the same reason.

Winterizing Your Air Conditioner

A window air conditioner will allow cold air to sneak into your home in winter. Take precautions by covering the air conditioner on the outside with rigid board insulation and plastic. However, the best precaution is to remove the unit entirely and insulate the window as you would all the others.

Insulating Basement Pipes and Ductwork

If your basement is cold in winter, be sure to insulate water pipes to prevent them from freezing. Also, the ductwork from your furnace should be wrapped with insulation to prevent heat loss.

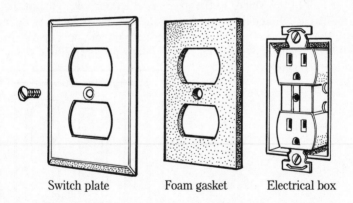

Switch plate   Foam gasket   Electrical box

Sealing Electrical Outlets

Electrical outlets are a common source of cold air entering the home. There is an inexpensive product on the market that can eliminate this problem—a foam gasket that fits behind the outlet's cover. When the cover is replaced, it holds the gasket and prevents cold air infiltration.

Weatherstripping Targets

Use caulk to seal cracks and holes in the places most likely to leak out warm inside air:

- At joints where door and window frames meet exterior siding.

- Where storm windows meet frames.

- At exterior siding corners.

- Where wood joists meet the house's foundation.

- At the joining of the original house to an addition.

- Around exterior openings such as water faucets.

- Where basement windows are set into a block wall.

- Around interior sashes and frames of windows.

- Around electrical outlets.

- Around doors and storm windows.

Insulating Windows

Don't be fooled into thinking that curtains and drapes provide good window insulation on cold nights. Curtains do help to trap air between themselves and windows, thereby reducing drafts. But if they are not floor-to-ceiling boxed drapes that seal the top and bottom of the window, they cut heat loss by only 10%. If they seal top and bottom, they can cut that loss by about 20%. Much better at reducing heat loss are tight-fitting insulated blinds, shutters, or rigid-foam panels that close over the window when the sun is not shining.

The Best New Windows

If you're looking for new windows that are really weathertight, choose thermal-break sashes that sandwich an insulating gasket between an inner and outer metal surface. Because metal is a far better conductor of heat than is wood, much more heat escapes through the ordinary metal sash to cold air outside. But even though a wood sash offers better insulation, it can rot if not caulked properly, it's heavier, and it costs more. The thermal-break sash gives you the best of both worlds.

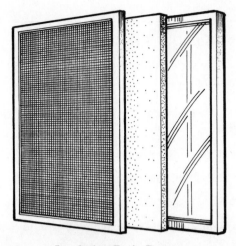

Insulating Patio Doors

Rigid-foam panels used in windows for insulation can also be used between existing patio sliding glass doors and their storm doors or screens for winter-long insulation.

Protecting Furniture from the Sun

Furniture in a solar home that has been designed with large south-facing windows is subject to extreme sunlight and may deteriorate rapidly. When shopping for upholstered furniture, buy a neutral color—fading

---

Solar Heating Rules of Thumb

- Your solar collector doesn't have to face direct south, but it should be oriented within 20° east or west of it.

- The collector should be tilted south as many degrees from the horizontal as your latitude.

- Tilt the south wall of your sunspace to local latitude plus 10° to 15°.

- For each 10 square feet of floor area in a house or room you want to solar heat, provide 1 to 4 square feet of south-facing glazing.

- For each square foot of south-facing glazing, a surface area of about 3 square feet of masonry thermal storage (walls and floors) is recommended to absorb heat for storage.

will be less noticeable. Synthetic fabrics and fiberglass curtains also tend to stand up to the sun better than natural materials; so do fabrics with woven, rather than printed, patterns. If your tastes fall outside these guidelines, buy clear solar control film, available at many hardware stores, to put on your windows. The film will cut your solar gain by 10 to 20%, but you won't have to replace your furniture as often.

Trees That Block Solar Heat

Which deciduous trees block solar gain the most? The ones with the densest branches. Beech trees are the worst offenders, blocking as much as 64% of winter sunlight; black walnut follows, with 45%; next comes the sycamore, which blocks 33%. The tree that keeps out the least amount of sunshine is the redbud, which blocks as little as 26%.

Wood Heat

Minimize Fireplace Inefficiencies

Don't forget to close chimney dampers if you have a fireplace (or stove) that isn't in use. An open chimney can let more heat escape than an open window can.

The common fireplace usually causes a net loss in heat. When a blaze is roaring, it takes your warm house air and sends it up the chimney (unless you have a fireplace insert device or tempered glass doors). When there's no fire, a loose-fitting damper will let warm air escape. To remedy this, force the damper closed as tightly as possible, then stuff the cracks with fiberglass batts. If you have no damper, cut a board of nonflammable material to cover the opening. This allows you to go to bed without waiting for the last embers to die out.

Fireplaces vs Wood Stoves

Trying to lower heating costs by burning wood? Remember that most fireplaces are grossly inefficient and are not suited for home heating. Wood stoves are better, especially airtight units.

Heat Exchangers

If you must use an inefficient fireplace or wood stove, consider buying and installing a heat exchanger. This device effectively reclaims much of the heat that would normally go up your flue and out of your house.

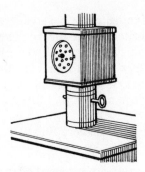

Wood stove heat exchanger

Don't Burn Green Wood

Burning green wood is a waste of energy. Because of the wood's high creosote content, it is also dangerous. Creosote buildup inside chimney walls may eventually cause a chimney fire, one of the leading types of fires in the home.

Increasing Humidity

Keep a pot of water on your wood stove while it is in operation. This will add humidity to the air and help you feel warmer.

Clean Chimneys Are Safer

Be sure to clean flues and chimneys at least once every heating season to remove the creosote that would otherwise be a fire hazard.

Dryer Lint as a Fire Starter

Dryer lint is an expensive commodity. It represents the life being worn from your clothes by the action and heat of the dryer. You can put this lint to use if you have a wood stove. The soft batts of lint ignite quickly and help set kindling ablaze.

Kindling for the Asking

If winter comes and you still haven't gathered a good supply of dry kindling, see whether your supermarket will give you some of the waxed cardboard boxes that are used to ship fresh vegetables to market. Cut them into strips of convenient size with a utility knife. You'll find that three or four 3 × 4-inch pieces are probably enough to ignite small logs. But use more and you take the chance of producing a very quick, hot blaze that could trigger a chimney fire.

A Simple Firewood Shelter

If you're not fortunate in having a spare outbuilding in which to store firewood, try setting up this simple shelter for sawed wood: Drive two steel poles into the ground approximately 10 feet apart. The poles should be placed deep enough and secure enough to take the considerable weight of a wood pile. For a cover that will slip down over the poles, cut two holes for the poles out of a 2 × 12-foot sheet of corrugated plastic. As the wood is used, the plastic sheet slips down to the posts. If the logs are removed so that the pile slants to one side or another, rain and melting snow will run off more readily.

Splitting Logs

A log will split easier if the maul hits it from the top down. You can probably tell which end is up by the difference in diameter (the top is slightly smaller) or by the direction of limbed branches. Most logs can be halved through the heart, but a few woods (such as elm) are bound by strands; the best technique for these is to work all around the edge of each log, taking off a narrow slab at a time.

Hot Water

Aerators Save

Aerators for faucets mix air pressure with water pressure and therefore reduce the water flow rate without reducing the pressure. If your faucets don't have aerators, install them; they are cheap and effective.

A More Efficient Showerhead

If you install a low-flow or water-saving head on your shower, you can cut hot-water consumption at shower time by 50%.

Showers vs Baths

A 4-minute shower uses less water than a bath. Save the bathtub for an occasional luxury soak.

When you use the tub in wintertime, don't drain the water immediately. The heat from the tub water will radiate into the bathroom, warming it. Most homes are too dry in winter, so the extra humidity will help also.

Cold-Water Washing

You can use cold-water detergents and cold water for most everything nowadays. Only the greasiest of clothing needs water warmer than 80°F. And it pays to do cold-water washing; you can save from $5 to $10 each month.

Drain Off Sediment from Your Water Heater

Drain your water heater two or three times a year. This removes excess sediment and allows the heating elements to operate more efficiently.

Turn the Water Temperature Down

Hot water probably is the second biggest energy expense in your home, often adding up to about 20% of your total energy bill. Most water heaters are set for 140°F—that's hot! Too hot, really, since water heated to over 120°F will need to be cooled down for most uses, which is wasteful. And there is more heat loss when hotter water sits in your storage tank. Water at 120°F will be fine for most people.

Automatic Hot-Water Thermostat

Install a thermostat that is set to switch your water heater off during the night when you aren't using the hot water and to switch it on a few hours before your morning shower. And remember to turn your water heater off when you leave for vacations and weekend trips.

Insulate Hot Water Pipes

Be sure to insulate hot water pipes, particularly those that travel through unheated areas such as cold cellars. Use tubular or wrap-on pipe insulation. Both are easy to install.

Insulate Your Water Heater, Too

Wrap your heater with batts of 6-inch fiberglass insulation. It should pay for itself after the first few winter months. One caution is needed, though: When insulating a gas water heater, be careful not to cover up the air inlet and outlet ports at the top and bottom of the tank.

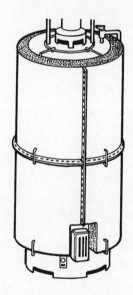

An Electric Ignition Saves Gas

If you have an old-fashioned pilot light on your gas water heater, try to have it replaced by an electric ignition, which fires up only on demand. This not only saves fuel, but is also safer, because there is no open flame burning all the time.

Tankless Water Heaters

As much as 20% of the energy used in heating water can be wasted because of heat loss from the tank and the long pipe runs between there and points of use. You might want to consider expanding the hot water system for a new bathroom by installing the new tankless heaters that provide instant hot water right over or under the sink, exactly where you need it—without heat loss from a storage tank or from long pipe runs.

In the Kitchen
(See also Appliances, in this chapter.)

Dishwasher Efficiency

Use the dishwasher for full loads only. Allow dishes to air-dry, rather than using the drying cycle at the end of the rinse. If your dishwasher has a cool-dry setting, use it, and remember to open the door so that the dishes can finish drying on their own.

Pilotless Ranges

Are you in the market for a new gas range? Look for one with an automatic ignition system instead of pilot lights. The old pilot system uses almost 50% of the total annual oven expenditure of gas.

Checking for Leaks

Halt the escape of oven heat. Check door gaskets on your oven for a snug fit by closing the door on a dollar bill. If the dollar slips out easily at any point, you're literally letting dollars of energy escape from your oven. You may be able to correct the problem by adjusting the latch, if your oven has one. If this doesn't work, get a new gasket.

Use the same dollar-bill test to check the gaskets on your refrigerator and freezer doors.

Refrigerator Efficiency

Don't stand in front of an open refrigerator trying to decide what to eat or prepare for mealtime. Instead, keep a checklist of your refrigerator's contents on the door and check them off as they are eaten.

Avoid positioning the refrigerator next to the oven or range; the heat given off will lower the refrigerator's efficiency.

If the coils are the in back of your refrigerator (and they are on most freestanding models), make sure there are at least 4 inches of space between the back of the refrigerator and the wall so that circulating air can carry off the heat buildup from those coils.

What Price for Frost-Free?

Automatic-defrost refrigerators use as much as 50% more electricity than the old-fashioned models. You'll have to decide if this extra expense pays for itself in convenience.

If you really want the frost-free convenience, look for a refrigerator with a "power saver switch." It turns off the defrost heater unit when humidity is low in the winter, thereby cutting your operating costs by possibly 10 to 15%.

Freezer Efficiency

Is your freezer too cold? Frozen foods need only be kept at 10°F. Put a household thermometer in your freezer and check the temperature. If it is colder than necessary, change the control setting.

Keep your freezer as full as possible. Foods retain the cold better than empty air does, and therefore make the refrigerator more economical. If you don't have enough food to fill the freezer, fill plastic jugs with water and freeze them until something better comes along to take up the space.

Allow most frozen foods to thaw in the refrigerator or at room temperature. (Be careful not to leave them at room temperature for too long after thawing, though.) Cooking frozen food wastes energy and is necessary only for certain foods.

Cooking Efficiency

Cook meals and desserts in quantity and freeze the extras. You'll save money on oven usage, and those extra pies and casseroles will save you time later on.

Cook several dishes in your oven at one time, or use the oven again immediately, while it's still hot.

Take advantage of any hot appliance to melt butter and warm rolls and other food.

Turn off the heat from a stove or appliance early and use the stored heat to coast to a finished meal.

Put aluminum foil under your stove's burners—especially if the appliance is electric—to reflect the heat.

Efficient Boiling

When boiling water to cook foods, turn down the heat as low as possible to maintain the boil. The water temperature will not rise higher than the boiling point, and too much heat creates excess steam and wastes energy.

When boiling anything on the stove, use the least amount of water possible to save both nutrients and energy. Also use a lid; water will come to a boil faster and will not escape the pan.

Pressure Cooking

A pressure cooker uses much less energy than a conventional pan because it does the job in less than half the time.

Lighting

Incandescent vs Fluorescent

Almost 10% of the electricity used in most homes goes for lighting, and most of us use more light than we really need. One way to cut back is to switch to fluorescent lamps whenever possible. These produce four times as much light per watt as do incandescent light bulbs for the same price. And you can now buy fluorescent bulb rings that fit into lamps designed for incandescent bulbs.

Task Lighting vs Overhead Lighting

In some cases, ceiling lights may be unnecessary. Lighting the individual spots where people are reading or working is less expensive than lighting an entire room—and it's also usually more pleasing to the eye.

One Large Bulb Is Better

If a whole room is to be lit, one large light bulb is cheaper than several smaller ones. It requires six 25-watt bulbs to produce the light of a single 100-watt bulb.

Dimmer Switches

Dimmer switches save energy by making it easy for you to reduce a room's lighting intensity when full lighting isn't necessary. They can also be used with lamps.

Turn Lights Off

It pays to turn off the lights when you leave a room for more than 3 minutes, say experts at the Center for Energy and Mineral Resources at Texas A & M University.

Natural Lighting

Use skylights and natural lighting through windows and glass doors whenever possible to allow the sun, rather than light bulbs, to provide your light. It's more pleasing, some claim more healthful, and free.

To reflect more sunlight into south-facing windows in winter, cover the outside ground beneath them with a light-colored material, such as white pebbles or light grey concrete.

Light-Colored Walls Cut Lighting Needs

Light-colored walls will reduce the amount of artificial lighting you need, because light is bounced off them, rather than absorbed.

Other Energy-Saving Ideas

Driving Efficiency

When driving at highway speeds, wind resistance is greater in an open car than in a closed one. To get the best fuel mileage, close the windows and keep cool with the fan or air conditioner. The amount of gas you save will more than pay for the power the fan consumes.

Before You Leave for Vacation

There are some things you can do before going on vacation to save energy while you're away. Turn down, or better yet, turn off, your electric water heater. If you want to leave lights on at home for security reasons, use timers that will turn them on and off at different times, and switch to low-wattage bulbs. If you'll be gone for any length of time, clean out the refrigerator, and turn it off. Be sure, however, to leave the door open a little to prevent mold and odors from building up.

6 Safe and Sound

Alarms and Locks

Lock Maintenance

To protect locks from dirt, rust, and unnecessary wear, spray them occasionally with a silicone aerosol. After treating the lock, turn the key to spread the lubricant.

Deadbolt Precautions

Some deadbolt locks operate by key only, from the inside as well as the outside. While this provides additional security, keep in mind that the lock may slow down your exit from the house in case of fire.

Deadbolt Your Doors

Use deadbolt locks with a rotating cylinder on all doors. They offer more security than lock-in-knob deadlatch locks. The deadbolt should be 1 inch thick and have a throw of 1 inch.

Smoke Detectors and Wood Stoves

Smoke detectors are a smart purchase for the home, but you may be irritated by false alarms if the units react to a smoky wood stove. Users of wood heat should look into photoelectric detectors, rather than those that operate by ionization. Photoelectric models are triggered by visible smoke particles, not by the gases that fires produce.

Traveling Lock

If you travel a good deal and don't trust the locks on motel room doors, bring along your own travel lock. One of these types of locks employs a piece that goes into the strike-plate hole; a keyed lock slides over it and

Before You Buy an Alarm System

Here are some points to keep in mind if you're thinking about investing in a burglary alarm system:

- Local systems are designed to send a signal from a sensory device directly to a light system or to a bell or siren. When a sensory device detects an intruder, the sounding device is activated and/or the house lights are turned on. Since the typical residential burglar is not a professional, a local system will usually scare him away.

- Many security companies can install a combination system that includes a local alarm plus a central reporting alarm. An advantage to the central reporting system is that it is constantly monitored by an alarm company. If the alarm goes off, the alarm company notifies the police department.

- There are usually two costs involved when dealing with alarm companies—an installation charge and a monthly service charge. Don't buy or lease a system from a company that doesn't offer a contract for continuing maintenance and service.

- The mere presence of an alarm is often enough of a deterrent to would-be burglars. Advertise the fact that your home is protected by an alarm by using warning decals.

holds the door fast. Another type simply is affixed to the outside door knob so that the door's keyhole is covered.

Outside the House

Doors and Windows

Lock Up

One-quarter of all household burglars gain entrance without breaking in—they enter through an unlocked door or window. Your house is only as secure as its most vulnerable point. Make sure you lock up!

Make Access Tough

Criminals are less likely to enter your home if access is difficult, visible, noisy, or time consuming. Window and door locks are good deterrents, especially when used in conjunction with other security measures, such as lighting and alarm systems.

Seal Up the Coal Door

If your home was heated by coal at any time in its history, the latch on the coal door could be a weak link in your home's security. Many coal doors are made to be opened from the outside by the person delivering the coal and may not require any type of key. Replace your door's unsafe latch, or better yet, if you're no longer using the door, seal it up.

Peepholes for Safety

As an extra security precaution, you may want to install a peephole or wide-angle viewer on the doors at all entrances so that you can see who is outside without opening the door. A short chain between the door and jamb is not a safe substitute because it can be easily broken or pulled off.

Chain-Link Ladder

For an inexpensive and inconspicuous fire escape, consider a chain-link ladder. It's anchored permanently on an inside wall and kept rolled up, then tossed out the window if there's a fire. Easiest to use are the ladders that come with a pair of bars (called standoffs) that hold the device away from the side of the building.

All about Doors

The most secure door is one made of steel. Second best is one of solid hardwood, without windows. Solid-core wood doors are more difficult to break than hollow-core wood doors. All-wood solid-core doors are stronger (and more expensive) than solid particle doors. Make sure wood doors are at least 1⅜ inches thick, preferably 1¾ inches thick.

Protecting Doors near Glass

If you have a door with a window in it or within 40 inches of it, use a double-cylinder deadbolt lock. This type of lock requires a key to open it from both sides, so even if a burglar breaks the glass, he cannot reach in and unlock the door without a key. An alternative to the deadbolt is replacing the glass with polycarbonate plastic, such as Lexan, which is much tougher to break.

Burglarproof Your Door

If a door swings out to open, use fixed rather than removable pin hinges for extra security. You can make the door even more burglarproof by removing the middle screw in both sides of the door's top hinge plate, drilling ¼-inch holes where the screws were and inserting a ¼-inch-diameter steel pin snugly into the hole that goes into the door frame. This pin should extend about ½ inch out from the hinge plate. It will go into the hole in the hinge plate on the opposite side when the door is closed. Repeat these steps with the bottom hinge. If the screws in the hinge plate cannot be removed, drill separate sets of holes near the top and bottom of the door for the steel pins.

Invincible Windows

Sliding windows can be broken into by lifting them up and out of their tracks. To prevent this, drill a hole through the top of the window frame, then insert a steel pin or a nail. For added protection, wooden slats or steel blocks may be used at the base of the window to keep the panels from sliding.

Landscaping

Save Your Trees

If you have lost small evergreens to Christmas-tree poachers, try this precaution next December. It'll make your trees look awful, but that's what you want them to look like to keep them from "walking away." Squirt purple or orange liquid tempera paint on the trees. This defaces them temporarily; the water-soluble paint will wash off in time. Squeeze bottles of tempera are available at art supply stores.

Low Hedges Discourage Burglars . . .

A hedge around your property may discourage would-be burglars from breaking into your home. According to a study at the University of Utah, a low, living wall provides a psychological barrier, even if it cannot physically exclude anyone intent on robbing you.

. . . But Keep Greenery Trimmed

A tall hedge provides less security than a short one that's trimmed to 3 feet or so. That's because burglars prefer to prey on buildings that aren't visible from the street. Low tree branches may also cut down on visibility, so keep your greenery trimmed, especially around doors and windows.

Goose Guardians

Geese have been used in Scotland to guard aging whiskey and have been employed by American troops as an alarm system. They can help you ward off intruders, too. While they might not be appropriate on an urban or suburban lot, they could be just the thing for a more secluded home. Geese are cheap, especially if you buy them as goslings. When left free to roam outside, the loud, 20-pound adults can intimidate burglars.

Make Your Yard Look "Lived In"

To avoid advertising that nobody's home, arrange to have your mail and newspaper delivery halted while on vacation. And get a neighbor to mow your lawn. If your travels take you away in snowy winter, have someone shovel the walk or driveway—or at least have them leave tracks.

Don't Hide a House Key

When you're going away for any length of time, don't "hide" your house key. There is no place you can think of to hide a key that a smart burglar hasn't thought of first. Leave a key with a trusted neighbor or a friend.

The Cost of Security

If you're weighing the costs of security measures for your home, keep in mind these sobering facts: The average burglar makes off with roughly $1,000 worth of goods, and only 14% of the thieves are caught and convicted.

Protecting Your Possessions

Bicycles

Lock Them Up

Bike locks aren't infallible, but a few lock companies will pay a limited sum if your bicycle is stolen in spite of the lock. Should your lock have such a guarantee, be sure to hold onto both keys; you must submit both of them, and a police report of the theft, to get your money.

To discourage bike thieves, take the extra effort to lock your bike up right. Pass your bicycle lock through the frame and at least one wheel, and attach it to as immovable an object as you can find.

Cars

Door I.D.

Chances are your car will never be stolen. But in the event it should be, how can you prove ownership if the plates and service numbers are removed and the body repainted? The next time your auto registration card expires and you get the new one to carry with you, take the old one, seal it in a small plastic sandwich bag, and drop it into the car door window well. Should you need to prove ownership, the interior panel can be removed.

Engraving Your Valuables

You can borrow an engraving device free from your local police department and use it to engrave your driver's license number onto your television, stereo equipment, and other valuables. An I.D. number makes these items difficult for thieves to unload—and easy for you to reclaim.

7 Mind Your Money

Banking

Speeding Up Your Loan

A common reason for delay in getting a loan approved is that all the questions on the loan application weren't answered or some responses were unclear. To speed up the loan process, make sure you fill out the form *completely,* answering all questions about employment, salary, assets, and debts. Include account numbers for your savings, investments, other loans, and charge cards. If there is something in your credit or work history that you know will cause a problem, attach a note to your application explaining the circumstances. Most of all, be honest. Lenders are very reluctant to deal with applicants who stretch the facts about their finances.

If Your Bank Machine Card Is Lost or Stolen

You are well protected against the unauthorized use of your credit cards—by law, you're not liable for any more than $50 per card. Bank teller machine cards are another story. Someone with access to your account could wipe out your checking account. You do have some protection, but the extent of your liability depends on how quickly you notify your banker of the theft. If you report your card lost or stolen within two days of finding out about it, your responsibility is limited to $50. Wait longer than that and you could be out up to $500 in fraudulent withdrawals.

A crook doesn't need your actual card to get into your account, just your access code. In that case, you won't know about a theft until your bank statement comes. You have 60 days from the mailing date of the statement to report the problem; otherwise, you may have to shoulder the entire amount that's been stolen.

Keep Your Bank Accounts Active

Don't forget about your infrequently used savings or checking accounts. That may sound silly; after all, who loses track of their own money? But according to the federal government, 10 million accounts worth $5 billion were sitting dormant in the nation's banks in 1983. Perhaps your children have small accounts that have been forgotten over the years. You may find an old passbook belonging to a deceased parent—or even to you. If an account is inactive for a long time—typically, that's one year—it's considered dormant. Many banks and savings and loan associations stop paying interest on such accounts and even charge dormancy fees. Your account may eventually dwindle to nothing. In addition, many states have escheat laws, requiring the bank to turn over dormant accounts to the state after a certain number of years. Should you find an old passbook or account ledger, don't automatically assume the money is lost. Contact the bank. If it still has the account, ask that all interest be computed and dormancy fees be reversed. If the funds have been turned over to the state treasury, that's where you'll have to go to reclaim your money. To play it safe, make a note of all your accounts so that you don't forget about one or two. And make a point of making at least one transaction on each account every year—a deposit or a withdrawal—so that it doesn't become dormant.

Choosing Money Market Accounts and Funds

Trying to decide which money market deposit account (MMDA) or money market mutual fund (MMMF) offers the best deal? You'll have to look beyond the advertised interest rate. Depending on various factors, one account may be far superior to another even though both tout the same rate. Ask your banker or funds manager what the effective yield is on the account and how often interest is compounded—daily, monthly, or quarterly. There are also other factors to consider: Some MMDAs cut the interest rate if your balance drops below a certain minimum amount, and MMDAs and MMMFs sometimes charge fees—either on a monthly basis or as a percentage of your investment. Ask about restrictions on withdrawals—how many can you make, and for what amounts—and how long you must leave a deposit in the account before withdrawals are allowed.

How Long Will It Take to Double Your Money?

Use the "Rule of 72." Divide 72 by an interest rate to find out how many years it will take to double your investment at that rate. For example, you have $5,000 in a savings certificate at 12%. In six years—72 divided by

12—you'll have $10,000 saved up. You can use the rule another way to see what yield you're getting for your investment. If stock you've owned for six years is now worth $10,000, and you originally paid $5,000 for it, you know that you're getting 12% a year—72 divided by six years.

Cosigning Loans

It may be hard to turn down a family member, friend, or business associate who asks you to cosign a loan, but don't let your urge to help someone get in the way of your practical thinking. Even though you're the secondary signer of a loan, you're equally responsible for repaying every dollar. If your friend or relative doesn't keep up with the payments, you could be forced to make them. Also remember that you must list that loan as an obligation of yours on a loan application. That will have a bearing on your ability to borrow. A lender may not want to grant you a loan if you're already tied up with someone else's. Should you want to help out someone in need, and trust him or her to meet the payments, here are some hints:

- Avoid putting up collateral of your own if you possibly can. Otherwise, if your friend defaults, your car or other property could be repossessed unless you make the payments yourself.

- See if the lender will allow you to be responsible for only the principal on the loan—the amount borrowed not including interest and late charges.

- Ask to be notified immediately if the borrower doesn't make a payment. You'll have time to try to resolve the problem before the situation gets out of hand.

- When you must borrow money yourself and have cosigned for someone, make a point of mentioning that person's credit worthiness and show a record of his or her prompt payments. That will help assure your lender that you will probably never be called on to cover that debt.

Budget

Your Nest Egg

Some so-called experts advise that the only savings reserve you need is the ability to borrow enough money to cover your expenses for three months. That's absurd; everyone needs a savings nest egg in case of an illness, job layoff, or other mishap that could leave you without steady income. A good rule of thumb to follow is keep the equivalent of three months' take-home salary in a savings account that you can cash in quickly without losing any of your investment. Good choices are money market savings accounts at a financial institution, or money market mutual funds. (See also Banking, in this chapter.) Once you have this reserve, you can go ahead and make other investments.

Making Your Own Yearly Financial Statement

Just as corporations must print out yearly financial statements showing their assets, liabilities, and net worth, so should your family. You can usually get a blank personal financial statement from your banker. Fill out a new one every year. Tax filing season is a good time to do it since you have your financial papers collected in order to do your tax return. Just total all the money you bring in from salary, investments, and debts owed to you, along with the value of assets such as your home and life insurance policies. Then total all your debts—mortgage, car loan, and other bills. The difference between the two is your net worth. Now, not only do you have the information on which to make your financial plans for the year, but with a few minor updates, you'll always be prepared with a current statement if you need to borrow money. Lenders require them.

Monthly Budgets

When you work with your monthly family budget, map out at least three months at a time—the previous month, the current month, and the upcoming month. Last month's budget will help you estimate what your current expenses will be, and you'll see if you have any items carried over into this month. By doing a preliminary sketch of next month, you won't be caught by surprise later with an unexpected bill. When next month comes, revise your projection to reflect your actual transactions. You can even sketch out a yearly outline with entries for insurance payments, car registration, children's tuition, or other expenses that occur only once or twice a year.

Credit

Don't Overdo the Credit Cards

Too much credit can hurt you in some cases. Lenders like to see that you have a credit history, but if you have too many credit cards, a lender may decide that you have access to too many potential debts. Most people need no more than a bank card like Visa or MasterCard, a business card like American Express, a gasoline card or two, and one or two department store cards. Also, by keeping your cards to a minimum, you have less to lose in case your wallet or purse is stolen. You can be liable for up to $50 of unauthorized purchases on *each* card.

If Your Credit Cards Are Stolen or Lost . . .

Do you know the exact contents of your purse or wallet? You should, in case it's lost or stolen. Make a quick inventory of your credit cards by making photocopies of them—eight cards fit well on one sheet of paper. On the back of the sheet, write down your driver's license number and checking account numbers; include a list of the keys on your key ring and other articles you carry with you. It would also be handy to write down the emergency numbers you are to call to report missing credit cards. Keep the paper in a safe place at home where you can get to it easily if you need to.

Credit Card Insurance?

Credit card users need not buy special insurance. Most credit card insurance companies have a $50 deductible clause under their coverage, and federal law provides this coverage for free. A cardholder's liability is limited to $50 per card on charges incurred before the credit card company is notified of the loss or theft.

The Importance of Individual Credit

Spouses should have their own credit histories. Under the present law, you should have your own listing at the local credit reporting agency. Joint credit accounts, like credit cards and bank loans, should be listed under each name so that both individuals accumulate a good record for those accounts. Until 1977, separate headings weren't required, so many married women who share accounts opened before 1977 with their husbands may not have a credit history of their own. To find out and correct the problem, call your local credit bureau—the number is in the Yellow Pages under "credit reporting agencies."

If you don't have a separate credit record, or if some accounts aren't listed under your name, write to the credit bureau with the correct information and ask that it be added to your records. It's a good idea to write creditors, too, and ask that from now on they report your activities under both names.

Women who apply for credit cards and other accounts should use their own first name, not their husband's; for example, use Mrs. Mary Doe instead of Mrs. John Doe. Because computer-based records often don't include titles such as Mr. or Mrs., your account could be incorrectly listed under your husband's name. Using your own name will protect you from missing out on the good credit history that you have established.

Don't Confuse Credit Cards with Debit Cards

You've been using credit cards for years—you present the card when you buy something, and pay for it when the credit card company sends a bill. Debit cards work more like checks—when you buy something, the money is taken directly from your checking account without any waiting period. Although the cards may look similar, be sure you know which

---

Cut Down on Finance Charges

The method a credit card company uses to bill you each month can make a difference in your finance charge. Suppose your account has the following activity:

> March 1 — Your account has a balance of $100 from last month.
>
> March 10 — You pay $50.
>
> March 20 — You charge $100.
>
> March 30 — Your ending balance for the month is $150.

Some credit card companies will charge interest on the entire outstanding $150, not allowing you any grace period to pay for your March 20 purchases. Other companies will charge interest only on $50 and give you the chance to pay off your March 20 purchases next month without charging you any interest on the amount. Even companies using the same finance charge interest rate may come up with drastically different dollar amounts. Your clue is in the credit agreement you should get whenever you apply for a new card. Shop around until you find a company that uses the most favorable method of billing.

one you're applying for and which one you pull out of your wallet when you make a purchase. With a debit card purchase, you'll also have to remember to write the amount in your checkbook register, just as if you had written a check.

Premium Charge Cards Are Usually Not Worth It

Unless you have a real need for some of the extras offered by prestige cards, an everyday Visa, MasterCard, and travel-and-entertainment card such as American Express (the green card) or Diners Club should do just fine. Annual dues for them range from free to $45 a year. On the other hand, status cards can cost up to $250 (for American Express's platinum card). For the extra fee, you're entitled to check-cashing privileges up to $10,000, higher credit limits, free traveler's checks, and credit life insurance. But on the bottom line, the regular cards are honored in just as many places as premium cards are.

Estate Planning

Where to Keep Your Will

A safe deposit box may not be the best place to keep your will. In some states banks must seal a box when one owner dies. It can't be opened without witnesses and authorities. Meanwhile, your survivors might need funds from the estate to meet expenses. Without your will, they'll run into trouble. First, check with your banker to see what the policy is on sealing safe deposit boxes upon death. Then think about keeping your will in a fireproof safe at home, with your lawyer, or with your named executor. You may keep a copy in your safe deposit box, but be sure your survivors will have instant access to at least one other copy.

A Living Trust

You can avoid probate—the lengthy and costly process of transferring property to your survivors when you die—by setting up a "living trust" now. You put all or part of your assets into the trust and appoint a trustee—it can be your spouse, banker, attorney, or even you. Name yourself as the trust beneficiary so that you receive income from the trust property as it's received. The nice thing about a living trust is that you still have control over your assets. You can change the terms any time you like, switch trustees, even cancel it altogether. When you die, the property will be distributed according to the trust, sidestepping probate. All your affairs can remain private, rather than being made part of a public record. You'll need an attorney to set up a living trust. Find one who is familiar with them.

Don't expect a living trust to help you avoid paying federal income taxes. That's not what it's meant to do. What's more, a living trust doesn't replace a will. The two should work hand in hand.

Writing Your Will

Paying an attorney to write your will is money well spent. You have a will so that you can arrange to have your assets given to your beneficiaries with as little trouble as possible. Don't risk having your will declared invalid because you wrote it out yourself and didn't know the correct terminology or procedure. A simple will can cost less than $100.

When you have your will written, notify the person you choose to be your executor, so that he or she won't be surprised later on. Being an executor is really not a privilege, and some people are not qualified to handle the administration of your estate. If you don't want to place the burden on your spouse, children, or family friend, your banker or attorney might be a good selection. Both should have financial knowledge and the ability to remain objective during a difficult time; moreover, they are legally required to act in a financially prudent manner.

Reviewing Your Will

Just because you've recently had your will drafted or revised by an attorney doesn't mean you can put it away and forget about it. Review it yearly to make sure your personal situation hasn't changed. You should review your will any time you:

1. get married or divorced

2. have children

3. move to a new area (you may need to name a new executor)

4. acquire a valuable asset

5. suffer the death of a person involved in your will

6. change your mind about something previously mentioned in the will.

Informing Your Heirs

It's not fair to your survivors for you to keep your estate wishes a secret. Although many people feel embarrassed to talk about inheritances, you should sit down with your family and other heirs, if any, and tell them what they can expect, and what you would like done when you die. It will save endless arguments and ill will later over who was entitled to that money or those heirlooms. Children old enough to be responsible should know who you want to be your executor, banker, and attorney, and how to reach them. They need to know how to find your safe deposit box, your will, and a list of your assets. When people are emotionally drained at the time of a death, they shouldn't have the added burden of searching out those important papers and other items.

Videotaping Your Will

It may be a good supplement to a written will, but videotaping your will shouldn't be a replacement. Many states won't honor wills that are not in writing. However, combined with a legally written document, a video-tape of you explaining your wishes can be a good way to show that your will is authentic, and its provisions would be difficult to dispute.

Insurance

When Collision Insurance Isn't Worth It

Collision coverage pays you for damage to your own car, but only up to its current value. If the book value of the car is only a couple of hundred dollars, that's all the insurance company will pay you no matter how much it costs you to have the car repaired because of an accident. And should you carry a typical deductible of $100, you'll actually be paying for only a small amount of coverage or perhaps none at all. However, make sure you keep your liability insurance up to date to cover any damage you may cause to someone else's vehicle or other property.

A Larger Deductible Equals Lower Premiums

For auto, health, or homeowner's insurance, the difference between carrying a $100 deductible—the amount you must shoulder yourself before the insurance company will pay a claim—and a $500 deductible can mean cutting your yearly premium by up to 30%. Keep the money you save as a cushion to cover the higher deductibles in case of a claim.

Keeping Records of Your Possessions

Without looking, can you make a complete list of everything in your home? Almost no one can, but if your home is destroyed by fire or flooding, that's what you'll have to do in order to file an insurance claim.

For a quick and easy record that no one else need see, rent a video camera and recorder for an evening—the cost is probably less than $75. Open all your closets, cupboards, and drawers, and lay out valuables on your bed, tables, and floor. Slowly pan the camera around every room in your home. Shoot the outside, too. Don't forget the garage and shed. After all your possessions have been photographed, store the video cassette in a safe place. It's compact enough to fit in a small safe deposit box. Back up your video recording with a written list including purchase dates, prices, models, and identification numbers, whenever possible.

Know What Insurance You Already Have

Companies, clubs, and unions often provide life insurance for employees and members. So do groups such as the American Automobile Association. When you use a charge card for airline tickets you may get life insurance protection during your trip. You may also be covered for lost or damaged luggage.

Check your homeowner's policy—it may cover items stolen from your car, a snatched wallet, or lost luggage. You will never know to file a claim if you're unaware that you are covered. By carefully reading each policy you have, and asking about coverage from other sources, you'll know where to turn if you suffer a loss.

Getting Replacement Value Homeowner's Insurance

For a small additional premium each year, your homeowner's insurance policy can cover the "replacement value" of your property rather than just its current or depreciated value. A typical policy pays only what your possessions are worth at the time of a loss, even if it costs much more than that to replace them. For example, if a fire destroyed your 5-year-old dining set, which cost $1,500 new but was worth $600 at the time it was destroyed, your insurer would pay you $600. But to buy a new one just like it would cost you $2,000 today. A replacement policy will cover your set for the whole $2,000. Your insurance company will probably require that your policy cover at least 80% of the home's current value—not including the land it sits on (since land can rarely be destroyed). You can also ask your insurance company to add an inflation clause to your policy, so that your coverage automatically rises as your home increases in value.

Discounts on Your Insurance

Want to pay less for your homeowner's insurance policy? Ask your insurer about available discounts for safety items such as smoke alarms, fire extinguishers, deadbolt locks, and permanent identifying marks engraved on your possessions. Older Americans who are often at home may also qualify for discount rates. If your current insurance company doesn't offer appropriate discounts, shop around for one that does. Not only will you save money on your policy, but by installing these safety devices, you could discourage a thief or even save your family members from harm.

Insuring Your Contact Lenses

Contact lens replacement insurance currently costs about $25 per year. Is it worth the charge? A $7 to $35 deductible per lost lens is average. Add the deductible plus the cost of coverage, and the total is more than the cost of a single lens replacement. Unless you lose a lens frequently, insurance makes little sense.

Investments

Treasury Bills

To save bank charges and brokerage commissions, you can purchase Treasury securities directly from the federal government. You can buy 3-month, 6-month, and 12-month Treasury bills (minimum $10,000) or longer term Treasury notes and bonds. Applications are available at the 37 federal reserve banks across the country and from the Bureau of Public Debt, Department F, Washington, DC 20226. For more information, call the Treasury at (202) 287-4113 (not toll free).

An added bonus with Treasury bills is that you receive what's called "original issue discount"—which amounts to your interest on the investment—within a couple of weeks after you send your application and money. But you aren't taxed on the interest until your Treasury bill matures. For example, if you buy a six-month T-bill in July, you'll get your interest by August, but you won't have to count it as income until the next year, when the bill matures.

Series E Savings Bonds

It's time to cash in any very old Series E savings bonds you've been holding for many years. Bonds issued between 1941 and 1952 fully mature after 40 years, meaning that time has expired (or will shortly expire) on many of them. It does no good to keep them longer; the government stops paying interest once the bonds reach full maturity.

Opportunities for Small Investments

Good financial opportunities aren't limited only to those people with lots of money. Even if you have only $100 or $200 to set aside at a time, you, too, can tap into high yields. Here are some of your better options:

- Money market mutual funds. The interest rate paid by these funds changes as market conditions fluctuate. You're always assured of the most current money market rate. Many of these funds require a deposit of as little as $100 to open an account. These mutual funds pool the money of every depositor and invest in lots of different securities. That way, your risk is lessened, yet you still earn a high yield.

- Your credit union. Interest rates paid to savers aren't restricted by the government and initial deposits are usually small. If you don't belong to a credit union, inquire whether you might qualify to join through relatives, your employer, union, local college, or other group.

- Zero coupon certificates. You buy these through a broker. Many are insured for safety. The way zero coupon CDs work is that you buy them at a very deep discount, and when they mature you collect the face value. For example, you might buy a $1,000 CD for only $250. When it comes due, say in 12 years, you get a check for $1,000.

What's more, the Internal Revenue Service says that you're supposed to report all the earned interest on your tax return for the year your E bonds mature, whether you cash them in or not. You can even buy new Series EE bonds with the money—they come in denominations as small as $50, which sell for $25, and they pay more than regular savings accounts.

Types of Mutual Funds

What's the difference between a load and a no-load mutual fund? "Load" is simply another word for sales charges and fees. No-load funds don't directly charge you any fees to invest in them, whereas load funds charge you a percentage of the funds you invest. Past track records show that load funds don't necessarily do better than no-loads. If you want to put money into a mutual fund, skip the sales charges, and go with a no-load fund.

Free Investment Advice

Investment newsletters that give advice on buying and selling securities can cost more than $500 a year, but you can often pick up free investment advice by looking for those same publications in your local library. Some trusted names that many library systems carry include Value Line and Standard's & Poor's.

Investment Clubs

If you're intrigued by the thought of playing the stock market but don't have the expertise or large cache of funds to invest by yourself, join an investment club. An investment club is a group of investors with similar goals that pools its money to buy and sell stocks that club members have researched. Historically, clubs boast a reputation of having done better than the stock market as a whole. For information about joining or starting a club, contact the National Association of Investment Clubs. It can guide you in choosing members of your club and explain the best ways to operate.

Who Should Hold Your Stocks and Bonds?

When you buy stocks and bonds, you can arrange to have them either sent to you or kept at your brokerage firm. Keeping them yourself gives you more flexibility—you can trade them with any broker you choose, not just the one who sold them to you. Also, dividend checks will be sent right to you instead of through your broker. However, if your broker holds your securities, you don't have to worry about storing them safely in a safe deposit box. And if you sell through the same broker, the transaction can take place immediately—just pick up the phone; you don't have to deliver the stock certificates. Finally, if you have a money fund that offers brokerage services, and the broker holds the stocks, your dividends can be placed directly in your account. The choice is yours and should depend on how often you buy and sell, whether you're pleased with your broker, and how concerned you are about finding a safe storage place.

Retirement

If You're an Older American, Speak Up!

Senior citizen discounts are available for the asking. If your parents are seniors, tell them about the numerous products and services available to them at discount prices. The key is to *ask*. Ask about discounts on airline tickets and train and bus fares, as well as price reductions on the services of beauty shops and barbers, health clubs, restaurants, and colleges and universities. Call your county government agency on the elderly, and ask about senior discounts. Check with all the merchants you deal with. Even the National Park Service offers a Golden Age Passport, which allows senior citizens and accompanying persons into the parks at no charge, as well as discounts on fees and charges within the parks.

Warning: Many times, the discount is applied against the list price or regular charge for a product or service. Ask about special sales rates or general discounts, such as super-saver fares on airlines. They may be lower than the senior citizen discount.

IRAs

You can have more than one Individual Retirement Account (IRA). The only limitation is that your total yearly contribution must not exceed $2,000 or 100% of your earnings, whichever amount is less. If you want four IRAs with $500 in each, you'll have no tax problem with the IRS. You can put your IRA money into savings accounts and certificates at your bank, thrift institution, or credit union; mutual funds; stocks and bonds; even annuities at insurance companies.

One advantage of owning multiple IRAs is that you spread your risk. All your money isn't at one place in the same investment. Another reason to consider multiple IRAs is a move to a new locale. Example: You have at your local bank a certificate of deposit IRA that won't mature for another five years. If you withdraw the money, you'll be charged a stiff bank penalty for early withdrawal. Instead, move to the new location and open a new IRA. When the old CD matures, transfer the funds closer to home if you wish.

The law says you can't contribute to your own IRA after you reach age 70½, even if you still work. But, should you have a nonworking spouse who isn't 70½ yet, you can put up to $2,000 a year into his or her IRA as a spousal contribution. Even in your later years an IRA makes good tax sense since the contributions are deductible from your taxable income, while its earnings can accumulate tax deferred until a withdrawal.

Getting a Perspective on Financial Needs in Your Later Years

Think of retirement planning as a three-legged stool: One leg is your company pension plan. The second is Social Security. And the third is your own investments, including your IRA and/or Keogh plan. If one leg looks short, find ways of either building it up or compensating by building up the other two.

You can always contact your nearest Social Security office for information about how to apply for benefits. And you can keep track of your own investments, IRA, and other accounts. But company-sponsored pensions require more care. It is quite common for a person to work for four or five employers during a lifetime. You may have pensions coming from all of them. None will seek you out just because you reach age 65. That's up to you. Keep a list of the personnel offices of all the companies you have worked for. Periodically check to make sure you are still on the books so that you can claim the retirement benefits due you.

Self-Employment after Retirement

When planning your finances for your retirement years, keep in mind an often-overlooked option: Continue to work. Retirement from your regular job doesn't mean you have to stop working altogether. Many companies welcome retirees who return as independently employed consultants. Another alternative is to take the hobby you've enjoyed over the years (or one you've always wanted to begin but never had the time) and turn it into a money-making operation—photography, artwork, gardening, sewing, electronics; the possibilities are endless. Work for others part-time or work for yourself. Not only will work help relieve some of your money concerns, but the tax breaks for self-employed individuals are very generous. If you're over age 70, you can earn as much money as possible without losing any of your Social Security benefits. Workers 65 to 69 can earn up to $6,960 (as of 1984) before Social Security benefits are reduced by $1 for each $2 over the limit that is earned.

Shopping

Service Contracts

Service contracts on appliances and other products often aren't necessary because the products may come with a thorough warranty. Before you sign a contract for your new washer/dryer, home computer, and so on, ask about the charges for repairs and what is covered under the warranty. You may find that the service contract will cost more than two or three service calls.

Off-Season Bargains

The middle of summer is the best time to buy firewood—suppliers aren't busy, you'll get quick delivery, and the wood is usually less expensive (you can get away with buying green wood since it will have several months to dry out). Summer is also the time to top off your heating oil tank, replace a dying car battery and balding snow tires, and upgrade your home's insulation.

During the fall and winter months, make needed repairs to your air conditioning unit. Stock up on swimming pool supplies, buy lawn furniture, and consider taking the family vacation (you can enjoy off-season rates at many resorts and vacation spots).

Buying a Car for Your Vacation

If you're planning a cross-country trip and also shopping for a new car, consider this option: Buy your new car at home, but take delivery at your vacation destination. You will save the expense of car rental and come home with one very large souvenir. Since delivery times vary and insurance and license plate arrangements need to be taken care of before you pick up the car, allow at least three months' lead time.

One note of caution: You will pay for the car and take ownership of it before you actually take possession, so be sure the dealership has insurance before you take possession.

Mail-Order Shopping

The Federal Trade Commission requires that mail-order companies ship orders within the time promised, or, if no time is stated, within 30 days. If you pay by check, the 30 days begin upon receipt of your check and order; but if you pay by credit card, the 30 days begin only after your card is charged. The FTC rule does not apply to telephone orders. The seller is required to notify you if shipment cannot be made within its advertised delivery time or within 30 days. Should a new delivery date be more than 30 days past the original, you may accept the new shipment date or cancel for a full refund. Either way, you must do it in writing. If you do not respond, the company assumes you accept the new shipment date. In the event that you decide to cancel, the FTC requires that refunds be issued within seven working days. For charged orders, adjustments must be made within one billing cycle.

Yes, you may refuse damaged mail-order packages at the time of delivery. Write "Refused" on the package and return it, unopened, to the seller. No new postage is necessary. If the damage is discovered after the package is opened, follow the company's directions for returns. You will have to cover postage costs, and the package should be insured.

If you are unable to resolve a complaint with a mail-order company, the FTC's Credit Billing Act allows you to stop payment of disputed charges. For orders paid by credit card, notify the credit card company within 60 days of the charge date; if you win the dispute, the unpaid amount will be removed from your account. The Better Business Bureau helps consumers with mail-order problems. Contact the BBB where the company is located. Or you can write with problems to Mail Order Action Line, at the Direct Market Association, 6 East 43rd Street, New York, NY 10017.

Taxes

Deductions for Students

One student can equal two $1,000 exemptions. To claim someone as your tax dependent, that person typically must not earn more than $1,000 in income. But that rule does not apply to your children under age 18 or to full-time students. That means your dependent student can work during summer vacation and school holidays and earn as much money as possible, and you will still be entitled to claim a $1,000 dependency exemption for him or her on your tax return. There is an additional bonus: When the student fills out a tax return to report wages, he or she gets to take his or her own $1,000 personal exemption. Your family gets two $1,000 deductions for the same person, all perfectly legal.

Credits for Summer Camp

Working parents who send their children to summer camp may claim at least part of the cost as a tax credit. The law allows you a tax break for child and dependent care expenses. If your young child (under 15) goes to camp during the summer so that you can work or attend school, the camp cost qualifies as child care, just as if you had sent him or her to a day care center or hired a sitter. Parents can claim a percentage of up to $2,400 in annual expenses for one child; $4,800 for two or more. The percentage depends on your income—it's 30% for those with incomes under $10,000, and decreases by one percentage point for every $2,000 in income up to $28,000. The minimum is 20%.

Social Security Numbers for Your Children

Each of your children should have an individual Social Security number. When you set up savings accounts for your children, you are asked for Social Security numbers. Many parents mistakenly provide their own numbers instead of their children's. Then, when the bank annually sends information to the IRS about the interest earned on the accounts, the IRS expects to see the money listed on the parents' tax return because it's identified under their Social Security numbers. Since the money is really their children's, they aren't required to pay income tax on it. If you have made this error, ask your banker to change the Social Security numbers on those accounts from yours to your children's. For every child who earns more than $1,000 a year in interest, make sure a tax return is filed. The tax owed won't be much; not nearly as much as you would pay on the interest income if the savings were listed on your return.

Social Security Up to Date?

Check on the accuracy of your Social Security earnings record at least once every three years. The amount of Social Security benefits you and your family are entitled to depends on the amount of your lifetime earnings subject to Social Security taxes. That's why it's important to make sure your earnings are being reported properly. Have your local Social Security office send you its Form OAR-7004. Fill it out and return it. You'll receive a printout of your earnings to date. Any error must be corrected within 39½ months after it occurs. Failure to correct mistakes could mean you lose benefits you're entitled to.

Keeping Receipts

Keep a bag or box handy to receive all your purchase receipts wherever you usually remove your coat, open mail, or empty shopping bags. The receipts will be valuable should you need to exchange or return something. And when tax time comes around, you'll have your receipts to tally so that you can itemize deductions or sales tax, as well as contributions to charities, volunteer work, energy conservation materials, and so on.

Make Note of All Your Income

Keep track of the sources of your bank deposits by making careful notes in your checkbook register. The IRS objects when people don't report all of their taxable income. On audit, you may have to furnish your checkbook registers and bank statements. There are plenty of valid reasons for not reporting some deposits as income. Gifts from family and friends aren't taxable; maybe you transferred money from your savings to your checking account or received Social Security benefits. It is important to write the source in your checkbook register whenever you make a deposit. Write "Birthday gift from Mom" or "Money from savings account #123-45." That will satisfy an IRS auditor.

Make Deductions Now, but Pay Later with Credit Cards

Running a little short of cash toward the end of the year? You can use a credit card to make tax-deductible purchases and claim them on this year's tax return, even if you don't pay back the credit card company until next year. The same rule applies to small bank loans. A bonus is that when you repay the loan or charge company, any interest payments are deductible on next year's return.

Use the Long Form

When you prepare to fill out your income tax return, always start by using the long form 1040. Although the IRS encourages taxpayers to use its shorter and more convenient forms 1040A and 1040EZ, neither includes space to report many important tax breaks such as work-related moving expenses, employee business expenses, the residential energy tax credit, and itemized deductions. You'll never pay more tax when you use the long form; it can only save you money by prompting you to claim tax breaks you might otherwise miss.

Don't Lend the IRS Your Money

Avoid tax refunds. Getting one usually indicates poor tax planning. It means that you have overpaid your taxes throughout the year. What's worse, you're not even collecting interest on the funds you're "lending" to the IRS. Adjust your withholding at work so that less is taken out each payday.

Deducting Job-Hunting Costs

Job-seeking expenses are tax deductible. Uncle Sam is willing to chip in with a tax break when you search for a new job. Just keep verifying receipts and records for long-distance phone calls, typed and mailed résumés, lunches with prospective employers, and transportation to and from interviews. The IRS says your expenses are deductible so long as you're looking for work in the same trade or business you're already in.

Your options will be wider if you list your occupation on your tax return as broadly as you can, such as "administrator" or "manager." You can claim the job-hunting deductions even if you don't land the new job.

Deducting Volunteer Expenses

While you can't deduct from tax returns the value of time you volunteer to nonprofit groups, you can include expenses incurred while volunteering. Be sure to keep a record of out-of-pocket expenses: stationery, postage, mileage, parking, tolls, lunches, and any other expenses directly related to volunteer work.

Choosing Your Income Tax Preparer

If you are looking for professional help with your income tax return, avoid anyone who promises that you definitely won't be audited. The IRS chooses some tax returns completely at random, so no one is totally exempt from the possibility of an audit. Also, the preparer may be too conservative with your return. A promise that you won't be audited is a sure sign that he or she won't dig hard enough for every tax break you may have coming.

Money-Wise Ideas

Bill Paying

If two of you are paying your household's bills, then both should be involved in the process of writing and recording checks, addressing envelopes, and filing receipts. You will find there will be less chance of unpaid or twice-paid bills if you split these jobs between yourselves, and neither one will lose track of what your real expenses are.

Emergency Cash

Stash a $10 bill or two somewhere in your house against an emergency. Everyone has experiences in which a check or credit card won't do; and automatic teller machines do go out of order now and then. (You might also stash a $5 bill in your car, in case you need gas or oil or a few groceries and are caught with an empty purse or wallet.)

Improving Resale Value

If you're about to buy a home with resale in mind, write down the aspects of the building or grounds that need improvement and that soured your

Don't Ruin Your Vacation by Running Short of Cash

Plan your money needs beforehand. Estimate how much you'll need for travel, hotels, meals, souvenirs, and emergencies. Then divide your funds among three sources:

- Credit cards. Use them for large expenses such as plane tickets, gasoline, lodging, and restaurant meals. That way you'll save your cash for places that don't accept credit cards. And you'll be able to put off paying until you get the credit card bill.

- Traveler's checks. They don't cost much, and because they're easily replaced, they can mean the difference between staying or going home should your money be lost or stolen. If you end up with traveler's checks left over once you get home, cash them in; don't bother to keep them because they don't earn any interest and are no more valuable than cash.

- Some cash and small change. These are necessary for things like vending machines, toll booths, and other incidentals that require cash. Don't carry all your funds in the same place, or at one time. And skip bringing your checkbook; it's one more thing you can lose. Many merchants don't accept out-of-town checks, anyway. To play it safe, keep your banker's name and phone number handy; in a real emergency, you can call and arrange to have money in your checking account wired to you.

first impression. Later, when it comes time to get the house ready for market, you can refer back to this list for top-priority improvements. Without such a record, you and your family will likely learn to live with the home's faults, and the resale value will suffer for it.

Should You Prepay Your Mortgage?

Would it be to your advantage to prepay your mortgage? That depends largely on your mortgage rate. If it is low (between 6 and 12%) and your money could be placed in savings vehicles that pay 13% or more, then you probably would be unwise to prepay.

But many homeowners have mortgage percentage rates *above* the levels of reliable savings plans and funds, and prepayments could benefit them.

Small prepayments are usually allowed without penalty. With compound interest, if you pay off just $50 extra at the end of the first year of a 14%, 30-year mortgage, the compounded savings would be over $2,200 (and your mortgage would be paid ahead of schedule). But remember to figure in your benefit from deducting the interest portion of your remaining principal.

A Progressive Yard Sale

In warm weather, when many families sell unwanted household items at garage or yard sales, you may be able to participate in a progressive sale. Combine forces with two or three other families; space your sales a week apart, and add items left unsold at one sale to the merchandise offered the next week. Your profits should be better than those from just one sale.

Save on Legal Fees

Mediators and legal clinics provide a money-saving alternative to legal fees. Middle-income families can save legal fees by having legal clinics

---

Gift Giving

It's nice to be generous but foolhardy to go overboard with holiday gift giving. To help keep spending in line:

- Prepare a holiday budget. Decide ahead of time how much you can afford. Consider the cost of extra food, entertainment, and decorations that always come with the holidays. Have a gift in mind before you head for the stores. That way you'll be less likely to buy on impulse.

- Beware of "buy now, pay later" offers. If a store says it will skip billing you for purchases until March or April, ask whether interest charges will accrue during that time. If it will cost you extra to put off paying, it's no bargain.

- Give freebies—gifts that don't cost anything. Be innovative: Offer a day of errands for an elderly friend or relative. Bake for a busy neighbor. Encourage your children to give their time to others. Give your skilled services, such as consulting, sewing, or gardening, for free. Often these gifts are appreciated more than anything you could buy at a store.

handle routine cases, such as uncontested divorces (the average divorcing couple requires approximately 14 hours of attorney's fees), bankruptcies, personal injuries, adoptions, wills, disability claims, landlord-tenant disputes, drunken driving charges, small claims, name changes, and Social Security and unemployment hearings. Some will handle criminal cases. Legal clinics also provide self-help services. If your problem is too complicated for the clinic to handle, the staff will refer you to other professionals.

Funerals

To some, preplanning a funeral may seem morbid. However, anyone who has made funeral arrangements after the loss of a relative or friend knows how difficult it can be to guess whether Aunt Harriet would have wanted to spend that much for a casket, whether she wanted a religious service, or whether she wanted to be an organ donor.

In 1983, the average cost of a funeral was between $3,700 and $6,800. Cremation is less expensive than a conventional funeral because it saves cemetery costs; the total cost is approximately $1,000. In many states, no casket is required, and in most states, ashes may be scattered over land or sea, or ashes may be placed in a columbarium niche at a cemetery.

Funeral services are not required before burial. Religious rules, custom, or personal wishes may indicate direct disposition. The body is transported directly from the place of death to the place of disposition (cemetery or crematory). With immediate burial many funeral home services are not required (embalming, viewing, casket), so the total cost is usually cut in half. A memorial service may be held later.

Planning Vacations

To spare yourself the expense of travel guides and maps, write the chamber of commerce, the bureau of tourism, and the National Parks Information Center at your planned destination for free maps, accommodation and restaurant guides, calendars of special events, historical background, guides to tourist attractions, and reservation information. You may receive as a bonus discount coupons for meals, lodging, and attractions.

Wiring Money from Out of Town

When you are due a large amount of money from someone who is out of town, consider having the money wired to you, rather than sent by check. Typically, bankers require up to three weeks of clearing time for sizable out-of-state checks before you can get to your money. If the money is sent by wire, you have immediate use of it.

To receive funds by wire, see the manager of the bank where the money is to be sent. You need to know the amount, the name of the bank it is coming from, the name of the person sending it, and the account number it is being drawn from. The fee for a wire transfer is minimal—$5 to $10—payable by the person sending the money.

Taking Pictures

If you're traveling with an untried camera, take advantage of a 1-hour film developing service and test a roll of photos. This precaution may spare you the disappointment of learning only after returning home that your camera was malfunctioning.

Unless you are a professional photographer or a talented amateur, only a few of the prints from each roll of film are truly memorable. It is much less expensive to have slides developed, review them for the best shots, and have these developed into prints than to have prints automatically made of the whole roll.

Second-Hand Stores

Clean out your closet and introduce yourself to second-hand shops. Many will accept used clothing on a consignment basis, which means that you will recover part of the stores' take for your items. Natural fabrics offer the best value for wear and appearance and typically bring more money. When shopping for yourself, stop in often: The inventory in thrift shops changes daily. When you find something you like, buy it, because it may not be there tomorrow, and a store usually has an inventory of only one such garment. Always try on clothes, and be sure to check for stains, worn elbows and knees, and broken zippers.

8 Gardening Indoors and Out

Fruits

(See also Controlling Pests and Diseases, in this chapter.)

Fruit Trees

Winter Protection

Cold winters can be hard on fruit trees, especially young ones. To help them make it through the winter, apply 4 inches of mulch in late fall after the ground has frozen. The mulch keeps the soil from alternately freezing and thawing, and it also reduces the loss of soil moisture.

Preventing Sunscald

Strong, early spring sun can also hurt fruit trees. Sunscald damage, as it is called, occurs when the sun heats the bark, causing the cambium to become active. The bark is then injured by the next cold night. To prevent it, coat the trunk and main limbs with white exterior latex paint in the fall. The white paint prevents sunscald by reflecting light and heat.

A Natural Brace for Old Trees

Do you have a fine old fruit tree with a V-shaped crotch that you want to preserve? Prevent it from splitting down the middle as it gets older by building a support bridge with water sprouts from each leg of the trunk. Tie them together with rope in the V space, letting the leafy ends of the water sprouts extend on opposite sides of the trunk. Wrap several bands of masking tape around the two sprouts to hold them tightly together. Within three or four years, they will grow together to form a natural brace. When the brace is about 2 inches in diameter, cut off the branch tips. This technique will add many years to the life of a heavy-bearing tree.

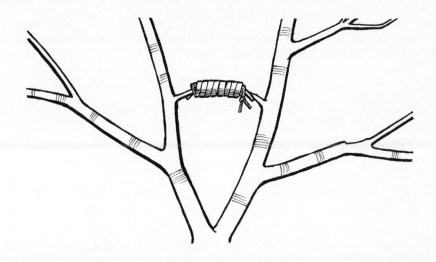

Pruning an Old Apple Tree

If you have an old, neglected apple tree that needs heavy pruning to restore it to production, spread the project over three years. Removing too many branches at once will result in an unproductive tangle of suckers and water sprouts.

Follow the rule of thumb that you can remove a third of the live wood each year. First, cut out and burn all dead, damaged, diseased, and insect-infested branches. Then gradually thin the healthy wood, removing all vertical growth like water sprouts, branches that grow toward the center of the tree, and branches with weak, narrow crotch angles (less than 35°). Encourage horizontal branches, since they are the most fruitful, and prune more heavily in the top of the tree so that sunlight reaches the lower limbs.

Berries

Storing Plants

If you can't plant your strawberries the day they arrive, keep them dormant by storing them in a plastic bag in the refrigerator. Once they break dormancy, every day out of the ground sets them back, reducing yields.

Southern-Slope Berries

Strawberries will fruit at least a week earlier on a south-facing slope than on one that faces north.

Narrow Rows for More Fruit

Strawberries grown in narrow rows produce more fruit than those grown in wide or matted rows, because the plants in the middle of wide rows suffer from shading.

Ready-to-Eat in Eight Weeks

By modifying cultural methods, you can pick strawberries eight weeks after setting out plants instead of waiting a year. Space your plants 4 inches apart in rows 12 inches wide, leaving enough room between rows to walk comfortably if you cultivate by hand or to accommodate your tiller. Mulch the plants and let them form flowers, but carefully remove all runners. The first year's crop will ripen two months later, and you'll get a second, larger crop the following year. With good culture and removal of all runners, the plants should produce well for three to five years. Tests have shown that this system produces heavier crops of larger, better-formed berries than the traditional matted-row system.

Winter Protection

To protect your strawberries over winter, too little mulch is better than too much. Tests at the University of Minnesota showed that 2 inches of straw is enough. Thicker layers may cause plants to suffocate because water percolates down through the mulch, freezes in a layer on the ground, and stays frozen all winter. The soil can't breathe, and carbon dioxide builds up and kills the roots.

Feeding Blueberries

Blueberries don't need heavy feeding, especially if they are kept well mulched. A mature bush needs only about 1 pound of cottonseed meal per year for good growth and heavy yields.

Pruning Bramble Fruits

The bramble fruits, namely raspberries (except for fall-bearing raspberry strains), blackberries, and dewberries, all produce their fruit on canes that grew the preceding year. It's important to understand this growth pattern in order to properly prune the plants. As soon as the crop of berries has been picked, cut the canes off at ground level and remove them from the garden. Do *not* cut off the new canes that are growing alongside the bearing canes—these will produce the next year.

Other Fruits

Winter Protection for Figs

To protect figs from frost, cover the branches that bear ripening fruit with plastic bags just before your usual frost date. Tie stone-filled tin cans to the bags to prevent them from blowing away.

Plastic Mulch for Melons

Black plastic is an excellent mulch for melons because they need warm soil to do well. Researchers have found that melons seeded or transplanted through black plastic yielded earlier and twice as heavily as those planted in bare soil. Black plastic absorbs heat from the sun, holds it in at night, keeps down weeds, and helps retain soil moisture.

Indoor Flowers and Plants

Preserving Cut Flowers

Cut flowers will keep longer if you add a little salt to the water in which they stand. The salt seems to slow the growth of decay-producing bacteria.

To prolong the life of fresh-cut flowers, add 2 tablespoons of white vinegar and 2 tablespoons of cane sugar to a quart of water and place the flowers in this solution.

Dipping cut flowers into a solution of baking soda and water also extends their life.

Nail Your Violets

Insert a few rusty nails into the soil around your African violets. The blossoms will be larger, more profuse, and brighter in color.

Starting African Violets

To start African violets, fill a juice glass with water and cover the top with aluminum foil. Poke a hole in the center of the foil with a pencil and, by handling the stem only, remove a healthy leaf from a violet plant (break the leaf stem off as close as possible to the trunk). Insert the stem into the hole so that it is almost completely submerged in the water. Be careful not to get the leaf wet, or a scar may form. Place the glass in a sunny window and leave it there until a good root system has developed. Plant the leaf in a small (3-inch) pot and water from the bottom only. Place the potted plant in an east window if possible. Avoid direct sunlight. After the roots take hold and a new plant has been established, the original leaf may be removed for balance. Water at least once a week but do not overwater.

Quarantine New Plants

When you purchase a plant, you're understandably anxious to get it home and into the right setting. But you shouldn't introduce a new plant to an area that already contains plants without first putting it in quarantine. Isolate the new plant for two to three weeks, inspecting it every few days for signs of insects or disease. Place it among your other plants only after you are sure it is not infested.

Avoiding Greenhouse Shock

Bringing a plant from a moist greenhouse environment into a warm, dry home may cause it to suffer "greenhouse shock." The leaves will quickly wilt, dry, and eventually drop off, and the plant will soon die. You can prevent greenhouse shock by enclosing your plant in a plastic bag. Open the bag gradually over a two-week span. The plant will slowly acclimate itself to the lower humidity level, avoiding the often-fatal shock.

Watering Tips

Don't water your houseplants with water straight from the tap. Chances are your water contains chlorine, which, while not deadly to plants, is a chemical they don't need to be exposed to. You can remove the chlorine by putting the tap water in an open container (such as a large, uncapped plastic jug) and letting it stand for 24 hours. After this time, the chlorine will have diffused into the air.

Another advantage to letting water stand is that it will be at room temperature when you're ready to use it. Cold water will shock plant roots, and repeated applications can stunt growth and invite disease.

Plants in clay pots need watering more frequently than those in plastic or glazed ceramic pots, since water evaporates through the porous walls of the unglazed clay. Keep this in mind when choosing pots for hanging plants or others that are difficult to water—a plastic pot can reduce the number of waterings you must provide.

In summer, water around noon time, since plants will lose more water through their leaves in the peak temperatures of afternoon. During the

Too Much Water

More houseplants are killed by overwatering than by any other single factor. This killing with kindness is easy to understand, since it is normal for people to worry about plants drying out. But the damage caused by drying out from underwatering is far less severe than that caused by an excess of water.

A plant wilted from dryness can usually be revived by giving it water, misting it lightly, and placing it out of direct sun. The symptoms of overwatering, on the other hand, are more difficult to detect and far less reversible. An overwatered plant will soon display wilted and yellowed leaves, which will eventually drop off. In some cases, the lower leaves and the base of the stem will begin to rot, the leaf tips will become brittle, or scablike bubbles will appear on the undersides of leaves. When this happens, you can be sure that root damage also has occurred. It is best to repot the plant, trimming away all the affected root and leaf portions, then put it in good light but out of direct sun. If the situation looks hopeless, take some tip cuttings and start over.

winter, watering in the early morning is best because it offers a full day of rising temperatures, allowing top-watered greenery to dry off before dark. Never water at night, since this will encourage soggy soil around plant roots and lingering moisture on leaves, both invitations to disease.

Glove Duster

Wash both sides of the leaves of houseplants at once by putting on an old cotton glove (or old sock), dipping it in tepid water, and running two gloved fingers along a leaf, one on top and one on the underside.

Plant Bath

You can clean small plants and help keep pests away by giving the plants a "bath." Wrap a cloth or piece of paper around the stem and over the edges of the pot to hold the plant and soil in place, and dunk the plant upside down in a bucket of mild soapy water. (Use 2 tablespoons of soap flakes such as Ivory or Octagon dissolved in 1 gallon of warm water.) Then dip the plant in clear water at room temperature to rinse.

Foam for Pebbles

Instead of using pebbles for drainage in flowerpots, use small pieces of expanded foam, such as those used as packing material for shipping. Just place a handful of them in the bottom of the pot. They do not decay, and they weigh less than pebbles, so you don't have to worry about adding too much weight to pots that you may want to hang from the ceiling.

Eggshells for Pebbles

Crushed eggshells also make a good substitute for pebbles. They promote drainage and add lime to the soil.

Controlling Pests and Diseases

Birds and Other Wildlife

Birdproof Berries

The most effective way to protect blueberries from birds is to build a frame that will hold birdproof netting about 6 inches from the plants. Since the fruit is borne on the branch tips, birds will be able to reach it if you just drape the bushes with netting.

Open up the seams of several mesh onion bags and sew them together to form one large piece of "netting" to protect strawberry or other berry patches from birds. Or use the uncut bags to protect peaches and grape clusters.

Birdproof Fruit Bags

Protect your ripening grapes from hungry birds by covering the fruit with grocery bags. To prepare the bags, place about 20 of them flat on a table and cut off two corners at the bottom of each with a sharp knife. This allows for drainage and ventilation, which keep the grapes from rotting. Use a stapler to fasten a bag around each grape bunch.

Can Your Corn

Keep birds and squirrels away from your corn with aluminum cans. Cut out one end of each can, and poke air holes all around the outside. As soon as the birds start to pick at your crop, put a can over each ear of corn. Neither the birds nor the squirrels will be able to get to the ears. Leave the cans on until the corn ripens.

Corn Socks

Save your old socks and stockings if you have trouble with squirrels stealing your corn. Cover each ear with a sock just before it gets ripe but after it's been pollinated. The squirrels won't bother the covered ears.

Thick-Plant Peas

If robins or other birds are eating your peas, try this. Plant peas in rows 8 inches apart, leaving 3 to 4 inches of space between seeds. Put several rows in a square patch of ground. The peas will grow together and the birds won't be able to walk between the rows. All they'll be able to get at are the peas on the outside rows, and you can harvest the rest.

Inner-Tube Snake

To keep jays and crows from stealing your corn seedlings, try putting an old bicycle inner tube in the patch. One tube protects about 12 square feet. Many birds will be scared away because the inner tube looks like a snake.

Reviving Mole-Chewed Plants

If moles are tunneling under your newly planted rows, cutting off the roots of seedlings, try this to fill in those tunnels and get your young plants growing again: Straddle a plant, with the front part of each of your shoes on either side of it. Shift your weight to the toes of both feet at the same time. If you do it right, the plant and the soil around it will sink down about 2 inches, caving in the tunnels. You can also do this with your hands. The plant should resume normal growth in a few days.

Deer Trellis

To keep deer out of your garden, try laying down trellis fencing or mesh with large openings between the rows and around the perimeter. Set the fencing on 3-inch-high strips of wood so that it's raised off the ground. Deer won't step on it because their feet will get caught.

Garden Ghost

Try spooking deer out of your garden with a "ghost." Tie three corners of a sheet to 4-foot poles set in the ground. It will snap and flap in the wind, keeping deer a safe distance away.

Soapy Repellent

Commercial apple growers in the Midwest have discovered that hanging bars of deodorant soap in their trees keeps the deer away; evidently they don't like the smell.

Cagey Melons

Keep animals from chewing on your ripening melons by caging the fruit with plastic milk crates. Place a milk crate over each melon. As the fruit ripens, move the crates to smaller melons.

Wire Wrap for Trees

Chicken wire wrapped around trees effectively keeps mice and other animals from girdling the trunks, but only if it extends above the normal snow line.

Cats and Dogs

Pepper Your Flowers

To keep cats and dogs out of your flower beds, sprinkle the beds liberally with black pepper. The animals dislike the smell, and if they get too close, they'll have sneezing fits.

Catproof Beds

If the neighborhood cats are scratching in your newly planted seed beds, try laying chicken wire over each bed. The cats can't get to the soil below, and many won't even walk on the wire. It doesn't interfere with sprouting seedlings and can be removed when the seedlings are a few inches high and the cats have lost interest in your beds.

Insects

Aphids

To get rid of aphids, mix nonfat dry milk with water according to the directions on the box, then put it in a spray bottle and apply it to the leaves of your plants. As the milk dries, the aphids get stuck in the milky residue and die. Nonfat dry milk is inexpensive and does no harm to your plants.

Aphids and whiteflies are attracted to bright yellow and can be trapped by placing yellow boards or other yellow objects—coated with heavy motor oil, petroleum jelly, or Tack Trap—near susceptible plants. Recoat the traps when they dry out.

The yellow plastic lids that come on some coffee and cat food cans also make good aphid traps. Paint them with honey or a commercial trapping solution. If washed regularly, the lids can be used over and over.

Plant kernels of garlic 5 or 6 inches apart around your fuchsia plants in the spring to keep away aphids.

Apple Maggot Flies

Apple maggot flies lay their eggs on apples. You can trap them by hanging 3½-inch red balls coated with Tack Trap or Tanglefoot in your apple trees when the flies become active in early summer. Use two traps per tree for dwarf trees and six to eight for standard trees, hanging them where they will be easily visible. Recoat the balls every two weeks.

Cabbageworm Moths

Protect your cabbages from cabbageworm moths and other pests by covering the heads with old pantyhose legs. The hose will let in light and will stretch as the cabbages grow.

Caterpillars

Researchers have found that bitter chemicals called limonoids in citrus fruits discourage certain caterpillars from feeding. If you want to try limonoids on your garden insect pests, grind up citrus rinds and seeds, soak them in water overnight, strain the liquid, and spray the extract on your plants.

Cherry Sawflies

Wormy cherries are usually caused by cherry sawflies. You can trap the adult flies before they lay their eggs in the cherries by hanging ammonia-scented, sticky, white boards in the trees at petal fall.

Codling Moth Lures

Codling moths, whose caterpillars feed on apples, can easily be lured into a pot of two parts vinegar to one part molasses hung from an apple tree limb. Clean out dead moths and replenish the mixture as necessary.

Cutworms

True to their name, cutworms feed by chewing through the stems of garden plants. These little devils can destroy a whole row of seedlings in one night. But you can outsmart them with this simple control: Cutworm moths seek out mulch and crop residues as egg-laying sites in early spring, so clean up the garden thoroughly every fall. Cutworm caterpillars depend on weed seedlings for the first week after hatching. By tilling the soil as soon as it can be worked in spring and delaying planting for 10 to 14 days, you can kill the weeds and effectively starve out close to 100% of the larvae.

A handful of hydrated lime (not ground limestone) sprinkled around plants in a circle 2 to 3 inches in diameter will keep cutworms away. Even if a spring shower wets the newly applied lime, the plants remain off limits to the pests.

Earwigs

Earwigs chew holes in plants at night and congregate in tight, dark places by day. Trap them by laying pieces of corrugated cardboard near susceptible crops. The bugs will hide in the corrugations. Then you can simply pick up the cardboard and burn it.

Fire Ants

The easiest, safest way to kill a fire ant colony is to pour 3 gallons of scalding water on the mound. Biologists at Florida State University killed 8 of 14 colonies this way. Hot water is most effective when ants are near the surface, so treat the mounds on a cool, sunny day after the soil has warmed. If you still see ants after a few days, repeat the treatment.

Flies

You can catch flies around the barn or compost pile by placing a bit of raw fish in a quart canning jar filled with ½ inch of water. Punch a few holes in the lid with a nail. The flies can crawl in but can't fly or crawl out. Replace the lure with fresh fish when the stench really gets to you or the jar is filled with flies—whichever comes first!

Grasshoppers

If your garden is overrun with grasshoppers, plant basil around the borders. The grasshoppers will munch on the basil and leave your other plants alone.

An easy way to destroy large numbers of grasshopper eggs is by shallow tilling in late fall. This exposes the eggs to the sun, weather, and birds and other predators.

Mosquitoes

If mosquitoes and other bugs attack you while you're gardening, make a portable smudge pot out of a metal bucket or small charcoal grill. Fill the bucket or grill with small kindling chips, light it, and add a handful of green grass or a piece of garden sod to make the smoke. Move the bucket around the work areas as you garden. Be sure to wear gloves to protect your hands because the bucket gets hot. (See also First Aid in the chapter, Here's to Your Health.)

Slugs

Slugs will avoid a garden ringed with a light sprinkling of moth crystals (not mothballs). This also discourages cats, dogs, and raccoons. (See also Cats and Dogs, and Birds and Other Wildlife, in this chapter.)

Try vinegar to destroy slugs. Mix it with water in a 50:50 solution in a plastic spray bottle. Go into the garden after dark, aim at the slugs on plants, and start spraying. If you spray the ground at the base of the plants, hidden slugs will appear and they, too, will die almost immediately. Don't make the solution stronger than 50:50. It has no greater effectiveness and can damage plant foliage.

Sometimes sprinkling slugs with salt doesn't work on the first application, and the pests just crawl away. Try this instead: Sprinkle salt into a moistened jar so that it clings to the sides as well as the bottom. Then just pluck up the slugs and put them into the jar. The salty sides will keep them from crawling up while you search for others. When the jar is full, put on the lid and throw the jar away.

Squash Bugs

Squash bugs, those brownish black, flat-backed insects that you find hiding under leaves, can seriously damage cucurbit crops. You can kill the adults and young by spraying them with insecticidal soap, rotenone, or pyrethrum. Check the plants daily, and spray when the adults first appear in spring. Crush the eggs, which are laid in geometric patterns on the undersides of leaves. If you've consistently had problems with squash bugs, avoid deep mulches like hay and straw, which provide hiding places for them. Plow under or burn all garden litter in the fall to eliminate shelters for the overwintering insects.

If you grow dill, make it work for you in the garden as a squash bug and cucumber beetle repellent. Plant the dill with all your vine crops.

Instead of hand-picking large populations of squash bugs or Mexican bean beetles, use an old household vacuum cleaner with a round upholstery brush attachment. The soft bristles won't bruise tender plants. When you're done vacuuming up the pests, shake a little rotenone inside the bag to kill the insects. Don't use a shop vacuum because the powerful suction could damage the plants.

Tomato Worms

If tomato fruitworms are a problem in your tomato patch, plant cherry tomatoes for several seasons to interrupt the fruitworm's life cycle. Researchers at the Department of Vegetable Crops at the University of California, Davis, have discovered that the thick skins and higher alkaloid content of the cherry tomatoes repel both the fruitworm and the sugar beet armyworm.

A generous pinch of snuff in the hole when transplanting tomatoes will prevent tomato worms and other insects from feeding on them. Be careful not to put it beyond the reach of the roots, but don't let the tobacco touch the roots when planting. A pocket-size tin of snuff will treat 12 to 15 plants.

Weevils

You can keep weevils from eating your stored dry beans by chilling or heating them after harvest. Freeze the beans at 0°F for a day or so, or put them in a 150°F oven for an hour. Either method will kill the insects and their eggs. Don't heat beans you plan to use for seed because it will destroy their germinating ability.

Yellowjackets

Here's a safe way to eradicate an underground yellowjacket colony: Press a small cone made from window screen over the hole on a cool night, and place a clear plastic shoebox over the cone. The workers will leave the nest, enter the trap, and be unable either to leave the box or reenter the cone. The colony will die in a week or two. Stuff rags and dirt around the base of the trap to prevent escapes.

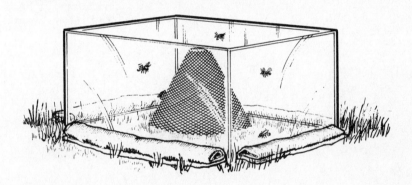

Weedy Attractions

Leave a patch or a few rows of mixed weeds near your garden crops during growing season. Weeds are often the preferred food for pests and can decoy them away from your crops. Weeds also provide food and shelter for beneficial insects.

Ammonia Jugs Repel Bugs

To protect fruit trees from insects, suspend empty plastic gallon jugs from lower branches and pour about ¼ cup of ammonia into each container. The rising fumes will keep the bugs away. Replace the ammonia after a rainfall because it will be too diluted then. Use this method only before blossoms are showing so that you don't chase away the bees.

Diseases

Blossom-End Rot

Water stress brought on by either drought or excessive rain is the most frequent cause of blossom-end rot, a common disorder of tomatoes, peppers, and melons. You can beat drought by providing at least an inch of water a week, keeping the plants well mulched, and maintaining high levels of organic matter in the soil. Calcium deficiency can also cause blossom-end rot, so keep your soil pH up around 6 to 6.5 by applying limestone as needed.

Celery Blight

To prevent late blight of celery, either soak the seed in quite warm (but not very hot—about 120°F) water for 25 minutes before planting, or store the seed in a cool, dry place for a year before using it. The seed will remain viable for up to five years, but the fungus spores that cause blight die after two years.

Fight Blight with Vinegar

Keep fire blight at bay in your apple orchard with vinegar—blight is acid-intolerant and vinegar is acidic. Even highly susceptible varieties like the Transparent apple will beat the blight when sprayed with a 50:50 mixture of water and apple-cider vinegar. Anytime you see leaves that look burnt, spray to keep blight from spreading. Respray after rain or at two-week intervals during the growing season.

Potato Scab

There are three steps you can take to prevent your potatoes from getting scab: (1) Plant scab-free seed potatoes; (2) rotate your crop, but avoid planting potatoes where other root crops like turnips, beets, and carrots grew the previous year, as these crops are also susceptible to scab; and (3) be sure your potatoes have enough water at the time of tuber set (one to two months after planting) because dry soil encourages scab.

Seeds and Seedlings

(See also Soil Preparation, and Vegetables, in this chapter.)

Germination

Water Seedlings at Room Temperature

Allow water to come to room temperature before using it on seedlings you start indoors. Water straight from the tap is usually too cold; it chills seedling roots, significantly slowing growth.

Thermos Soak

Soak seeds in warm water for 24 to 48 hours before planting to soften the seed coat and promote quicker sprouting. This can be done conveniently by placing the seeds in a wide-mouthed thermos bottle with warm water. The thermos keeps the water warm, and the wide mouth makes seed removal easy.

Steep Hard Seeds

While warm water is good for soaking seeds, many hard seeds benefit from being soaked in strong tea overnight as well. It's the tannic acid in the tea that works to soften the outer covering.

Light Bulbs for Beans

Beans won't sprout unless room temperature is 68°F or higher. You can grow bean sprouts in a colder room, however, by placing the sprout jar near a 75-watt light bulb. The bulb gives off a good amount of heat. Wrap the jar in a dish towel and leave one end open for air circulation.

Roll Your Beets

If you have trouble getting your beet seeds to germinate, try spreading the seeds on a piece of wax paper and rolling them with a rolling pin. This crushes the outside husks, giving the seeds a head start.

Soilless Germinating Mix

To avoid the bother of pasteurizing soil for seed starting, use a soilless germinating mix consisting of equal parts of milled sphagnum, perlite, and vermiculite. It is free of disease organisms, and seedling roots penetrate it easily. But it contains no nutrients, so transplant the seedlings as soon as their first true leaves appear.

Paintbrush Sowing

When you use a trowel or your hands to cover small seeds with soil, you sometimes bury them too deep, inhibiting germination. Try using a paintbrush instead. It lets you better control the amount of soil you put on the seeds.

Citrus Planters

After you've eaten or juiced half an orange or grapefruit, use the skin as a "pot" for germinating seedlings. Scoop out the remaining pulp and fill the half with soil, then plant your seeds. When you're ready to put them in the ground, plant them, citrus half and all. The citrus will decay, adding nutrients to the soil.

Water-Heater Germinator

Place germination trays or seedling flats on top of your water heater for even bottom heat and quicker germination. If the water heater is wrapped with insulation, make a removable cover by cutting around the top. The insulation can be replaced and fastened with tape when the seeds have germinated.

Fluorescent Tubes for Grow Lights

If you want to start seeds or grow houseplants under fluorescent lights, it isn't necessary to buy grow lights. Cool white or warm white fluorescent tubes are as effective, less expensive, and longer lasting than grow lights.

Cool white tubes are rich in light from the blue end of the light spectrum — the light that seedlings need for best growth. The red light given off by warm white tubes encourages flowering and bright colors. Use one tube of each to grow the widest range of plants.

Storage

Bag Your Seed Flats

To prevent planted seed flats from drying out, keep them in clear plastic bags until germination occurs. Check them often to make sure there isn't too much moisture inside the bags, which could foster disease.

Keeping Seeds Dry

If you keep them dry and at room temperature, seeds such as beet, cucumber, muskmelon, mustard, and tomato will maintain their germination rates for over five years. Seeds that will keep up to five years are asparagus, bean, broccoli, Brussels sprout, cabbage, cauliflower, celery, chicory, endive, okra, pea, pepper, spinach, and watermelon. To ensure dryness, keep seeds in tightly sealed jars along with ½ cup of flour or dry milk.

Prepackaged silica in your seed jars will also keep seeds dry. Pharmacies use these small, tissue-wrapped packets to keep medications dry until dispensed. Ask for them at your drugstore.

Refrigerate Cuttings

To protect cuttings when you can't get around to planting them right away, store them in a plastic bag in the vegetable crisper of your refrigerator. Spray a little water in the bag, insert the cuttings, and tightly tie the top of the bag. Cuttings will stay fresh for at least one week this way.

Soil Preparation

Compost

Sawdust

Compost sawdust before adding it to the garden. Because it is a high-carbon/low-nitrogen material, raw sawdust can cause a nitrogen deficiency in the soil as it decays. If you must use it fresh, be sure to add a rich nitrogen source like blood meal, cottonseed meal, or manure.

Put Sowbugs to Work

Sowbugs much prefer decaying matter to growing plants, so put them to work in your compost pile. Gather up all of the sowbugs you can find and introduce them to the pile. Punch a deep hole and drop them in. Then cap the hole with soil. The sowbugs will start to eat their way out, aerating the pile with their tunnels. To encourage the sowbugs to reproduce, lay wooden boards on the damp surface of the compost pile, and they'll breed underneath.

Quick Composting

If you have animals or have access to manure, you can start a compost pile in little time. Put a wheelbarrowful of manure mixed with sawdust in the middle of the compost pile. Within 24 hours the pile should be heating. (The composting process is activated by the nitrogen content of the manure.) Instead of rotating the entire pile every few days, which is a lot of work, replace a small portion each day, putting the top of the pile off to one side and moving some of the pile from the opposite side to the top. Rotate a different part of the pile like this every day or so. The heating

Easy Composting

Making compost is not difficult. The basic method calls for layering natural ingredients in heaps in mixed proportions, providing necessary air and moisture, and turning the heaps to provide bacterial action in all parts of the pile. Just about any organic material can be used. Some of the most common are:

- Leaves: Rich in minerals, they should be chopped or finely shredded for best results. Mix with weeds, lawn clippings, or plant residues.

- Hay: Green legume hay will break down quickly in a compost heap, though any hay or straw makes a worthwhile addition to the heap. Shredding hastens decomposition.

- Garden residue: Dried or green tomato or squash vines, cornstalks, flower stems, and weeds can be shredded or added whole to the heap.

- Grass: Grass clippings can be used dry or green.

- Kitchen garbage: High in nitrogen, kitchen vegetable trimmings can be used for green matter in the heap.

- Paper: Unprinted paper and cardboard are suitable for composting if shredded.

Sawdust, wood chips, nutshells, peanut hulls, coffee wastes, and dried blood are all good compostable materials, not to mention animal manures. In short, any decomposable organic material can be used for composting, except human feces, diseased animals, plant debris impregnated with pesticides or herbicides, and other toxic materials.

There are several methods of composting that can be used on the small farm or in the home garden. The Indore method, devised by Sir Albert Howard, was the first scientific method of composting. Using this method, compost can be made either in open piles or in will continue, and after three weeks, the compost should be ready to go. To keep the water content high, prevent leaching, and maintain the high temperature, cover the pile with a plastic sheet.

Here's another quick and easy compost method if you don't have manure but do have a good supply of grass clippings. Grass is also quite high in

bins. The average pile is 6 feet wide, 3 to 5 feet high, and 10 to 30 feet long. First, spread a 6-inch layer of plant wastes over the area to be covered by the pile. Then add a 2-inch layer of manure and bedding. Follow with a ⅛-inch-thick layer of topsoil. Finally, spread a sprinkling of lime, phosphate rock, granite dust, or wood ashes to increase the mineral content of the heap. (Lime should not be added if you want an acid compost.) Water the pile and continue layering in the same manner until the desired height is reached. Do not trample on the heap; if it is matted down, aeration will be impeded, and a compost heap needs plenty of oxygen to aid decomposition.

Within a few days the heap will begin to heat up and start to shrink. Turn the pile with a pitchfork two or three weeks after it is made and again at the five-week mark. Take care to place the outer parts on the inside so that they can decay fully. The heap will probably heat up to almost 150°F at the outset. After the first turn, the temperature will rise again but will then settle to a steady 130°F. The compost will be finished in about three months.

Another composting technique is called the 14-day method. If you choose this method, you must first grind or shred all materials going into the compost pile. The reasons for this are several. First, the surface area of material on which microorganisms can multiply is greatly increased. Second, aeration of the mass is improved because shredded material has less tendency to mat or pack down. Third, moisture control is improved. Finally, turning of the heap is much easier.

Material is not layered in the 14-day method. It is mixed either before or after shredding, then piled in heaps no more than 5 feet high. After 3 days, the heap is turned. Turning is continued at 2- or 3-day intervals. After 12 to 14 days, the heat of the pile will have dropped, and the compost will be sufficiently decayed to use.

Quick-Start Gardens

It doesn't take much to start a small garden in an existing grassy area or in rocky soil. It just takes a bit of planning and one of the following schedules:

In a Grassy Area

- Mark the boundaries of the area you'd like to garden in the fall. Place a layer of two or three newspaper sheets on the grass and cover it with a thin layer of mulch or dirt.

- By the end of the spring you should see a thin layer of dark humus at the surface of the soil under the mulch, and there should be plenty of earthworms, too. The rain goes through the newspaper, and the mulch keeps watering to a minimum and controls weeds. The decaying grass underneath eliminates the need for organic matter, though you may want to sprinkle on some wood ashes.

- At the beginning of the summer, you'll have healthy, friable soil ready for planting.

nitrogen. Mix one part of sawdust with four parts of fresh grass clippings. Turn and mix the pile thoroughly every third day for three weeks. Do not make layers, and do not add water—the fresh clippings will produce enough moisture. The heat will go down by the fifteenth or eighteenth day, and the compost will be ready to use.

Measuring Tips

Keep in mind these weight-volume equivalents when you need to measure quantities of compost or manure: One bushel basket will hold about 46 pounds of compost. That's enough to cover 4½ square feet of garden 3 inches deep. One thousand pounds of compost will fill 21½ bushels and cover 100 square feet to a depth of 3 inches.

When using compost or manure to fertilize your garden, apply 2 bushels per 100 square feet every year. That amount will keep the soil in good condition and should supply all the nutrients your plants need. Very hot summers burn up organic matter quickly so gardeners in the Deep South and Southwest may need to use twice that amount, applying half in the spring and half between crops in midsummer.

In Rocky Soil
Here's a method that eliminates the need for rotary tilling or spading.

- Start by blocking off the area you'd like to garden with railroad ties or other wood borders in early spring. As soon as the ground thaws, wet down the area and lay down a double layer of newspaper, tucking the sheets under the ties along the edges. Then water the newspaper so that it doesn't blow away.

- For the next several months, add all kinds of organic material (strawy manure, kitchen scraps, grass clippings, autumn leaves, weeds) and some compost and soil. Whenever you spot an earthworm, gently transport it to your new garden bed.

- At the beginning of the summer, lay black plastic over the entire bed area. In the fall, remove the plastic and put in a layer of dead leaves. By the spring, you'll be ready to plant.

Cultivation

Too Wet to Work

Working the soil when it is too wet can ruin its structure for the season. Pick up a handful of soil and squeeze it. If the soil doesn't crumble easily when pressed, it's too wet to work.

Keep Off the Soil

Avoid walking back and forth over a wet garden. Repeated steps compress the soil, and compacted soil is inhospitable to plant roots. Provide paths either around beds or between rows.

Hoe to Control Weeds

If you cultivate to control annual weeds, don't hoe deeper than 2 inches. As you cultivate, you'll force all the weed seeds that are in the top 2 inches of soil to germinate. Once all the seedlings have been killed, few additional weeds will appear because most seeds buried 2 inches deep or more won't germinate.

N-P-K Content of Common Composting Materials

Material	% Nitrogen	% Phosphoric Acid	% Potash
Alfalfa, hay	2.45	.50	2.10
Apples, fruit	.05	.02	.10
Apples, leaves	1.00	.15	.35
Blood meal	12.0–15.0	1.30	.70
Coffee grounds	2.08	.32	.28
Coffee grounds, dried	1.99	3.60	.20
Corn, green forage	.30	.13	.33
Cottonseed meal	7.00	2.0–3.0	1.50
Cowpeas, green forage	.45	.12	.45
Crabgrass, green	.66	.19	.71
Eggshells	1.19	.38	.14
Feathers	15.30		
Field beans, shells	1.70	.30	.35
Fish scrap, fresh	2.00–7.5	1.50–6.0	
Freshwater mud	1.37	.26	.22
Garbage rubbish	3.4–3.7	.1–1.47	2.25–4.25
Gluten feed	4.0–5.0		
Grapes, fruit	.15	.07	.30
Hair	12.0–16.0		
Incinerator ash	.24	5.15	2.33
Kentucky bluegrass, green	.66	.19	.71
Kentucky bluegrass, hay	1.20	.40	1.55
Lemon culls	.15	.06	.26
Oak leaves	.80	.35	.15
Orange culls	.20	.13	.21
Peanuts, shells	.80	.15	.50
Pigweed, rough	.60	.16	

Material	% Nitrogen	% Phosphoric Acid	% Potash
Pine needles	.46	.12	.03
Potatoes, leaves and stalks	.60	.15	.45
Potatoes, tubers	.35	.15	.50
Prune refuse	.18	.07	.31
Pumpkins, flesh	.16	.07	.26
Pumpkins, seeds	.87	.50	.45
Ragweed	.76	.26	
Red clover, hay	2.10	.50	2.00
Redtop, hay	1.20	.35	1.00
Rhubarb, stems	.10	.04	.35
Rockweed	1.90	.25	3.68
Roses, flowers	.30	.10	.40
Salt-marsh hay	1.10	.25	.75
Salt mud	.40		
Seaweed	1.68	.75	4.93
Silkworm cocoons	9.42	1.82	1.08
Spanish moss	.60	.10	.55
Sweet potatoes	.25	.10	.50
Tea leaves	4.15	.62	.40
Timothy, hay	1.25	.55	1.00
Tomatoes, fruit	.20	.07	.35
Tomatoes, leaves	.35	.10	.40
Waste silt	8.0–11.0		
Wheat, bran	2.65	2.90	1.60
Wheat, straw	.50	.15	.60
White clover, green	.50	.20	.30

Mulch

Grass Clippings

Grass clippings are a good source of nitrogen and should be put to work in your garden and flower beds. Use them as a mulch, turn them into your garden as green manure, and add them to the compost heap to create the necessary heat for good decomposition. (See also Compost, in this chapter.)

Thick and Thin

How thick should a mulch be? Fine organic materials such as sawdust need be only 1 to 2 inches thick. Coarse materials such as straw should be at least 4 inches thick.

Soil Warmup

To encourage soil to warm up quickly in the spring, pull all mulches back from the planting beds. Replace the mulch as soon as the ground is warm.

Seed Coverup

If your soil is very dry and you doubt there is enough moisture for your seeds to sprout, try this. Make small holes in your soil for sowing seed and pour water into each hole until the soil is saturated. Sow the seeds and cover them lightly with soil. Immediately lay down old boards, burlap, or any material that will keep the wind and sun out and the moisture in. After three or four days, remove the covering only in the evening. (By doing so during the day, you may bake the soil.) If you get rain, remove the covering at that time also. This method will persuade even the hard-to-get-started seeds like beets, carrots, chard, and parsnips to sprout.

Soil Miscellany

Testing pH

A quick and inexpensive way to test garden soil pH is with blue litmus paper (you can find it at a pharmacy). Water your garden as usual, wait a few minutes, then press the paper to the damp earth. Do this in several spots, because the pH may vary from place to place. Blue litmus turns pink when brought into contact with acid. If the paper shows little or no change, your soil probably isn't acid.

Determining Soil pH

The pH of a large area can often be determined by the natural plant growth there, even though plots within that area can be quite different. The following are some clues to determining pH:

- Hard water in area springs and wells usually indicates abundant calcium carbonate (lime) in the soil, making it alkaline.

- Native trees of hemlock, white pine, red spruce, oak, and black spruce in relatively large numbers usually mean the soil is fairly acid.

- Native trees of Eastern white cedar and white spruce in quantity usually indicate alkalinity, especially in the subsoil.

- Wild blueberries, most ferns, wild orchids, rhododendrons, and bayberries are all signs of soil acidity at crop-growing depths.

- White and red clover in abundance mean the soil in the growing area is rich in alkaline materials as well as high in fertility.

Wheelbarrow Sterilizer

A wheelbarrow and a sheet of clear plastic make a great sterilizing chamber for potting mixes. Mix together and sift the soil, compost, and other amendments, then put a 2- to 3-inch layer of the mix in the wheelbarrow and cover it with the plastic. Leave the wheelbarrow in the sun for at least 8 hours, turning the mix two or three times. If you do this in mid- to late summer, the sun should be strong enough to heat the soil to a temperature more than adequate to kill bacteria and weed seeds. After each batch has "cooked," store it in jugs or jars until transplant time in spring. (See also Structures and Tools, in this chapter.)

Fishy Gardening

Do you have an angler in your family? Take advantage of the refuse left over after the fish cleaning. Bury the scraps in your garden about 6 inches deep. If they are covered well with soil the neighborhood cats won't find them, and they'll add rich nutrients to your garden.

Correcting Acid or Alkaline Soil

If your soil tests show that your soil is too acid, it may be brought back to a favorable pH by applying limestone. Ground limestone is the commonest and safest liming material. Of the two types of ground limestone, calcitic and dolomitic, the latter is preferred because it contains magnesium in addition to calcium, thus fertilizing the soil as well as neutralizing it.

To increase pH by one unit, spread 30 pounds of limestone on every 1,000 square feet of sandy soil, 50 pounds on sandy loam, 70 pounds on loam, and 80 pounds on heavy clay.

Another good material with which to lime soil is unleached hardwood ashes. If you have a fireplace or wood stove, save the ashes. If you can't put them on your soil right away, store them in a dry place, since rain quickly leaches out the lime and potash they contain. (Coal ashes are of little or no value.)

Spread your liming material on top of the soil in the fall after you have plowed, rotary tilled, or spaded deeply. Lime should not be plowed under, because it leaches down into the soil too rapidly. On lawns and pastures, spread lime in late summer. Lime should not be applied with other fertilizers and should not be used around acid-loving plants.

Do not expect dramatic results the first year you use ground limestone. The year after will show improvement. Liming should be repeated every fourth or fifth year, depending on the indications of soil tests. Be careful not to overlime—a pH of 7.5 means you've overdone it.

If your soil tests show that your soil is slightly alkaline, a little borax and manganese may help. A good way to acidify soil is to add naturally acid materials—acid muck from swamps, oak leaves, oak sawdust, ground-up oak bark, cottonseed meal, or acid peat moss. Increasing the organic matter content can be beneficial, too. Organic matter contains natural acid-forming material and produces acids directly on decomposition. These acids combine with excess alkali and neutralize it. Organic matter can be applied in great quantity without damaging the soil. It acts as a buffer against both excess alkalinity and excess acidity.

Give Your Plants the Soil pH They Need

The majority of common plants prefer a soil pH of 6.5 to 7. (On a pH scale from 1 to 14, 1 is extremely acid and 10 or more is extremely alkaline.) In the 6.5 to 7 pH range, all the essential mineral nutrients are available to plants in sufficient quantities. Incorporating good compost will help correct an adverse soil pH to the range where the most common plants will thrive. Even where the pH is less than optimum, plants will do well if there is sufficient organic matter present. The following tables show soil pH preferences for common plants:

Acid-Loving Plants (soil pH of 4 to 6)

azalea	marigold
bayberry	mountain laurel
blackberry	oak
blueberry	peanut
butterfly weed	pecan
cardinal flower	potato
chrysanthemum	radish
cranberry	raspberry
flax	rhododendron
heath	spruce
heather	sweet potato
huckleberry	trailing arbutus
lily	watermelon
lily-of-the-valley	yew
lupine	

Acid- to Neutral-Loving Plants (soil pH of 5 to 7)

apple	gypsophila
balloon flower	nicotiana
blazing star	pansy
cornflower	pumpkin
gardenia	redtop grass
gloxinia	rice
gold-banded lily	turnip

(continued)

Give Your Plants the Soil pH They Need—Continued

Alkaline-Loving Plants (soil pH of 7.5 to 10)

alyssum	lettuce
asparagus	mignonette
bean	nasturtium
beet	onion
cabbage	parsnip
cantaloupe	pea
carnation	phlox
cauliflower	rhubarb
celery	salsify
cucumber	squash
geum	sweet pea
iris	

Structures and Tools

Plant Protection

Inner Tube Heaters

Old inner tubes make great solar heaters for young plants, helping to ward off a late frost. Simply place the tube on the ground with the plant in the middle. Cut a hole in the tube just large enough to accommodate the nozzle of a garden hose; then insert the hose and fill the tube with water. Pinch the hole closed with a clothespin or two. The black rubber absorbs solar heat and stores it in the water.

Hot-Cap Anchors

If you've had bad luck using plastic jugs as hot caps because they won't stay put, here's a way to anchor them. Cut off the top and bottom of the jug and run a sharpened stick through the hollow handle. Put the jug over your plant and drive the stick into the ground. Even a good gust of wind won't disturb the hot cap.

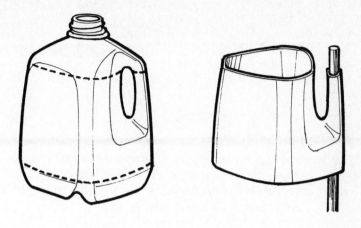

Window-Screen Tent

Propping two old wood-framed window screens like a tent creates a shady canopy for vegetables like lettuce and Chinese cabbage and provides a simple and easy way to blanch celery. If more shade is desired, drape the sides of the screen "tent" with gunny sacks or other porous material. In a windy location, you may want to secure the frames at the top.

Mirrored Transplants

When it's time to start transplants indoors, make double use of the light you get by putting all the plants on a large-mirrored dresser with the mirror facing the window. You won't have to turn the plants because the mirror will reflect the sunlight, preventing the plants from getting leggy as they stretch toward the light.

Plant Starters

Eggshell Planters

Whenever you break a raw egg for cooking, try to crack just one small portion of the end of the shell. Then rinse out the shell. While the shell is still wet, poke a small drain hole in the bottom end. Collect several and use them as pots for starting vegetable seedlings. When you transplant the seedlings, crush the shells so that the roots can get out. Eggshells add lime to the soil.

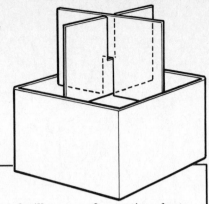

Milk-Carton Dividers

Many gardeners use the bottoms of milk cartons for starting plants. What they may not know is that the rest of the carton can be put to good use by cutting it into dividers so that up to eight plants can be started without danger of the roots intertwining.

Start by taking a half-gallon milk carton and cutting off the bottom 2½ to 3 inches to use for planting. Take the remainder of the container and cut apart the four sides. Cut each side into two rectangles the same height as the bottom planter (2½ to 3 inches). Then cut a slit in the middle of each rectangle, about halfway up. Fit two rectangles together at right angles, with one slit fitting into the other. These dividers then slip into the bottom of the carton to make four growing sections. To make eight smaller planting sections, use four rectangles and cut them down to size.

Grow Bag

Grow bags make it convenient to start seeds or young plants and later transfer them to the garden. Cut holes in the top of a bag of peat or other plant medium and poke small holes in the bottom of it for drainage. Plant your seeds and plants right in the bag, then water them and set the bag in a warm, sunny location. When your plants are ready to be set out, just carry the bag to the garden and transplant them by placing the bag in the ground and cutting it away from the plants.

Planting Beds

Post-Hole Digger for Even Spacing

To make evenly spaced holes of uniform depth in your raised-bed garden for transplanting plants, use a post-hole digger. It digs down deep into the subsoil quickly and easily.

High-Rise Beds

Heap the topsoil and compost higher in your raised beds each year; then as you grow older, less stooping will be required to plant and harvest your crops. One way to do this is to add a railroad tie each spring, along with another 6 to 8 inches of composted soil.

Straw Borders

Rectangular bales of straw make great borders for your raised beds. They provide insulation, and when a plastic sheet or a storm window is laid over the bales in the spring and fall, your growing beds become mini-greenhouses. In late fall the partially rotted bales can be used to cover root crops or added to the compost pile.

Easy-Reach Beds

When planning to build raised garden beds, remember that the width is more critical than the length. Beds between 3 and 5 feet wide make efficient use of space, yet are easy to work. Beds over 5 feet wide make it hard to reach the center for planting, picking, and weeding without stepping on the bed. Four-foot beds are the most comfortable for people with average reach.

Same-Size Beds

Fertilizer, yield, and planting calculations are easy if your planting beds are each 100 square feet (4×25 or 5×20). Making all of your raised beds the same size enables you to build trellises, cloches, cold frames, shading laths, and other accessories that can be moved from bed to bed as needed.

Beds for Tillers

If you're constructing raised beds and you know you'll be using a rotary tiller to work them, make the beds about twice as wide as the tiller so that you can keep one foot on the path while operating it. Don't build wooden sides on the beds.

Row Guides

For ease in planting straight rows in wooden-framed raised beds, measure off intervals along the long edges and make ⅛-inch-deep notches in the frame with a wood saw. A board or rake handle laid across two opposite notches indicates the position of a row to be planted.

Sink Your Garden

To reduce the effects of high-velocity, dry desert winds on your garden, use lowered beds, and set the beds crosswise to the prevailing winds. Try beds 8 to 16 inches below the surrounding earth surface, 3½ feet across, and up to 15 feet long.

Tools

Preserving Wood Handles

You can preserve the wood handles of garden tools by coating them with boiled linseed oil. If you leave your tools outside, the oil will be gradually weathered out of the wood by the sun and rain, but a coat each spring will protect the handles throughout the year.

Sandy Storage

Use a pail of clean, dry sand as a storage place for small garden tools. Push them into the sand in the pail when you're not using them and it will help keep them rust-free.

Polyurethane Protection

You can keep your gardening tools looking new and make them last longer by spraying the handles with clear polyurethane before their first use.

A Wicket Hose

Use old croquet wickets to route your garden hose around flowers, shrubs, and vegetables, and you'll never again have crushed plants.

Tire-Rim Rack

An old car tire rim makes a convenient rack for your garden hose. The rim can be welded to an iron stake and placed at the spigot or nailed right to the wall. Your hose won't unwind and it will stay neat and kink-free.

Apron Caddy

A handy and step-saving device for gardening is an apron. Buy or make one with large, deep pockets. They're great for holding seedlings, seed packets, small trowels, and other tools.

Glove and Hat Hanger

Damp gardening gloves will dry faster if they're hung up rather than thrown down on a table or shelf. An easy, space-saving method for hanging gardening gloves and hats indoors is to tie plastic clothespins along a string at intervals, then tie the string to a hook. The clothespins have holes in the tops, so just knot the string through one hole. Install the hook near the back door or in your garage, barn, or tool shed—wherever it's within easy reach en route to the garden.

Tool Bag

An old golf bag on a golf cart makes a great tool caddy. Fill it with the tools you use most in the garden and yard—rake, shovel, hoe, and so forth. You can put hand tools in the bag's pockets. There's even a ready-made ring for a hand towel on most golf bags. When you go to the garden, just pull the cart with you.

Jug Waterer

Here's an efficient watering device for any garden plant. Take a plastic gallon jug and remove the cap, cut out the bottom, turn it upside down, and force the neck of the jug into the ground close to the plant. When the plant needs water, just use your garden hose to fill the jug. You may put fertilizer, including compost, into the jug, and the water will carry the fertilizer into the ground, right where the plant can make best use of it.

A Homemade Soaker Hose

Make your own soaker hoses for a drip irrigation system out of 8-mil plastic. Cut the plastic into long strips 2 inches wide. Then, with a heavy needle for a fast drip or with a light needle for a slow drip, sew up the tubes on a sewing machine. Use tape to connect the plastic hoses to store-bought tees and elbows. Water leaks out the holes made by the needle. This system cannot be used to make just one water hole for each plant, but it works well when a whole row, such as carrots or spinach, needs gentle soaking. The cost per foot of hose is far less than the store-bought variety.

Pantyhose Powder Sifter

A foot from a pair of old pantyhose is a great applicator for *Bacillus thuringiensis* or rotenone. Just fill the toe area with the powder and shake it over the plants.

Tiller Tips

Most of us remember to check the gas and oil before starting our tillers and heading for the garden. But there are several important things to do when stopping your tiller at the end of a day's work. These tasks can help prolong its life:

- Idle your tiller on a level surface for a few minutes before shutting it off. This cools the engine evenly to prevent warping and allows the oil to splash around and lubricate the insides.

- If your tiller is equipped with a manual choke control, move it to the "full choke" position. This will help keep damp air from entering the engine through the carburetor.

- If your tiller has a pull starter, pull the rope slowly until you feel strong resistance. This indicates the valves have closed for the compression stroke, which helps prevent damp air from entering the engine through the exhaust.

- When your tiller is due for an oil change, do it after tilling, when the engine is still warm and dirt is still suspended in the oil. Don't change oil in a cold engine because the impurities will have settled to the bottom of the crankcase and won't drain out.

- If your tiller has a fuel shutoff valve, close it all the way so that gasoline won't seep into the engine or leak in your storage area.

- Before putting your tiller away, take a moment to clean it up. Clear away debris caught in the tines. A heavy buildup reduces efficiency and tilling depth, may overheat the shaft and gear housing, and can be forced into the seals and bearings, causing permanent damage. Brush off any soil sticking to the tiller. Soil holds moisture, which causes rust.

- While cleaning your tiller, look for loose nuts and bolts and for oil leaks around shafts, axles, and seals. Check again for slow leaks after the tiller has been out of operation for several days.

Clam-Shell Trowel

A hand-size clam shell serves as an excellent trowel and is better than the cheap tools you find in most garden supply stores. It fits the curve of your hand and is great for weeding, transplanting, and hilling young plants.

Coffee-Can Ash Applicator

A coffee can makes a handy shaker for applying ashes to your garden. Simply punch holes in the plastic lid with a leather punch, fill the can with ashes, and you're ready to go. Keep an extra, unpunched lid to use as a cover when storing the ashes.

Cardboard Rolls for Transplant Pots

Make individual transplanting pots from cardboard tubes such as those from paper towels, bathroom tissue, and wrapping paper. Cut the longer ones to the desired length and wrap the tubes with aluminum foil to prevent the cardboard from falling apart when it gets wet. Stand the tubes on waterproof trays, on plastic lids, or in shallow pans. Add soil and one seedling to each tube. When it's time to transplant, just remove the foil and plant the tubes.

Plastic-Bag Greenhouse

Plastic sandwich bags supported by Popsicle sticks make good greenhouse environments for small potted plants.

Venetian-Blind Markers

Reusable garden markers can be fashioned from old venetian blind slats. You can make three stakes from each slat by cutting the slat in thirds and cutting one end of each into a point. Use a permanent marking pen to label your markers, then clean them off at the end of the season with lacquer thinner.

A Produce Wash Box

Make washing fruits and vegetables from the garden easier by spraying them outdoors with the garden hose in a mesh box. Make the box in any dimensions with 1 × 4s, then staple wire mesh on the bottom. Lay your produce on the screen and hose it down.

Pantyhose Ties

Instead of using ties to support your vines, try 2-inch strips of pantyhose. They're sturdy and flexible and won't cut into delicate vines.

Plastic Ties

Adjustable ties such as these make great plant ties. They're better than paper-coated metal ones because they won't injure fragile plants and they won't corrode. You can use them year after year. Plastic ties are included with many brands of plastic trash bags.

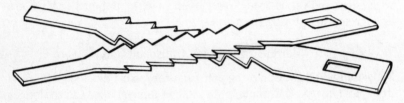

Shoe Coverup

Plastic food storage bags make great shoe covers when you're working in the muddy garden. Slip two bags over each shoe and secure them with rubber bands around your ankles. Instead of dealing with muddy boots, just discard the bags when you're done outside.

Seasoning-Jar Sower

An easy way to sow tiny seeds like carrot, lettuce, or radish is to use a seasoning jar with a shaker lid. Choose one with the right size holes for the size of your seeds, then just shake it along the garden row. A salt or pepper shaker works well, too.

Saw-Blade Cultivator

You can make a good garden cultivator with a piece of band saw blade. Cut a piece of blade about 12 inches long. Drill holes at each end and bend the blade into a U shape. Fasten it to a handle of your choice.

Fishnet Fencing

If you have access to plenty of fishnet, use it as garden fencing. It doesn't rust, and the soft, pliable netting doesn't hurt growing plants or your fingers. Trim the netting to the length you want. To keep the netting taut, feed a wire through the top loops. Then hang the wire from large-head roofing nails set 2 inches from the tops of wooden posts. Anchor the netting by burying the bottom 6 inches of mesh.

Bleach-Bottle Sifter

Here's a handy soil sifter. Cut the bottom off a bleach bottle at a slant to make a scoop and insert a 6-inch-diameter piece of ¼-inch hardware cloth so that it rests right above the handle hole. Hold the bottle upside down to scoop up the dirt, sifting the stone-free earth out the narrow top opening. The stones remain inside on top of the hardware cloth and can be easily tossed away.

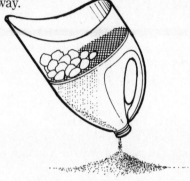

Minnow-Trap Soil Sifter

A minnow trap also makes a durable, easily handled soil sifter. Unlike the mesh on most homemade soil sifters, the ¼-inch steel mesh on the minnow trap extends all the way up the side and all over the bottom. Because of the additional mesh area, sifting goes fast. You can buy these traps at most fishing-tackle shops.

Clothes-Rack Tomato Cage

A wooden clothes dryer rack can be turned into great tomato cages. Place the rack on its side on the ground and plant the tomatoes between the bars. The dryer keeps the tomatoes off the ground and eliminates the need for wire cages.

Clothesline Ties

Loop plastic clothesline over stakes to hold up raspberry canes. It is easy to slide off when cutting canes, and it stands up to the weather better than twine.

Vegetables

Beans

Quick and Easy Bush Beans

Here's a time- and space-saving way to grow bush beans. On tilled ground, mark off an area 18 inches wide and as long as you want. Dig out the soil to an even depth of 2 inches and distribute the seeds 4 inches apart in all directions. Carefully shovel the soil back over the seeds, rake the bed smooth, and soak the area thoroughly. Except for watering, the beans will almost care for themselves until harvest. The closely spaced plants shade out weeds and help keep the soil cool and moist; what's more, the beans stay clean. Yellow or purple snap beans work especially well because they're more visible among the leaves than green ones, making it easier to harvest them.

Pick Beans Early

To make snap beans produce over a longer period, pick the beans when they're pencil width and the seeds are barely visible. If you let them get bigger, the plants will put their energy into seed production rather than more flower production, and it's the flowers that give you more beans.

Plant between Corn Rows

Try planting pole beans between corn hills or rows. The beans will climb the corn, saving the bother of setting poles.

Beets

Young and Tender

If you like beets only when they're young and tender, sow a short row every two weeks starting four weeks before the last frost in spring until about mid-August.

Keep Them Cool

Spring and fall beets are usually sweeter than those harvested in summer because beets grown in cool temperatures store more sugar in the roots. If you do raise summer beets, mulching helps keep them sweet by keeping the soil cool.

Carrots

Increasing Your Yield

Do you tend to get patchy stands when you grow carrots? It's probably because your soil crusts over, preventing the delicate seedlings from emerging. Cover the seed with vermiculite, sawdust, peat, or sifted compost instead of soil, or plant some radishes with the carrots. The radishes will sprout before the carrots and break the crust, but be sure to pull them before they crowd the carrots.

Fast-Sprouting Carrots

Tired of searching through weeds for slow-sprouting carrots? Here's a way to get the carrots growing before the weeds catch up. Soak carrot seeds in warm water for a day, then spread them thinly and evenly on damp paper towels. Lay the towels in a large glass baking pan. Add a layer of plastic wrap, then another layer of paper towels with seeds, and so on. As you add each layer, wet the towels thoroughly. Cover the pan with plastic wrap, leaving about 2 inches of air space between the top seed row and the plastic.

Keep the pan in a warm place and in about a week, check the seeds for small white spots. Plant the seeds as soon as the white spots appear. To plant, prepare a row the width of the paper towels. Lay the towels down and cover them thinly with soil and compost. Most of your carrots should be up before the weeds are. (See also Seeds and Seedlings, in this chapter.)

Cole Crops

Growing from Seed

If you would like to grow cole crops from seed but can't start your seeds indoors, try sowing them in the garden about the same time you would normally set out transplants in the spring. The seedlings will mature their crop two to three weeks later than the transplants would.

Bag Your Cauliflower

Instead of tying up the leaves over cauliflower plants to bleach the heads, gather up the leaves and place a grocery bag over each plant. This allows air to circulate around the plants and prevents the rotting that often occurs when the leaves are tied over the heads in wet weather. The bags are easily lifted to check for maturity. You will probably need to replace the bags after a rainfall.

Tomatoes

Choosing Plants

Should you buy tomato plants with or without flowers? For early tomatoes, buy plants with flowers. Even if the flowers fall off after transplanting, more will soon be produced because the plants are in their reproductive stage. But these plants may not yield well after the early crop. Young plants without flowers will fruit later but will bear more.

Quick Planting

A quick and easy way to plant tomato plants is to use a bulb planter. It makes a nice, deep hole with little effort on your part.

Improve Yields

You can improve your tomato yield by fertilizing with dry cow manure at the rate of 100 pounds per 100 square feet and by spacing plants 3 feet apart in each direction.

Other Vegetables

Windowsill Chives

Want windowsill chives to cut during the winter? Start seeds in pots in late summer. Within two or three months you'll have vigorous young plants ready for cutting.

Don't Remove Corn Suckers

If your corn develops suckers (the side shoots that grow out at ground level) don't remove them. Research at the University of Minnesota has shown that leaving the suckers on won't decrease ear yield, and during moderate stress, such as a drought, the suckers will send nutrients to the main stalk, increasing the harvest. Careless removal of suckers could also cause weakening of the main stalk and provide entryways for disease. Some corn varieties don't produce suckers, but even in those that do, suckers usually don't develop if plantings are closely spaced. Suckers are often a sign of excess nutrients per plant, so suckering could mean you're spacing your corn rows too far apart.

Improve Okra Germination

The hard outer seed coat of okra can inhibit germination, resulting in a patchy stand. Here are four preplanting seed treatments that improve germination: (1) Nick the seed coat with a sharp knife; (2) rub the seeds lightly between two sheets of fine sandpaper; (3) soak the seeds for 24 hours at room temperature; or (4) place the seeds in the freezer overnight, then soak them in hot tap water for 30 minutes before planting. (See also Seeds and Seedlings, in this chapter.)

Grow Your Own Onion Sets

You can grow your own onion sets for less than it costs to buy sets in the spring. You'll also have a wider choice of varieties. Buy seeds of an onion variety that keeps well, and sow them on 1-inch centers in a weed-free bed 4 to 6 weeks before the frost-free date in the spring. Gently dig them up about 15 weeks later, shake off the soil, and cure the little bulbs in a dry, well-ventilated place. After about a month, trim the tips and sort the bulbs. Keep the dime- or nickle-size bulbs for sets, storing them until next spring in a cold, dry, airy place.

Onion Hammock

When it's time to dry and cure your onion harvest, just put it in a mesh hammock at night; if it rains, use a sheet of plastic. Once the crop is dry, bring the onion-filled hammock inside and hang it in your attic or storage room. Air will continue to circulate through the crop and keep the onions firm for use all winter.

Pea Partners

Plant a row of peas 2 inches in front of a row of sunflowers. The sunflowers grow faster than the peas and provide shade. Better still, you don't have to build trellises for your peas because they will climb the sunflower stalks.

Front-Page Peppers

When planting peppers, wrap each plant stem in a 5 × 5-inch square of newspaper that has been dipped in water. This keeps plant roots moist and discourages cutworms.

Pumpkin Protection

To keep soil-borne fungi and bacteria from attacking maturing pumpkins and squash, place a board under each fruit. (See also Controlling Pests and Diseases, in this chapter.)

Radish and Parsnip Partners

Plant radish seeds along with parsnip seeds in the same row. This not only conserves space, but the radish seeds "break the ground" for the parsnip seeds, which sometimes do not come up easily. The radishes are up and long gone before the parsnips begin to mature.

Lead-Free Vegetables

If your garden is near a road, you've probably worried about auto emissions that can contaminate your vegetables. Lead and cadmium, the most hazardous components of auto exhaust, can be washed off your crops with a dilute vinegar or soap solution, according to research at Cornell University. Use about 2½ tablespoons of vinegar or half that amount of dishwashing liquid per gallon of water.

Vegetables can also *absorb* lead and cadmium *from the soil,* and then you can't wash them away. But if you increase the content of organic matter in your garden soil and keep the pH above 6.5, the lead and cadmium will be unavailable to the plants.

Green Manures Choke Out Weeds

In a large vegetable garden, weeds can be a real problem. Try planting buckwheat or other green manures in fallow areas to choke out weeds. Buckwheat can be sown in the summer, then plowed down in the fall so that you can plant on clean soil. For fall seeding, try spring oats, spring barley, annual sweet clover, or annual rye grass. You can till them under in the spring. Plant your vegetables where the green manure crops were. This method will keep down the weeds and add humus to the soil.

Planting by the Moon

For centuries farmers have heard the folklore of coordinating farming activities with the phases of the moon to give crops an extra boost, supposedly due to the moon's ever-changing light and gravitational pull. Though the moon's effect on plant growth hasn't been substantiated, here's a look at the moon's phases, and some of the lore that surrounds them:

- From New Moon to First Quarter: At new moon, nights are darkest; the moon exerts a gravitational pull in the same direction as the sun. As nights become brighter, the moon's pull increases to 90° away from the sun. Germination, leaf growth, and root growth are all stimulated. Plant quick-sprouting and extra-slow sprouting seeds—those that germinate in less than a week and those that take about one month.

- From First Quarter to Full Moon: As the moon approaches fullness, nights become much brighter; the gravitational pull is increasingly opposed to that of the sun. Leaf growth is stimulated, root growth is suppressed. Do not plant or transplant; seeds that have failed to sprout in the past seven days are most likely to germinate during this period.

- From Full Moon to Last Quarter: Nights darken as the waning moon rises later and later; its gravitational pull narrows to 90° away from the sun. Root growth is stimulated, leaf and stem growth suppressed. Transplant seedlings and larger plants. Plant slow-sprouting seeds, those that take about two weeks to germinate.

- From Last Quarter to New Moon: Nights are increasingly dark as the moon rises shortly before the sun, and its gravitational pull narrows until it finally comes from the same direction. Leaf growth and root growth are both suppressed. This is a good time for shipping dormant plants. Two days before the new moon, plant quick-sprouting and extra-slow sprouting seeds so that they will germinate in time to benefit from the moon's initial waxing.

9 Yard and Patio

Flowers

Potato Rooters for Roses

Rose bush slips will take root if you insert the stems into white potatoes.

Clothespin Holder for Thorns

When cutting thorny roses and other prickly plants, hold on to the stem with a spring-type clothespin to avoid pricking your fingers.

Cinnamon Fights Peony Mold

If you're troubled with slime mold, toadstools, or mildew around your peonies, try a light dusting of cinnamon around each plant. There is a naturally occurring fungicide in cinnamon called ortho-methoxyanna-maldehyde. Researchers in Tokyo have found that fungi refuse to grow on cinnamon even under optimum temperature and humidity.

Selecting Annuals

Flats of annual flowers in full bloom are tempting buys in spring, but they aren't the best deal around. Those masses of flowers too often hide yellowing leaves and stunted, pot-bound roots. Select instead young, stocky plants with dark green leaves that are just forming buds or beginning to show color. They'll grow faster and bloom sooner once they're set.

Edible Flowers

Don't just grow pretty flowers—grow flowers you can eat. Here are some flowers that not only add beauty to your landscape, but add pizzazz to your salads as well: carnations, chives, daylilies, marigolds, nasturtiums, pansies, roses, squash blossoms, sunflowers (for seeds), and violets.

Lawn Care

Seeding and Feeding

Plant in the Fall

When seeding a new lawn, keep in mind that grasses are cool-weather plants and grow fastest during the cool, moist months of spring and fall. In hot weather they become dormant. By planting in the fall, you'll give your grass two favorable periods of growth—fall and spring—before it has to withstand summer heat.

Germination Time for Common Lawn Grasses

Grass	Days
Kentucky bluegrass	20–28
Merion Kentucky bluegrass	20–28
Park Kentucky bluegrass	14–21
Bentgrass	7–12
Redtop	8–10
Chewing's fescue	10–21
Creeping red fescue	10–21
Meadow fescue	7–14
Common ryegrass	7–14
Perennial ryegrass	7–14

Spring Feed

Feed your lawn regularly every spring. Use a spike-tooth aerator, then spread a mixture of compost and bone meal. Rake this into the holes made by the aerator. You can use a fairly thick covering of compost, but make sure it's not so thick that it smothers the grass.

When to Fertilize

Applying fertilizer to speed midsummer growth can lead to lawn trouble. Young leaf blades are particularly vulnerable to fungus diseases under summer temperature and moisture conditions. But fertilizing in early spring and fall stimulates growth during seasons when the danger of disease is greatly reduced.

Lawn Seed Mixtures

- Open, Sunny Location: Merion Kentucky bluegrass, 40 to 65%, and Kentucky bluegrass, 35 to 60%. Seed at 2½ to 3 pounds per 1,000 square feet. Or Kentucky bluegrass, 100%. Seed at 3 to 3½ pounds per 1,000 square feet. Or Pennlawn red fescue, 35 to 65%, and Kentucky bluegrass, 35 to 65%. Seed at 3 to 4 pounds per 1,000 square feet.

- Shaded and Partially Shaded Areas: Pennlawn red fescue, 60 to 70%, and rough bluegrass, 30 to 40%. Seed at 4 pounds per 1,000 square feet (good for heavy shade). Or Pennlawn red fescue, 50 to 60%, Kentucky bluegrass, 15 to 25%, and rough bluegrass 15 to 25%. Seed at 4 pounds per 1,000 square feet (good for moderate to partial shade).

Cheap Grass

Instead of buying expensive grass seed, just use oats, rye, or wheat. They provide a beautiful green grass at one-tenth the cost.

Maintenance

Don't Water at Night

Don't water your lawn *late* in the evening. The grass will remain wet through the night, encouraging mold and fungus growth. The best time to water is right after the sun goes down, so that water has a chance to reach the roots instead of evaporating quickly in the hot sun.

Mow Long Grass in Stages

If your grass has gone for a long period of time between cuttings, it is better for the appearance and vigor of the turf to cut the grass gradually in successive mowings rather than all at once.

Mow Less in the Shade

Grass in shady areas should be mowed less frequently and kept at a greater height than recommended for other areas. The reduced amount of light available to shaded grass makes it more difficult for the plant to produce enough food for healthy growth. Higher and less frequent mowing will permit grass to survive in many areas where it would die if cut more heavily.

Mowing Tips

When mowing the grass, there are three practices you should follow to maintain a healthy, attractive lawn:

- Mow high, as high as 3 inches or more if you can. Keeping grass high keeps weeds and crabgrass out by robbing them of sunlight.

- Mow regularly, as often as grass growth requires.

- Never cut more than one-third of the total length of the grass blade at one cutting. The health and growth rate of your grass depend on the food manufactured in the blades, not the roots. And the depth and vigor of the grass roots are determined by the top growth of the blades. If you cut more than one-third of the blade's length at one time, you'll be slowing down food production.

Directional Mowing

Avoid creating patterns across your lawn by trying to mow in a slightly different direction each time.

Revive an Old Lawn

To renovate an old, patchy lawn, dig up the bare spots about 2 inches deep, work in plenty of finished compost, then tamp and rake well. Sow grass seed after thoroughly soaking the patches.

A Strong Lawn Foundation

One of the best ways to build up poor soil where you want a strong foundation for permanent lawn growth is with green manure—an inexpensive cover crop that does a concentrated job of incorporating plenty of needed humus. Start with a winter rye or wheat crop sown any time from early September to mid-October. Turn this under in the spring and follow it with a planting of soybeans, barley, vetch, or clover, dug in during late summer. You're now ready to sow a good lawn seed mixture.

Mixed Grasses Fight Disease

The most effective way to keep turf diseases out of your lawn is to plant a mixture of grasses. Different diseases attack different varieties, so when a single grass is planted, there is little to halt the spread of a disease once it has started. But in a mixed turf, the disease organisms soon reach a species of grass that is resistant, and further progress is halted.

Weed Control

Rake Out Poison Ivy

If you're overrun with poison ivy, rake it out. Use a sturdy rake and carefully tug at the ivy. Most of it will come right up, roots and all. When you're done, rinse off the rake to get rid of any plant oils. Wash your hands well, too, if they came in contact with the ivy or the bottom of the rake.

Boil Away Ivy

Small patches of poison ivy can be safely eradicated from your yard by dousing them with boiling water.

Killing Unwanted Grass and Weeds

You can also kill grass or weeds growing between sections of cement walk with salted boiling water.

Hammer Those Weeds

Try a straight claw hammer for removing clumps of weeds such as plantain and dandelion from your lawn. Just grab the weed between the claw and pull.

Ornamentals

Ground Covers

Spacing Your Ground Covers

Because ground covers cost more initially than lawn seed, some gardeners try to economize by setting the plants a good distance apart. You'll use fewer plants this way, but you'll have to battle weeds until the plants establish themselves. The ideal method is to set small plants close together. The correct distance for most ground covers is 3 to 8 inches apart, though some vines can be planted up to 3 feet apart.

Planting on Banks or Slopes

When planting on a bank or slope, cut pockets into the bank at different heights along its length and wedge stones deeply into the holes. Then cover with a good rich soil and plant the ground cover. The stones help anchor the young plants' roots, keeping them from being washed away during rains.

Off to a Good Start

Water your ground cover occasionally during the first season. Top-dress it with compost, humus, or well-rotted manure to supply the nitrogen needed for the dense growth that will cover the ground without any "holes." As the plants grow, they will strangle any crabgrass or plantain. Once established, ground covers need no special care.

Keep Off the Ground Cover

No ground cover can cover the soil as closely as a good grass turf. Ground covers are therefore not recommended for any area where there is traffic—none of them will stand up to wear. Walks should be built through areas covered by plants other than grass, because almost any ground cover will succumb to trampling.

Ground Cover under Shade Trees

Dense shade trees cut out enough sunlight that grass has a difficult time growing under them. One solution is to keep trimming off lower branches as the trees grow taller, so that sunlight can angle to the ground under the branches. An alternative is to grow a shade-loving ground cover, such as ivy or pachysandra, under these trees instead of grass.

Landscape with Blueberries

Blueberries are choice edible ornamentals for the home landscape. They need an acid (pH 4.2 to 5.5), highly organic soil to do well. Dig a hole 3 feet around and 12 inches deep for each plant, and backfill with a mixture of half soil and half sphagnum peat. The fluffy peat aerates the soil and holds water for the shallow roots. After planting, cover the 3-foot circle with 6 inches of mulch. Add fresh mulch each year, extending the circle to keep up with the dripline. (See also Fruits in the chapter, Gardening Indoors and Out.)

Trees

Save Your Trees

Use grass barriers or metal edgings around your lawn trees. This will reduce tree damage from your mower and eliminate the need for hand trimming around the trunks.

Minimize Transplant Shock

Transplanting a tree invariably involves injury and shock to the tree. To keep these effects to a minimum, trim all injured roots and limbs, but keep the tree in balance while doing so, cutting back the roots to keep their volume and extent in line with the branch system, and vice versa. Do not cut back the central leader of the tree.

Small trees can be transplanted more easily and will adjust themselves to their new environment more quickly than large trees. A tree must build up its root system to balance the top before it will continue to grow. For example, a tree 6 to 8 feet tall will adjust itself more quickly than a tree 16 to 18 feet tall. At the end of four or five years, the 6-foot tree probably will be as tall as the 16-foot tree, and it will be more vigorous.

Reusable Tree Support

You can make a simple, reusable tree support with no lines to trip over and no stakes to mow around. Simply mount a 2 × 2-inch piece of wood lengthwise on a barbed-wire U-shaped fence post. Position the post and drive it into the ground with a maul or heavy hammer. Open the eyes on two TV-antenna wire guides, drill holes in the piece of wood 4 to 6 inches apart, and mount the guides, with one guide hooked to the right and one guide hooked to the left. Protect the supported section of tree trunk with a cut piece of garden hose, then slip the guide hooks around the trunk. The tree will be secure but cannot bind if you forget to remove the support when the tree grows.

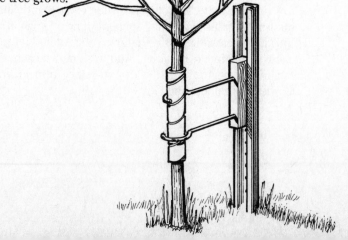

Evergreens for Windbreaks

A double row of evergreens spaced between your house and the prevailing winter wind can cut heating bills significantly. Your yard will be more comfortable in windy weather, too. Red cedar, Canadian spruce, Norway spruce, red spruce, Austrian pine, western yellow pine, pitch pine, white pine, Scotch pine, Japanese black pine, and hemlock are good choices for windbreaks. Good deciduous trees for windbreaks include Amur maple, boxelder, Osage orange, white mulberry, white poplar, balsam poplar, and pin oak.

Winterize Your Evergreens

Evergreens, especially newly planted ones, can be damaged by winter sun and winds, which dry the foliage. Shield them with burlap stapled to stakes set 6 inches away from the plants on all sides. You can prevent them from spreading or breaking under the weight of snow by tying sturdy string around them.

Plant for Noise Reduction

Highway noise can be reduced by combining plants with slopes or earth mounds that rise above the edges of the highway. The most effective way to screen highway noise is to plant buffers of trees and shrubs, 25 to 35 feet in width. Hedges and other narrow plantings are relatively ineffective in controlling noise.

Plant to the South

Large decaying trees can be a hazard if close to your roof. In windstorms, they are liable to topple onto the house. Trees planted directly south and southeast of the house are less likely to hit the roof than trees planted to the southwest because strong winds come most often from westerly directions.

Stratify Tree Seeds

The seeds of hardy trees and shrubs need to be stratified (a simulation of winter conditions) in order to break dormancy before planting. First, clean the seeds, and soak those that have a hard coat for two to four days. Next, place the seeds in moist sphagnum moss, vermiculite, or old sawdust. Then mix the seeds with one to three times their volume of medium, or alternate layers of seeds and medium. Put the mix or layers in a container that allows aeration, such as a plastic bag or can with small holes in the lid. Store at 35° to 45°F for about four months, or until you can plant the seeds in spring. (See also Seeds and Seedlings in the chapter, Gardening Indoors and Out.)

Pests and Other Wildlife

Ammonia Keeps Dogs Away

Discourage dogs from ripping apart your plastic trash bags when they're put out for pickup by sprinkling them with ammonia. The fumes will keep the dogs away.

Hot Spray Deters Cats and Dogs

To keep cats and dogs off your lawn, put two or three cloves of garlic and three or four hot red peppers into a blender and grind them up. Then combine the mixture with a bucketful of water and add a few drops of dishwashing liquid. Mix well. Sprinkle the solution around the edges of your yard and garden and along sidewalks. Repeat often, especially after a rain.

Swinging Trash Cans Foil Invaders

Suspend your garbage cans to keep dogs and raccoons out. A simple frame made of five 2 × 4s will do the trick. Suspend the cans about 18 inches above the ground. If an animal jumps up and leans against the can, it will simply swing away, foiling the invader.

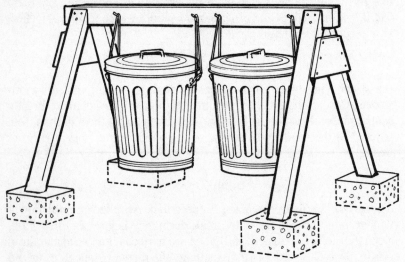

Cricket Weather Watchers

Crickets can be used to determine the approximate temperature. Just count the number of chirps in 14 seconds and add 40 to get the present air temperature in degrees Fahrenheit.

Basil Repels Flies

To keep flies away from outdoor dining areas, grow a pot or two of basil. Put the potted plants on the table. When you sit down to eat, pinch some leaves off and crush them in your hand. The released oils will repel the flies. Repeat as needed.

Feed the Birds

Save your old net onion bags and use them as "hanging baskets" for suet. The holes in the bags allow the birds easy access to the suet.

Feed wild birds sunflower seeds right off the flower head. Just slip the entire sunflower head into a rope plant hanger usually used to suspend plastic or ceramic pots and tie it on a tree limb. The birds love it.

You can make your own bird seed. Save the pulp and seeds from squash and other vegetables and spread it thinly on a plate or tray. Then leave the tray in a gas oven overnight. The pilot light generates just enough heat to dry the pulp and make it easy to pick out the seeds. If you have a pilotless gas oven or an electric one, you can dry the seeds by setting the oven at its lowest temperature and heating them for several hours.

Instead of lugging out heavy bags of bird seed to your feeders, use an ordinary watering can to carry the seed. It holds enough to fill several feeders in one trip, and the spout directs the seed so that it isn't spilled. If your bird feed contains especially large seeds, this may not work because they'll clog the spout.

Store bird seed in a trash can with a tight-fitting lid. Have the can filled before winter arrives, and locate it near your bird feeders so that you don't have to carry scoops of seed far in bad weather.

10 Auto Advice

Maintenance
(See also When Things Go Wrong, in this chapter.)

Brakes

Checking Wear

If you suspect your brake rotors are worn to the limit but don't own an expensive caliper, you may have a substitute right in your tool box. Let's say the limit is 6 millimeters. Take your 6 mm open-end wrench and see whether it fits over the rim of the rotor. If it does, it's replacement time. Should you find that there's a lip on the edge of the rotor and the worn shiny part lies beyond, simply take the smallest wrench that will fit over the edge, slip it on, and insert feeler gauge blades between the wrench jaw and the rotor surface. Subtract the total thickness of the blades between the wrench jaw and the rotor surface and you have the measurement.

Checking Performance

You can performance-test your car's brakes on a long gravel driveway or a straight and level dirt road. First, make sure there is no traffic in sight. From a speed of 10 to 15 mph, gradually depress the brake pedal until the brakes lock and the car slides to a stop. Then get out of the car and examine the skid marks left on the ground by the locked wheels. The front wheels should lock first and then the rears. Both fronts and both rears should leave skid marks of equal length. Finally, make the same test with the hand brake; the rear wheels should lock and leave equally long skid marks. (On a few front-wheel-drive cars, the hand brake is on the front wheels.)

When Working on Brakes

Use wooden golf tees to plug brake or fuel lines that have to be removed when you work on your carburetor, fuel pump, or brakes. The plug keeps out dirt and keeps fluids from dripping.

Electrical System

Splices

When splicing a car's electrical wires, you can get by temporarily with crimp-on solderless connections. But these are subject to corrosion and may not make good contact for long. For best results, twist the wires together, solder the joint, and then insulate the connection with electrical tape or a piece of shrink-on insulating tubing.

Battery Care

All electrical circuits in your car start and end with the battery. You can avoid a host of troubles by making sure the battery can work at its best by keeping the connections tight and clean.

If your battery has cells caps, remove them and check that the electrolyte is up to the full level and that the cell plates are covered. Then remove each terminal and clean it with a special brush (the kind with a plastic housing is best and can be purchased inexpensively at auto supply stores) both inside the terminal and on the outside of the post.

If you have a side post battery, wire brush the screw thread post and the wire terminal until both are bright and shiny. Replace the connections and coat them with anticorrosion grease or a special spray made to protect battery terminals.

Rather than buy a commercial product to keep battery terminals from corroding, you can coat them with either Vaseline or an acid-neutralizing paste of baking soda and water.

Timing Marks

Here's an easy way to highlight the timing marks on an engine's pulley: Clean the area, and dab on a bit of the white correction fluid used by typists. It dries quickly.

Fuses

When you last replaced a fuse, did you notice corrosion on the bracket that holds it? If so, here's something you can do to clean it off: Cut a piece of ¼-inch dowel as long as the fuse. Then cut a piece of sandpaper large enough to wrap around the dowel, and curl it into shape and glue it on with rubber cement. Gently tap a nail into the dowel and, using the nail as a handle, plug the dowel into the fuse bracket. Rotate the dowel a couple of times to sand away the corrosion.

D.I.Y.

Most routine maintenance procedures for your car were designed by mechanical experts to be performed by mechanical novices. So, if you're willing, you can take on several basic tasks—oil changes, lubrication, tune-ups, brake jobs—without expensive tools. Since you don't have to charge yourself $30 per hour, and can purchase oil, filters, and spark plugs at discount prices, doing your own work pays very well indeed. As a bonus, should something simple go wrong with the car, your familiarity with it will better your chances of fixing it.

Spying on Sparks

Occasionally open the car's hood in the dark and study the engine. If you see any arcing along wires, plugs, or fittings, you have electrical leakage that could stall your car. Replace the leaking parts to avoid getting caught out on the road.

Don't Oil Plugs

When installing spark plugs, never oil them. Oiled plugs go in more easily, but the oil will eventually bond the plugs and the cylinder heads, making them that much harder to remove the next time.

Nuts and Bolts

Starting Them

When a nut does not thread easily onto a bolt, back it off a full turn until you hear it click. The threads then will be correctly seated, and you can proceed to tighten the nut onto the bolt.

If nuts are rusted or stripped and must be replaced, how do you determine the size? Find the wrench that fits them, and note the size of the wrench. Similarly, you can determine the size of a bolt by removing it and finding what size wrench will fit around the shank.

To hand-start a bolt in a hard-to-reach spot, hold the bolt in the socket with a wad of wax or heavy grease.

Removing Them

If a screw is rusted tight, clamp locking-grip pliers to the head and turn it out.

When trying to remove a stubborn nut, screw, or bolt, try tightening it a hair before loosening it.

A screw that's rusted fast can be coaxed in this way: Hold a sturdy screwdriver with the blade in the slot; apply counterclockwise pressure; then strike the head of the screwdriver handle with a hammer.

Apply anti-seize compound when working on your car, and auto repairs will be easier next time around. You can buy it at any auto supply store, in spray cans or in cans with a brush inside. Use it on threaded fasteners that might rust together—wheel lug nuts, exhaust pipe U-bolts, and so on.

Oil

Oil Changes

To make a clean job of an oil change, catch the oil in a cardboard box that's lined with a heavy-duty plastic garbage bag. Drape the bag over the top of the box. (If the engine is cold, let it idle for 10 minutes to allow for more complete drainage.) When the oil is drained, tie the bag shut and take it, still in its box, to the nearest service station that recycles oil.

More than once, a driver has taken to the highway in a car that had only half an oil change: he or she drained the old lubricant but, through an oversight, didn't add the fresh oil. Avoid the consequences of such a mistake by placing the filler cap on the driver's seat as a reminder. (Protect the seat with a rag or newspaper.)

Automotive Leak Finder

If you notice liquid dripping from beneath your car, here's a quick guide, based on the substance's appearance and characteristics, to what the leak is—and where it's probably coming from.

- Dark, smelly, slippery fluid: Oil, usually from the engine, oil pan, or transmission.

- Green or rust-colored, slightly scented, slippery fluid: Antifreeze, from the cooling system. Green when it first leaks out, it turns rust-colored within a few minutes.

- Honey-colored fluid: Depending on the location of the drip, either hydraulic fluid (from the steering column) or brake fluid (from the master cylinder, wheel cylinder, brake lines, or brake fluid reservoir). Both fluids are corrosive; avoid contact with skin.

- Honey-colored, slightly scented fluid; not as slippery as oil: Automatic transmission fluid, from the reservoir.

- Clear to yellowish, strongly scented, slightly slippery fluid; evaporates quickly: Gasoline, from the tank, fuel lines, fuel pump, gas filter, or carburetor.

- Yellowish, odorless, nonslippery fluid; leaks from battery directly above: Battery acid, which is highly corrosive. Avoid contact with skin.

- Clear, odorless, nonslippery fluid: Water, from the heater-air conditioner, windshield sprayer, or—if you don't use antifreeze—cooling system. (Water, a by-product of gasoline combustion, will also drip from the tailpipe briefly about a minute after you start up a cold engine.)

Oil Recycling

An inconvenience of doing your own car maintenance is disposing of the spent oil. People usually dump it in a hole in the backyard, in the trash can, or down a drain, but this practice may eventually pollute the ground and water. Many service stations will accept used oil for recycling, so keep on hand a sealable plastic container large enough to transport the contents of your car's crankcase.

Used engine oil can be mixed with turpentine to make a preserving finish for fences and sheds. It can also be painted on garden tools to keep them clean and rust-free.

Keep Extra Oil on Hand

Buy motor oil by the case when it's on sale. Oil won't deteriorate with storage, and you are more likely to change oil regularly and conscientiously if you keep a supply on hand.

Check Your Oil

For the sake of your car engine's longevity, it's best to check the oil level frequently. But many drivers are apt to put this off simply because they don't have on hand a rag to wipe off the dipstick. Tie a rag in the trunk, making sure that it won't come in contact with things stored there.

Maintenance Miscellany

Tune-Up Time

How can you tell when your car needs a tune-up? Road test it when newly (and properly) tuned to establish performance norms. After a major tune-up, take it to a steep hill and accelerate up it briskly, noting the speed you achieve at a couple of landmarks along the way. Later, when the car seems sluggish, match its performance with the previous record to see whether it really isn't running up to par.

Plug Diagnosis

Pull a spark plug for an indicator of what's wrong with an ailing engine.

Appearance of Electrode	Problem
Damp, smelling of gas	Faulty plug or ignition wire; flooded engine
Black soot	Gas-air mixture too rich
Discolored pale yellow	Gas-air mixture too lean
Discolored white	Cooler plug needed
Dark bits of carbon	Hotter plug needed
Oily and black	Worn rings or valve guides

Each time you take a compression reading, record the results on a clean spot on the underside of the engine hood with a felt-tipped marker. This creates a running medical history of the engine in a place where it won't be lost.

Weaning Your Car from Lead

Unleaded gas can damage the engines of older cars. Without the lubricating effect of the lead, valve seats get worn down. A machine shop can install special hardened steel valve seats. This is a routine task that only adds about $50 to the price of a valve job, and it will let you run your car on unleaded gas without problems.

Parts for Less

Where should you buy repair parts? Some items are cheapest when bought through a discount store: spark plugs, fan belts, radiator hoses, oil, filters, and cheap tools to carry in the car for emergencies. But for rebuilt parts like brake calipers, alternators, and starters, you'll usually find better quality at professional parts stores that sell primarily to service stations. Perhaps you can knock down the higher prices by negotiating for a mechanic's discount.

Junkyards can be a good source of parts—or even the only source, in the case of older models. As a general rule, used body parts should sell for about half or less than the price of new parts. Because they come off an existing car, you may get a complete assembly rather than a lone item. For example, a front fender may be complete with headlights.

Windshields and rear windows may not be much cheaper than new parts because of the labor and risk of removing them from the dead car, but major mechanical assemblies like engines, transmissions, and rear axles are often a very good deal. They may come with a guarantee that they work and, if so, can be exchanged if they don't (although you will be out the labor of installing and removing the part). Electrical parts, such as alternators, are usually better bought as rebuilts or new parts.

Coolant

That's not just water flowing through your car's radiator. Coolant also contains ethylene glycol to prevent freezing, rustproofing additives, and lubricant for the moving parts of the water pump. Top off the radiator as needed with distilled water, but use commercial coolant if a substantial amount of fluid must be replaced.

Keep Vinyl Looking New

The sun can turn your parked car into a greenhouse, and vinyl trim and dashboard padding may become brittle as a result. Protect interior plastic parts with one of the silicone sprays intended for this purpose.

Cleanup Tips

To easily lift stickers from car windows, rub on a little nail polish remover.

After washing and drying the windows of your car, try buffing them with dry, crumpled-up newspaper for optimum sparkle.

Spoked hubcaps dress up a car but are hard to clean with a sponge and garden hose. Instead, pry off the caps, rinse them to get off the major dirt, and then place them in the dishwasher.

Rustproofing

Should you consider rustproofing your car? Yes, if you plan on keeping it more than five years; if the manufacturer does not have a guarantee against corrosion; or if that particular make has been riddled with rust in the past. Note that a new car's rustproofing guarantee may be invalidated by an aftermarket treatment.

Best Investments for a Longer Life

The two most important tips for getting a long life from your car are: (1) Change the oil and oil filter frequently (every 3,000 or 4,000 miles, regardless of the manufacturer's recommendations), and (2) conscientiously flush the underside and wheel wells (to remove road salt and moisture-holding dirt that will prematurely rust the body).

Touch-Ups

Paint chips and minor scratches can be repainted using a toothpick for a brush. First, use a typewriter eraser to clean away the rust from the damaged spot. Then, using either touch-up paint or leftover paint from a past body repair (always ask the body shop to give you any leftover paint after having work done), fill in the scratch with several coats applied a drop at a time from the end of a toothpick. The results will not be cosmetically perfect, but the rust will be prevented from spreading under the paint and further damaging the body.

Fuel Economy

When Shopping for a Car

Smaller Engine, Better Gas Mileage

If fuel economy means more to you than jack-rabbit starts, shop for the smallest engine that gives you adequate and safe performance. Typically, a 10% increase in engine size is paid for by 6% poorer mileage.

Small Axle Ratio, Better Gas Mileage

The role of axle ratio of a car means little to most car shoppers, but it has a real effect on performance, engine life, and gas mileage. As a rule, the lower the ratio, the less strain on the engine and the better the mileage. A 10% decrease in axle ratio translates to a 4% improvement in mileage.

Manual vs Automatic Transmissions

In choosing between automatic and manual transmissions when ordering a car, keep in mind that the convenience of the automatic will cost you, on average, 5% poorer gas mileage. An overdrive gear can improve mileage and is especially economical when used with an automatic transmission.

Things You Can Do Now

Lighten Your Load

Car trunks tend to collect all sorts of heavy things, and this weight depresses mileage. If you can take out as much as 100 pounds, you might gain 1 mpg.

If your car has a roof or bicycle rack, remove it when not in use to cut air resistance and save gas.

Increase Tire Pressure

Another mile or two per gallon can be coaxed from your car by seeing to it that tire pressure doesn't drop below the recommended figures. Run tires up to 2 pounds above the recommendation for even greater economy. A caution against making tires too hard: Overinflation can wear tires prematurely, shake your hind teeth loose, and cause the car to be more apt to skid in rain or snow.

Drive Slower

Obey speed limits, and you'll use less fuel. A car operates more efficiently at lower speeds because air resistance increases—as does impact force—at the square of the increase in speed. For example, at 60 mph you have more than twice the air resistance you do at 45 mph.

Keep Your Car Tuned

An advantage of computing your mileage every time you fuel up is that if you notice a mileage drop over several tanks of fuel, you'll know it's likely time for a tune-up. And a tuned-up car gives better gas mileage.

Safe Driving

Belts and Bags

Buckle Up

How can you make yourself safer than 89% of other car passengers? Just use your seatbelt. Although seatbelts are mandatory for all cars sold in the United States (and actually using them is mandated by law in several states), only 11% of passengers bother to use them. By buckling up, you increase your chances of escaping death or serious injury by 60%.

Once children have survived the trauma of birth and the first few weeks of living out in the world, the greatest threat to their survival is a car accident. Invest in car seats for your children and use them. Almost 60% of child fatalities could have been prevented with the use of car seats or, for older children, seatbelts. The use of car seats, too, is now mandatory in some states.

When carrying a heavy or fragile object in your car, hold it down with a seatbelt. Should you get into an accident, the object might otherwise injure you or someone else in the car.

Has it occurred to you that a seatbelt does more than keep you from injury in an accident? The very act of fastening your belt may remind you that driving a car is a risky exercise and that the stakes are high whenever you take the wheel.

Airbags

Seatbelts give good protection against injury in a car accident, but airbags are even better. Compared to cars having standard seatbelts, cars equipped with airbags cut deaths and serious injuries by half. The bags work by cushioning passengers and spreading the force of impact over the head and body. They are particularly effective in head-on crashes. Although airbags have been on the market only a short time and are currently available on very few models, they are worth your serious consideration.

Heavier Means Safer

You can greatly increase your safety on the highway by driving sober and by using a seatbelt. Not so well known is the importance of the weight of your car. According to fatality-rate studies conducted by the National Highway Traffic Safety Administration, a car weighing 2 tons generally will be twice as safe as a car weighing half as much. There are exceptions to the rule: Good engineering may render a car less vulnerable in a crash.

Bad-Weather Driving

Misty Windows

Keep a chalkboard eraser in your glove compartment. When the windows steam up, just wipe the moisture away.

Staying on the Road

If you're about to drive into some snowy weather in a car with rear-wheel drive, top off the fuel tank. The added weight over the drive wheels will improve traction.

What's the best strategy for making it up snowy hills? Choose a higher-than-normal gear and keep a light foot on the gas.

You can improve your traction on ice by removing a spark plug lead. By making one cylinder drag instead of push, you reduce the horsepower of the engine, and the tires are less likely to slip.

When rounding a slippery corner in a rear-wheel-drive car, the rear end may swing around suddenly if you goose the accelerator. A front-wheel-drive car, on the other hand, tends to "understeer" in a corner, which means that it typically heads straighter than aimed.

On-Board Tools

In years past, a few cars were manufactured with a small tool box designed to fit under the hood. Look at your car's engine compartment for a place where you can bolt a small tool box, possibly a steel ammunition box from a surplus store. Apply antirust compound between the box and the car before bolting the box in place. Store an old towel or diaper in the box to keep loose tools from rattling.

The items you choose to pack away in the box will depend both on the model you drive and the extent of your mechanical ability: slot-head and phillips-head screwdrivers, wrenches in the sizes most useful for your car, a small roll of duct tape to temporarily patch leaking hoses, and spare fuses and points, to suggest a few. One tool with several uses is a pair of locking-grip pliers; it will serve as an adjustable wrench, clamp, and even a lightweight hammer. Also consider a flare or flag, to warn other motorists in case you have to do roadside repairs.

Keep a pair of inexpensive leather-palmed or plastic gloves in the glove compartment or trunk. They'll come in handy should you have to change a tire, scrape the windshield, or push a fellow motorist out of a ditch. If you pump your own gas, the gloves will help keep your hands from taking on the persistent odor of the fuel. Finally, any driver will benefit from stashing away an inexpensive flashlight.

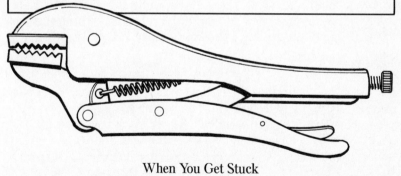

When You Get Stuck

Here's a tip for drivers in snow country who have rear-wheel-drive cars: Next time you go to the supermarket, pick up a bag of cat box filler, the larger the better. Keep the bag in the trunk for added weight over the drive wheels; should you get stuck, open the bag and sprinkle a few handfuls of the granules around the rear wheels for better traction.

Shopping for and Selling a Car

Look for Little Signs

Small indicators may tip you off to the overall condition of the car. Are the window handles tight? Is the dashboard vinyl showing signs of cracking? Are the carpets worn and frayed? Are the rubber gaskets around the doors and windows intact? Wear and tear on these items suggests that the rest of the car may be suffering as well.

Get a Mechanic's Okay

If you have little knowledge of the particular model you are considering buying, have it checked out thoroughly by a garage specializing in that type of car. Its mechanics will be familiar with the serious problems unique to that model.

Check the Oil

Check the oil on the dipstick. Although clean oil will tell you only that the oil has been changed recently, filthy oil will tell you that the engine may have a less-than-normal life expectancy. Other signs like shabby hoses in the engine compartment, oil spray patterns on the underside of the hood, and worn fan belts should be viewed as warning signals that the car has not received the best of care.

Arriving at an Offer

Know the Blue Book value of the used car you are considering. From the value of the car in good condition, deduct the cost of problems you uncover from the asking price and base your offer on the result.

Listen to Your Intuition

Pay as much attention to who is selling the car as to the condition of the car itself. If you get the feeling that you wouldn't buy a used car from the person, then you probably shouldn't, regardless of how good the deal seems to be. In shopping for a used car, intuition matters.

A seller who attempts to pressure you into buying may be hoping for a sale before you discover problems that turned off other buyers; his fast talk may well stick you with a slow ride. Don't allow yourself to be bullied.

Is Front-Wheel Drive Better?

In shopping for a new car, keep in mind that both front- and rear-wheel-drive models have their advantages. If the engine powers the front

Simple Mechanical Checks When Inspecting a Car

- Look under the bell housing (where the engine and transmission meet). If there is even a hint of dripping oil, suspect either a blown transmission seal or a blown rear seal in the engine. To replace either requires the removal of the transmission and probably the replacement of the clutch plate. An oil leak may also signal excessive wear on transmission parts—people are apt to neglect their transmissions. Have someone with a good nose for the smell of transmission oil (it has a sharper odor than engine oil) check the drip to identify it.

- Carefully remove the radiator cap, allowing steam to slowly escape if the engine is warm. Check the cap and the filler neck for oily grey foam. Its presence may mean the head gasket is leaking oil into the coolant.

- Closely check the alignment of the body parts. A crooked bumper or a fender that doesn't quite match up suggests the car experienced a nasty bump that may have bent the frame. Such a car should be considered for purchase only with extreme caution.

- Do the doors open and close with ease? Should there be any need to lift the door to latch it, you may be dealing with door posts so rusted (externally or internally) that they no longer support the weight of the door. Lift the door and watch to see whether the post flexes. If it does, quietly close the door and bid the owner adieu.

- Lift the floor mats and carpets to see what's going on below. Dust and gum wrappers are fine, but anything soggy is potential trouble. Look closely for rust, and check brake lines running through the afflicted area for signs of corrosion—a small but potentially life-threatening matter.

- Look at the wheels, tires, and brake hubs for dark or damp spots that might indicate leaking brake fluid. If you're suspicious, look closely at the bottom of the brake backing plate (with your head stuck under the car looking up, it's the inboard side of the wheel). There, between the (stationary) backing plate and the (movable) wheel, you may find a drop of brake fluid; if in doubt, smell it, and compare it to the liquid in the brake fluid reservoir. Its presence means replacing brake wheel cylinders on the axle, and most likely the brake shoes. If the car has disk brakes, check for wet spots around the calipers, particularly along the bottom surfaces.

wheels, both weight and space are conserved because there's no need for a drive train down the center of the car; also, traction is superior on slushy, slick surfaces. The traditional front-engine, rear-wheel-drive configuration gives better general handling and performance, and service is cheaper and simpler. One car maker recently introduced a model with front-wheel drive on the more sedate sedan and rear-wheel drive for the sporty coupe.

Will Its Fuel Become Illegal?

When shopping for an older used car, don't forget to consider the availability of leaded fuel. Expect federal legislation to increasingly restrict its distribution. Local restrictions may also come into effect; in 1984, Chicago became the first municipality to ban the sale of leaded gasoline.

A Heavy-Duty Battery for Cold Weather

A tiny spare tire isn't the only way in which car manufacturers are sneaking weight and raw material from new models. Puny batteries are another concession to mileage improvement and cost cutting. If you're concerned about cold-weather starting, ask your dealer about replacing the standard battery with a heavy-duty one.

Avoid Costly Upkeep

The sticker price of a car doesn't reflect the cost of maintenance over the vehicle's lifetime. Generally, the most expensive cars to keep on the road have been diesels and German makes.

Frequency-of-repair statistics are reported annually in the April issue of *Consumer Reports.* The magazine compiles the experiences of hundreds of thousands of readers, and the results are vital reading for car shoppers. Also consult back issues of *Money* magazine for their annual lists of cars that hold their value best over the years.

Is It a Safe Car?

Before you buy a car, new or used, you might benefit from a call to the toll-free Auto Safety Hotline sponsored by the National Highway Traffic Safety Administration. Be prepared to give the year, make, and model of the car. Call 800-424-9393 (or in the Washington, D.C., area, 426-0123).

Before You Sell

When is the best time to sell an older car? Have a mechanic give the car a thorough checkup, and ask for a rough estimate of what major repair and replacement jobs can be anticipated over the next several years. Couple this information with the fact that most cars depreciate rapidly for the first eight years or so and then remain at a fairly constant, low value for a few years; after that they begin to appreciate. Cars in demand by collectors (consult Hemmings Motor News, Box 380, Bennington, CT 05201, or other old-car publications) begin to appreciate faster and may reach their original sticker price 18 to 25 years after the year of manufacture. Convertibles regain their value much quicker than sedans.

Tires

Rotate for Maximum Wear

You'll extend the life of your tires by rotating them—changing their location every six months or 6,000 miles. If your car has radials, switch tires from front to back, not from one side to the other.

Checking Tire Wear

To gauge tire wear, insert a penny into the shallowest tread on the tire. If you can't hide the top of Lincoln's head, you need a new tire.

Tire Pressure

Follow the manufacturer's recommended tire pressures for maximum tire life. But you may choose to deviate from these pressures in a couple of cases. Increase pressure by a few pounds to decrease the tires' rolling resistance and thereby increase mileage. Or, to increase the size of the tires' tread prints on a slippery, near-impassable stretch of road, bleed a few pounds of air; do not, however, travel at highway speeds on tires with low pressure.

Keep a tire pressure gauge in your car. Most of those on air pumps at service stations are woefully inaccurate, and service station operators can't afford to lend you their hand gauges. By checking on pressure about once a month, you'll have safer handling and an improved ride. Correctly inflated tires also last a lot longer than those running just a few pounds soft.

Checking tire pressure is one of the most neglected routines of car maintenance. To make the job easier, buy valve caps that visually indicate whether the tire is at a proper pressure all the time. All you have

Tire Changing Made (Relatively) Easy

If your tires were bolted onto the wheels by power tools, you're apt to have to struggle in coaxing the lug nuts back off when changing a flat tire—especially if dirt and rust conspire against you. Here are four steps to take, followed by a somewhat desperate measure for budging a stubborn nut.

- Ask the person mounting the wheels to tighten the nuts by *hand power,* using a torque wrench if possible.

- Ask him or her to put a few drops of oil on the wheel lugs before turning down the nuts to discourage rusting.

- Carry a hand impact driver and hammer in the trunk; the driver will loosen frozen lug nuts.

- To remove a wheel that was installed by what seems to have been a gorilla with an air gun, first strike each lug nut with a ballpeen hammer.

- If you are stranded because you can't apply enough force with the lug wrench, place a rock beneath the wrench's shaft to serve as a fulcrum. Step on the arm to the left to loosen the lug nut. Apply your weight gently at first, as the wrench may give way suddenly under this strain. It's safer to use this simple device: a short length of 2×4 with a groove cut in one end. It serves as a lug wrench fulcrum, supporting the wrench in the notch. Once the lugs are loose, you can use the block to chock a wheel or to support the jack when raising the car.

to do is walk around your car and glance down at the valves to see if you need more air anywhere. They're available at auto supply stores.

Checking Wheel Alignment

You can check your own wheel alignment by feeling the tires. Slide your hand back and forth across the tread, feeling for the telltale trace of ratchet-tooth wear: If the tire feels rougher when you slide your hand in one particular direction, then you need to get the wheels aligned.

When Things Go Wrong
(See also Maintenance, in this chapter.)

Low on Coolant

Loss of coolant is a common cause of auto breakdowns on the highway. If your cooling system develops a small leak, you can increase your chances of completing the trip by releasing the pressure in the cooling system. Simply loosen the radiator pressure cap; cover the cap with several rags, and turn it slowly to avoid being scalded by a geyser of steam.

If the Radiator Hose Springs a Leak

Keep a roll of duct tape on hand so that a radiator hose leak won't strand you on the highway. Before removing the radiator cap, allow the engine to cool to relieve pressure on the system; or cover the cap with a heavy rag and carefully back it off just enough to allow the pressure to escape. Clean and dry the hose. Apply the tape over the leak at a slight angle to the hose, so that the successive windings will overlap. The tape should cover 3 inches of the hose on each side of the leak. Remove the cap and add water, if available, to the radiator. Then put the cap back on, but leave it loose so that pressure won't build up. Drive at moderate speed to the nearest gas station.

Out of Gas?

Should you need gas to start a stranded car or a dry lawn mower, you may be able to pump it directly from your car—if it has an electric fuel pump. Disconnect the fuel line between the filter and the carburetor, and have someone turn the key while you catch the gas as it streams steadily out.

Don't try to siphon gas from a car by sucking it up a hose with your mouth. Gas not only tastes awful but is extremely hazardous to your health. Try cupping your hands over the tank opening and siphon hose and blowing into the tank. If you can pressurize the tank slightly you'll start the siphon without having to suck the hose.

While you should never carry a container of gasoline in your trunk because of the fire hazard, you can benefit from taking along an empty plastic or metal container. Should you run out of fuel or have a cooling system leak, you can fill it with fuel or water. A plastic gallon milk jug serves the purpose and costs nothing.

Fuel Line Leaks on Diesel Models

Diesel cars often fail to start because of a leak in the fuel line. If the car takes a bit more cranking than usual to start and the glow plug system is functioning properly, suspect this cause. The fuel flows back down the lines unless held in place by vacuum. To check out diesel fuel lines, install at least one section of clear line in the system. A trail of bubbles points to a leak—usually a poor hose connection or leaky filter fitting. Check the fuel return lines as well as the main fuel lines.

Expensive Sounds

If you experience a deep noise that sounds like a knock in the bowels of the engine, suspect either a worn main bearing or a worn camshaft bearing. Drive the car up a hill. If the noise is loud when going uphill and ceases when you let up on the gas, you may be facing worn main bearings. You may not be inclined to tackle any of the repair work yourself, but you now have an idea of what repairs (and expense) you are in for.

An engine noise that sounds like a light tap-tap-tap could be caused by loose valves or a worn connecting rod bearing. To determine whether it's the former or the latter, run the engine at idle and remove each spark plug wire in turn. If the cause is a loose valve, there will be no change in the noise. If it's a worn rod bearing, the noise will cease when the afflicted cylinder is deprived of spark.

A Broken Fan Belt

Should a broken fan belt strand you, try replacing it with a nylon stocking. Stretch the stocking around the pulleys and tie it as tightly as possible. Trim the loose ends close to the knot, and head for a service station right away.

Emergency Tune-Up Tips

Here are two emergency car tune-up checks you can make with "tools" you probably have on you right now: You can use a paper match as a feeler gauge to set your ignition points; the thickness of a match just happens to be close to the proper gap for most cars. And a quick check for ignition timing can be accomplished with a piece of thin paper, like cigarette paper or a credit card receipt. With the points closed on the paper, turn the engine by hand while tugging lightly on the paper. (If you can't turn the engine by hand, put the car in gear and rock it back and forth.) When the paper begins to slip, the static timing marks on the engine should be aligned.

A Short in the Electrical System

If you are experiencing a short that blows fuses as quickly as you can replace them, take an old but functioning blinker relay box and attach two pieces of electrical wire to the "hot" terminals. Attach alligator clips to the other ends of the wires, and connect the clips to each end of the fuse bracket. The relay will act like a self-resetting breaker box, giving you an audible signal until you find the source of the electrical drain.

To begin tracking a short in the electrical system, remove and reinstall each fuse. When one sparks upon being replaced, you have found the faulty circuit (note that the sparks are small and apt to be hard to see in daylight). Consult your owner's manual for a list of accessories governed by the fuse, and check each in turn.

The Alternator Light Comes On

When the red warning light for the alternator comes on, first check the fan belt.

What if the light goes off as you begin driving, and then comes on again at high speed? On a high-mileage car, suspect worn brushes on the alternator; they tend to fail to maintain contact at higher rpm. The cure is to replace the brushes. In some alternators this is a simple job of removing a holder and replacing it with another. Other types of alternators have the newer brushes that have springs and braided copper pigtails, and these must be soldered.

Battery Problems

Does your battery go dead when the car sits awhile? To determine whether the current is draining because of the battery or a short in the car's electrical system, disconnect the battery ground strap and lightly touch it to the battery terminal, after turning off all accessories and closing the car doors. If there is a spark, electricity is being drained through a short in the system.

Start-Up Trouble

If your car won't start on a warm wet morning after a few days of cool weather, look for a simple cause. In these conditions, moisture condenses on the cool metal surfaces of the ignition system parts. Spray the entire system with a light coat of moisture-displacing aerosol oil (WD-40 is one brand name), following the directions on the can. The oil displaces moisture from metal surfaces and should enable the car to start.

Jump-Starting Tips

Store jumper cables in any car that's prone to electrical problems. Here are a few suggestions for using them more effectively.

- Be aware that long, light jumper cables often won't carry enough current to start a car.

- If the sick battery isn't too far gone you can start the functioning car, connect the cables, and wait 5 to 10 minutes for a charge to build up in the stalled car before trying to start it again.

- Two sets of cables work better than one. If another pair is available, hook it up as well to double the current delivered to the ailing car.

- When cables don't do the trick, try bypassing the battery. Disconnect the car's lead from the positive terminal and connect the lead straight to the jumper cable. A bad battery may be shorted out so that it won't pass current to the starter.

- If the stalled car is lodged so that you can't reach it with cables, try parking the helper car so that the bumpers of both cars touch and create a ground connection. (The bumpers must be metal, of course.) Then connect the two jumper cables end to end and affix them to the two positive battery poles. Be sure that both cars operate on negative ground—that is, the negative post of the battery (it will be marked) is connected by a cable to the car body.

In the Garage

Cleanup

To clean automotive grease or engine oil from your hands, keep a bottle of baby oil in the garage. It will remove any oil-based substance, without the burning, drying feeling caused by heavy-duty cleaners or solvents.

If you do your own car repairs, you may be cursed with permanent deposits of grease under the fingernails. Try this *before* getting into the grease: Scratch your fingernails along a bar of soap, then work the soap around the nails. At wash-up time your hands will clean up far more easily.

You may be tempted to clean dirty automotive parts with gasoline, but don't do it; this is a dangerous practice. A spark can ignite the fumes; furthermore, the vapors are unhealthy to inhale. Instead, buy a nonflammable solvent that emulsifies grease so that it turns to soap when rinsed down with water.

If You Don't Have a Garage

Not everyone has a clean, well-lighted place in which to do car repairs after dark. If an electrical socket isn't handy, attach a 12-volt fluorescent trouble light to the car battery. It will use far less electricity than an incandescent bulb yet provide the same amount of light. (The light will also come in handy should you have to stop for repairs along the road.) If you'll be using the light for a few hours, plan against the battery going flat by parking on a hill steep enough for a roll-start.

Hooks for Hanging

For a row of handy hooks on which to hang rakes, garden hose, and other items, saw down through the rungs of a worn-out ladder, and attach the halves to the garage's studs with lag bolts.

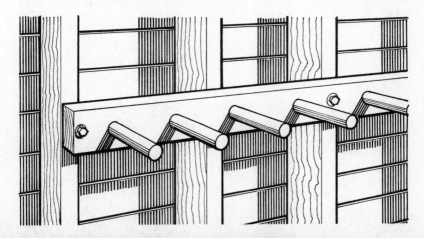

Keeping Track of Small Parts

When you are disassembling a gadget with lots of small parts, use an egg carton or plastic sandwich bags to hold the pieces. By organizing the parts, you'll be more likely to reassemble them correctly.

Use strips of masking tape to hold tiny parts to your workbench.

Label Wires

To avoid frustration when working on electrical appliances or car wiring, label the wires as you remove them. Simply fold a piece of masking tape in half around the wire to serve as a label. With the wires clearly identified, there will be no guesswork when it comes time to plug everything back in.

Homemade Wheel Chocks

All home mechanics ought to have at least a pair of wheel chocks to keep a car from rolling when it is jacked up. These can be made easily by splitting a short log into wedges.

Safety First When Jacking Up a Car

When raising a car to work under it, always support it on jack stands. Make certain the car is solidly supported by trying to rock it first, before you begin any serious work. Removing a tight nut from a shock absorber or exhaust system may involve considerable movement. Further, place a wheel or other solid object under the car to catch it should the stands tip and let the car fall. This will ensure that you still have living space.

11 Here's to Your Health

Aches and Pains

(See also Sportsmedicine in the chapter, Keeping Fit.)

Rx for Leg Cramps

Ever wake up the middle of the night with shooting Charlie horse pains? If you do, try sleeping on your back, and keep the bed covers loose or use a foot cradle to keep the weight of the covers from forcing the foot into an exaggerated bending position. You might also try resting the foot against a pillow at the foot of the bed. If you sleep on your stomach, let your feet extend over the edge of the mattress so that the muscles of the foot are in a neutral position.

The quickest way to get relief from a Charlie horse pain is to flex the cramping muscle. Try this remedy: Stand up facing a wall about 3 feet away. Hold your arms out in front of you and lean forward, resting on

your hands, with arms bent, while you keep both your heels on the floor, with legs and body straight. Hold this position for a count of ten, relax for a count of five, then repeat the stretch. This stretching will also work well for daytime cramps. If the cramp still doesn't go away, massage the area to ease the contraction.

Headaches

Relieving a headache may be as easy as swinging your arms. It's the basis of a treatment called Li Shou, which in Chinese means "hand swinging." Li Shou works because it counteracts the swollen cranial blood vessels that cause your head to throb and ache. By swinging your arms, you shunt the flow of blood to your limbs and reduce the flow of blood to your head.

Migraine Headaches

Sometimes migraines are brought on by food allergies. If you suspect this might be the cause of your attacks, see what effect eliminating these foods from your diet has: foods that contain sodium nitrates, like luncheon meats, frankfurters, ham, bacon, and cured sausage; monosodium glutamate (often in egg drop soup and other Chinese dishes, and in some meat tenderizers and seasoning mixes); red wines; hard and semihard cheeses; salted pretzels, nuts, potato chips, and popcorn; chocolate; coffee; and tea.

Migraines can also be triggered by stress, fatigue, automobile exhaust, sun glare, tobacco, and skipping meals.

Sore Thumbs

If you hit your thumb (or any finger) accidentally when hammering a nail, immerse it right away in cold water. The coldness of the water eases the pain almost instantly and helps to prevent swelling, soreness, and a nasty black nail. (For black nails see First Aid, in this chapter.)

Muscle Strains

Right after a muscle strain injury, take any weight off the affected area and raise it up. The pain is due not only to a muscle tear, but also to a muscle spasm. Spasm means that the muscles around the injured area contract and sometimes stay that way for days. Spasms are painful, but they are the body's way of protecting the injured tissues.

If You've Got a Bad Back

It's been estimated that 8 out of 10 Americans will experience the agony of back pain, especially lower back pain. What can you do to ward off the pain?

- As your mother said, "Stand up straight; stop slouching." Bad posture exaggerates back curvature and puts extra strain and stress right at the curve in your lower back. You should stand so that the back's curves can take their natural arc: First, lengthen your neck without thrusting your chin forward; keep your chin tucked into your chest. Second, contract the muscles in your buttocks, letting your pelvis thrust forward.

- When standing, ease the pressure on your back by standing with one foot elevated in front of you; rest it on a stool, the rim of a chair, a low shelf, or anything that's above floor level.

- Wear low-heeled shoes; they don't require you to arch your back as much as higher heeled shoes do.

- The majority of people who suffer from back pain have weak abdominal muscles. Sagging stomach muscles put strain on the back, which is forced to bear the weight that the abdomen can't handle. Exercise can often help to reduce lower back pain by strengthening the stomach muscles.

- To reduce strain on your back while sitting, raise your knees ½ to 1 inch higher than your hips by resting your feet on a footstool.

- After a long workday don't slide the car seat back for a "winding-down" ride home. This will actually put unnecessary strain on your lower and upper back muscles. Instead, bring the seat forward so that your knees are higher than your hips.

- Sleep with your knees raised if you sleep on your back. If you sleep on your stomach, put a pillow under your pelvis. And if you sleep on your side, bend your legs in a semifetal position and put a pillow between your knees. All these positions will help to take the pressure off your back.

Place ice on the sore area to stop internal bleeding, reduce swelling, and induce numbness, which will ease the pain. If there's a great deal of swelling, wrap the area snugly but not tightly. Heat helps strained muscles only when the pain and swelling are gone, by bringing in nutrients and new cells that accelerate healing. The heat also loosens the muscles. You can apply heat by using a hot water bottle or heating pad.

Emergency Cold Pack

If you need a cold pack in an emergency, use a plastic bag of frozen vegetables from your freezer. Just tap the bag on a hard surface to loosen and separate the frozen vegetable pieces, then lay it on the affected area; the bag easily conforms to the contours of your body.

Ice for Arthritic Knees

Swollen, arthritic knees can be very painful, to say the least. But relief may be here. There is a simple treatment that has worked wonders for many arthritis sufferers: ice. Fill two small plastic food storage bags with ice, seal, and hold or secure one over and one under the knee. Do this for 20 minutes at a time, two or three times a day.

Allergies

Allergenic Foods

The least allergenic foods are lamb, rice, carrots, potatoes, apples, lettuce, and gelatin. Among the foods that most commonly cause allergic reactions are cow's milk, corn, wheat, eggs, and chocolate.

Milk Allergy Sufferers Take Note

If you are allergic to milk and are wondering where you get the calcium you need in your diet, you should know these facts: Calcium is obtained from certain leafy green vegetables (such as turnips, mustard and collard greens, kale, and broccoli) and from hard water. And calcium leaches into the water from the soup bones when you make acidic stocks (those that contain tomatoes or vinegar). Other sources of calcium are the bones in canned salmon and carob. Gram for gram carob has three times more calcium than does milk.

Selenium, Good for Some Allergies

Selenium, an essential trace mineral for the body, may be the remedy for your allergies, particularly if your allergens are environmental ones such as pollution, pesticides, and industrial solvents, or even if you're allergic to preservatives. A California researcher, who cured his own hypersensitivity to chemicals with selenium, believes that selenium works because it protects us from free radicals, those nasty substances that are believed to bombard and break down cells. To increase your selenium intake, eat tuna fish packed in water, liver, kidneys, and Brazil nuts.

Allergy Signals in Children

If the phrase "Jekyll and Hyde" describes your child's behavior perfectly, suspect a food allergy. Great mood swings can be related to diet, with sugar being the biggest culprit. Other foods that often cause problems in children are wheat, milk, corn, eggs, citrus fruit, chocolate, and peanuts.

Dark circles under the blue eyes of your blond child (who happens to be getting plenty of sleep) could point to allergies. Although the cause is not understood, it's often observed that blond, blue-eyed children are more susceptible to allergies and develop the dark bluish circles under the eyes called "allergic shiners." Other signs that would point to allergy, especially food allergies, are loose bowels and gas.

Indoor Pollution

Allergy sufferers may find great relief in literally leaving home. California researchers who monitored the levels of pollutants inside some homes found air pollution to be worse inside than outside. Two of the major sources of pollution were cigarettes and gas stoves.

If that sounds like your house, then now is the time for the smokers at home to give up cigarettes. Also, be sure to use an exhaust hood for your gas stove; better yet, ask your utility to come out and turn off the gas to the pilot light so that the stove doesn't give off fumes even when it's not being used. In most stoves it's not much trouble to light the stove with a match each time you use it, especially if it'll make a difference in your health.

Air Conditioners Can Foster Allergens

Your car's air conditioner could set off an allergy attack. One study of 14 various makes of air-conditioned cars found that 11 of them contained one or more kinds of mold. The doctor who ran the study had a patient whose allergy manifested itself only when the patient drove his wife's car. His symptoms stopped when the air conditioner in her car was cleaned.

Your Water Supply Could Be the Culprit

Tap water can contain allergens, too. So if you've eliminated all the allergenic foods from your diet but your sinuses are still stuffy, have your water analyzed. The water from your faucet may very well contain intentionally added chemicals such as chlorine or fluoride, or even industrial wastes or agricultural chemicals that inevitably find their way into local water supplies and irritate you.

Parakeets, Canaries, and . . .

Pet birds are often overlooked as the cause of allergies. Birds regularly shake off microscopic feather particles into the air that can cause serious respiratory problems.

Vitamins for Hay Fever

Hay fever sufferers, if you tend to run to the drugstore for an antihistamine when the pollen season hits, make it vitamin C. Vitamin C is Mother Nature's own number one antihistamine. (Other nutrients with hay fever-fighting abilities are the B-complex vitamins and bioflavonoids.)

Food Cravings

A food craving could be your body's signal that you have a food allergy. Recognizing the craving as such and eliminating the offending food from your diet could end those mysterious headaches or bouts of depression.

A food allergy can become a craving in a curious way: When you are frequently exposed to a food that causes severe symptoms, the body is forced to adapt to the problem and reacts by suppressing the symptoms. This stage may give way to a period of no symptoms or to one of chronic symptoms like headaches or depression. The result is that you crave what makes you feel miserable because your body has grown used to working with that food around!

Allergy-Free Baking Powder

Are you allergic to aluminum or wheat? You can make your own baking powder that is free of these ingredients. Combine 2 teaspoons of cream of tartar, 2 teaspoons of cornstarch, and 1 teaspoon of baking soda. To make it corn-free, use arrowroot powder instead of cornstarch.

Dark vs White Chocolate

If you crave chocolate but can't eat it because it gives you headaches, try substituting white chocolate. Many people find that they can tolerate the white but not the dark. One possible explanation is that white chocolate has no theobromine, a substance that is irritating to some individuals.

Burns and Sunburn

Vitamin E for Burns

Cover a burn, scrape, or cut with vitamin E squeezed from a capsule or with vitamin E ointment to speed healing. Skin researchers have finally confirmed what some laymen have known for years—that vitamin E is soothing to damaged or problem skin when applied topically. Why? Because, say the scientists, vitamin E fights inflammation and tends to counteract the swelling that accompanies it.

Aloe Vera for Burns, Too

And don't forget the juice from the aloe vera plant for burns and sunburns. Cut off a leaf and squeeze the juice on the affected area. It'll lubricate and soothe the skin as it soaks in, without leaving a greasy or sticky film.

Milk Protein for Sunburns

Sunburned skin can benefit from the protein in milk. Make a milk compress as follows: Mix together one part of skim milk with four parts of water. Add some ice cubes and then soak a cloth in the mixture. Lay the cloth on the sunburned area for 15 to 20 minutes. Be sure to keep the cloth moist by soaking it in the milk solution as often as necessary. Repeat this every 2 to 4 hours.

Sunburned Skin Heals Slowly

Sun seekers should be aware that their skin doesn't take kindly to being burned twice in the same summer. Even though you may feel as if your skin has quickly recovered from a burn, it actually takes your skin three months to return to normal. The top layer of skin peels off, and the newly exposed skin is extremely sensitive to more sunburns.

Vinegar and Water for Sunburn Relief

You can treat sunburn pain by spraying on a water and vinegar solution kept in a clean spray bottle. It soothes on contact.

A Sunscreen from Vitamin E

If you can't decide which sunscreen to buy, buy vitamin E ointment instead. Applied topically, vitamin E makes a pretty good sunscreen because it reduces the amount of ultraviolet light reaching the skin. And biochemical action induced by the vitamin helps reduce injury-related inflammation and further skin damage.

Caffeine, Tobacco, and Alcohol

Caffeine Content of Coffees

Do you want to reduce your caffeine intake? Then the following information will be important to remember: Decaffeinated coffee beans have half the caffeine of typical coffee beans. Use the perk method of brewing rather than the drip, which extracts about 25% more caffeine. Regular instant coffee has about three-fourths as much caffeine as regular brewed coffee, while instant decaffeinated coffee has about the same amount of caffeine as brewed decaffeinated coffee.

Caffeine Withdrawal

Are your lovely, long-awaited weekends usually accompanied by a headache on Saturday afternoon? Many working people's weekends are. This is because people whose first task at work during the week is to get a cup of coffee often don't drink it at home on the weekends. Because coffee constricts blood vessels, withdrawal from the brew for more than 18 hours causes the blood vessels in the head to dilate too far and produce pain.

Alkalinizing Foods for Kicking the Smoking Habit

If you're having a tough time breaking the cigarette habit, you ought to know about certain everyday foods that can help. These foods work by shifting the body's chemistry from an acid one to an alkaline one. The more alkaline we make our body chemistry, the less we crave nicotine. These alkalinizing foods include almonds, apples, berries, carrots, celery, grapefruit, lima beans, milk, mushrooms, onions, peas, raisins, spinach, summer squash, sweet potatoes, and tomatoes.

Some people find that sunflower seeds provide the same pick-me-up and calming effect that tobacco does—without ruining their health.

Effects from "Passive Smoking"

Even if you're not a smoker yourself, you might be suffering from passive smoking—the inhalation of smoke that's in the air from a nearby smoker. Many tests have shown that nonsmoking spouses and other family members of smokers are about 60% more likely to develop lung cancer than nonsmokers whose spouses don't smoke.

The Drink with the Least Alcohol

Which do you think has the least amount of alcohol: a bottle of beer, a glass of wine, or a jigger of scotch? Most think beer, but the answer is wine. The most popular beer in America contains 17.6 grams of pure alcohol in a 12-ounce bottle, a jigger of 80-proof scotch has 15 grams, and a glass of table wine has only 9.9 grams.

If You Drink

Be a wise alcohol consumer by following these tips:

- When pouring liquor, don't pour straight from the bottle; use a jigger to measure out your drinks. You'll usually pour out less this way.

- Resist pouring in a little extra for "good measure."

- Make your mixed drinks as healthy as possible by mixing them with fruit or vegetable juice.

- Mix your wine with carbonated water or mineral water to make a wine spritzer; the drink will last longer and you'll find yourself consuming less alcohol. Make the second drink a spritzer, too—without the wine.

- If you like bloody marys, try a virgin mary next time. Because this is a hearty, spicy drink, you'll hardly miss the liquor.

- Instead of taking a drink to give yourself a lift or to relax, try something that is equally effective: a shower, a brisk walk, or a short nap.

Don't Mix Smoking with Drinking

You'll be more likely to set yourself up for a hangover if you smoke while you're drinking. This is because you'll be getting a double dose of acetaldehyde, a hangover-causing substance that's in both tobacco and alcohol.

Smoking and Alcohol Can Dampen Your Sex Drive

Putting some spice in your life and your spouse's can be as easy as putting down that after-dinner cigarette or drink. Heavy cigarette smoking causes carbon monoxide to accumulate in the blood, which interferes with your cells' ability to get a good supply of oxygen. A result of this is decreased sexual capabilities. Alcohol drowns sexual desires because it tends to reduce the body's production of sex hormones.

Colds

(For sore throats see Ear, Nose, Mouth, and Throat, in this chapter.)

Catching a Cold

Colds are not caused by a chill or a draft, but either one can leave you susceptible to the virus that really causes the cold, because such environmental stress will help the virus to multiply in your body. The cold virus goes through a one- to six-day incubation period before symptoms even appear. It's during this period that colds are often most contagious.

Preventing Colds with Room Humidifiers

A humidifier in your home and workplace may significantly reduce your incidence of winter colds. Studies show that when work environments are humidified, absenteeism is substantially lower. Because greater relative humidity results in shorter survival time for many bacteria and viruses, winter colds may actually have more to do with low indoor humidity than low outdoor temperatures.

Warding Off Colds

Did you wake up in the morning with a scratchy or thick throat that you recognize as the beginnings of a cold? Take vitamin C after your breakfast (but not on an empty stomach, since it is acid and might give you discomfort). You maximize your chances of fighting a cold with vitamin C if you take generous doses at the very earliest sign of coming down with one.

Moisturizing Your Mucous Membranes

Steam by itself can relieve cold symptoms by moisturizing the mucous membranes. Adding chamomile or peppermint to the water may offer further relief because the mildly antiseptic effects of these herbs can help destroy bacteria in the nose. Also, peppermint contains menthol, a substance found in many commercial cold products, which penetrates mucous membranes to unblock nasal passages.

Soups for Colds

Chicken soup does indeed help cure a cold. Its warmth and aroma not only make you feel good, but they also give you a runny nose, thereby reducing the time the germ-infested mucus stays in contact with your nasal passages.

The Chinese may have one over mother's chicken soup for colds. Oriental hot and sour soup contains the same soothing chicken broth, but its hot spices do a better job of stimulating and clearing the nasal passages than does mother's milder version.

Special Tea for Cold Sufferers

Whenever anyone in Rodale's Test Kitchen has a cold or feels a cold coming on, Debra Deis prepares this special tea.

In a medium-size saucepan, mix 4 cups of water with 1 tablespoon of anise or fennel seeds and bring to a boil. Remove the pan from heat and add:

8 thin slices unpeeled ginger root

1 lime, squeezed and dropped in

2 teaspoons dried mint

2 teaspoons dried rosemary (optional)

2 teaspoons blueberry leaves (optional)

1 teaspoon dried sage (optional)

Steep for 10 minutes and then grate the brown skin only of 1 nutmeg into the tea. Sweeten with honey to taste and strain as you serve.

Stuffy Noses

A stuffy nose can develop when the mucus becomes dry and thick and clogs the sinus ducts. In addition to hot herbal teas and chicken soups, beef liver is excellent for the sinuses. It's loaded with vitamin A, which keeps mucus thin and fluid.

You can also sprinkle a few drops of eucalyptus oil on a handkerchief and inhale it a few times to clear a stuffy nose.

Nasal Decongestants

A nasal decongestant will also provide temporary relief from a stuffy nose, but be careful not to use it for more than about three days. Using it longer than that could make your nose more stuffed up than before.

Exercise Off the Sniffles

Exercise can be a natural decongestant when you have a stuffy nose due to a cold or allergy. Do some light exercising that gets your head and upper body up and moving. When you relax, your blood vessels take it easy, too, and this can lead to nasal congestion.

Honey for Coughs

Putting a dab of honey on the back of the tongue can bring relief from a nagging cough.

Cloves for Coughs

Another simple cough remedy is a whole clove. Pop one in your mouth and suck on it, and you'll find that it produces a slight burning effect that quiets lots of tickles in the throat better than the sugary cough drops on the market.

Coughs Due to Stress

A nagging throat tickle that makes you cough frequently may be due more to stress than a cold. Many people involuntarily tense their throat muscles, which causes a cough. To relieve the problem try relaxing your throat muscles by breathing deeply through your mouth.

Lots of Fluids for Coughs

Water, fruit juices, and chicken soup may work better for your cough than an expectorant. Expectorants are supposed to increase the watery excretions produced by cells in the upper respiratory tract. Theoretically, those secretions loosen mucus and phlegm, making them easier to cough up and out of the lungs. But expectorants often don't work as advertised. What your system really needs is fluids to moisten the mucous membranes and loosen the mucus.

Postnasal Drip

A cough that is related to postnasal drip can keep you up half the night. Try sleeping on your stomach.

Cough Suppressants

Suppressing a cough with either an over-the-counter drug or a home remedy is okay for a dry, hacking kind of cough. But don't try to suppress a wet, phlegm-producing cough; it is actually doing your body good because it is helping to clear your lungs.

Doctors and Hospitals

Talking with Your Doctor

Ever leave your doctor's office dissatisfied with the amount and kind of information you got? You're not alone; one of the biggest complaints among health consumers is that their doctors don't spend enough time with them and don't explain things carefully enough during visits. Granted, the bedside manner of many doctors leaves something to be desired, but the fault could be partially yours. Preparing for each visit can substantially improve what you get out of it.

Take with you a list of questions you want to ask the doctor; keep them short and to the point. (You may find it very useful to read up on your problem before your visit.) Don't hesitate to ask your doctor to repeat his or her responses to your questions if you don't understand the answers. You can also call your doctor later if you're confused about what he or she said.

Explaining Your Health Problem

You'll probably be a lot more successful in helping your doctor or other health provider understand your problem if you can explain your symptoms in detail. Define your symptoms in terms of character (what they are, i.e., pain, ache, soreness), intensity (how strong), duration (i.e., continuous, once a day, at bedtime), location, influences on symptoms (i.e., gets worse after a meal, after standing a long time), associations with other symptoms (i.e., bright light brings on dizziness along with the pain), and recurrence (how often it's happened in the past).

Since it's very easy to mix up times and events and forget just what happened when, keep a daily log of the symptoms, being as descriptive as you can. Keep in mind what activities you were involved in, what you ate, the times that you noticed the problem, and so on. It's also a good idea to be familiar with your health history and family background and with what medications you have taken in the past.

Taking Medications

Always ask your doctor to explain just what medication he or she is prescribing for you: its brand, generic name, and strength (since some medications come in different strengths); just what it is supposed to do for you; what side effects, if any, you should expect or look out for; what precautions you should take when using the drug (i.e., not mixing it with another medication, not driving or drinking when taking it, taking it with meals, and so on); how often it should be taken daily and for how many days. This may seem like obvious information, but don't assume that your doctor or pharmacist will explain it all to you without your asking. With such information from your doctor you can check that the pharmacist gave you the correct prescription.

Paying for What You Got (and No More)

Ask that your hospital send you an itemized bill, even if you're fully covered by health insurance. A 1984 nationwide survey of 41 hospitals done by Equifax Services of Atlanta turned up some startling results: There were errors in 98% of the 3,000 bills that were reviewed. And this is not the first survey that made such a discovery. Nor will it be the last; Blue Cross/Blue Shield plans to do more of such audits.

Ear, Nose, Mouth, and Throat

Vitamin A for Middle Ear Infections

Chronic middle ear infections may be a sign of vitamin A deficiency. Vitamin A is necessary for the normal function of the middle ear because it stimulates the production of mucus, and mucus in the ear automatically traps dirt and bacteria and flushes it away. In animal studies, researchers found that animals deprived of vitamin A suffered a breakdown in the ear's cleaning mechanism that resulted in an ear infection. Good food sources of vitamin A are apricots, broccoli, and winter squash.

Nosebleeds

To treat a nosebleed, squeeze the nostrils firmly enough to stop the bleeding, but not so strongly that it becomes painful, and continue applying pressure for 15 minutes. If the bleeding continues, pinch the nose closed for 5 more minutes. Lean forward during this time; do not lie down. Place a cold cloth or ice bag on the nose and face to constrict the blood vessels. If the bleeding persists, get medical attention. Do not blow or touch the nose for several hours after the bleeding has stopped. You may want to apply petroleum jelly inside the nose twice a day to keep the tissues from drying out, opening, and bleeding again.

For Irritated Gums

If your gums are temporarily irritated and swollen, you can make yourself a pleasant ice pack: pineapple sherbet. It tastes good, the cold reduces the swelling, and, according to some studies, pineapple has curative effects.

Care for Healthy Gums

Periodontal disease, also referred to as receding gums, is the most common reason for loss of teeth in later life. But it can be controlled with regular hygiene if it is caught early enough. If your gums are tender or inflamed, or if you notice some bleeding when you brush your teeth, you may have the beginnings of this problem.

Be sure to brush your teeth at least twice daily and floss them once a day. When you brush your teeth, do so with an up and down—not sideways—motion, holding the brush at a 45° angle. Be careful to *gently* brush the gumline so that you push the bristles in between gums and teeth to remove all traces of food and to massage the gums. Thorough brushing and flossing will remove plaque, which is what causes pockets to form between your teeth and gums.

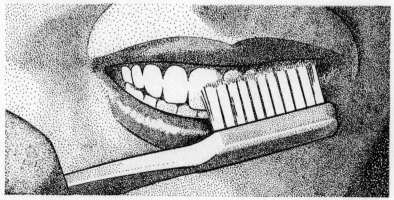

Apples, carrots, and other raw foods also help to give your gums important massages. And you can dry brush your teeth to massage the gums any time—like while you're reading or lying down to rest.

Temporary Toothache Relief

If that cavity is just killing you and the dentist can't see you right away, try putting a cold or warm compress on your cheek or jaw closest to the trouble spot. One or the other seems to work well as a temporary relief for many people because it induces numbness. You can also soak a small piece of cotton in oil of cloves (which you should be able to get at most pharmacies) and pack it into or around the cavity. However, do not let the oil come in contact with your gums because it can cause nerve damage and permanent loss of sensation in the affected area.

Hold onto That Loose Tooth

Should your child knock out a permanent tooth, drop it in a jar of milk and get your offspring—and the tooth—to the dentist immediately. He or she may be able to save the tooth.

Cleaning Dentures

Soak your dentures in white vinegar overnight. It's an inexpensive and effective way to clean them.

Canker Sores

You can treat a simple canker sore by touching it with the tip of a styptic pencil. An alternative is to rinse it with a mild solution of baking soda and water.

Cold Sores

If you're bothered by cold sores, try *Lactobacillus acidophilus* capsules. Many people find them effective for treating cold sores caused by the herpes simplex virus I, the very common variety of cold sore. Acidophilus restores and nurtures the natural bacterial flora in the mouth.

At the first sign of a cold sore you might also try rubbing it gently with an ice cube for a few minutes. This treatment is preferred by some physicians and is claimed to be more effective than any drug treatment.

Sore Throats

For a sore throat, gargle with warm water mixed with a little vinegar, cayenne, or hot pepper. The vinegar creates a mild acidic environment in your throat to kill bacteria, and the heat from the warm water and cayenne or hot pepper speeds extra blood to the irritated tissues.

Energy and Stress

Perk Up with Folate

If you constantly feel tired, despite a check of your iron levels that showed they were normal, then maybe folate is what you're lacking. Folate is necessary for the production of normal red blood cells. Folate deficiencies are not unusual, particularly if you've been avoiding vegetables and liver. Lentils and other beans are also good sources of folate.

Morning-Booster Breakfast

Load up on protein in the morning. Your body can't store protein the way it does carbohydrates and fats, and a high-protein breakfast keeps blood sugar levels up so that you're more alert and more energetic. Mix yogurt or cottage cheese with any combination of nuts, seeds, wheat germ, bran, or fresh fruit in season for a quick protein boost.

Light Lunches for Alert Afternoons

There are ways to beat that afternoon slump or, as scientists call it, the postprandial (after-eating) dip. It's the slump that hits people somewhere between 1 and 4 P.M. Physically, it involves a drop in body temperature and blood sugar, which in turn lowers your mood and work efficiency.

To stay alert and prevent the slump, eat a light lunch. Avoid heavy foods and overeating, which can drag you down. Instead, try to eat a 100% raw, light lunch. A salad containing nutritious foods like watercress, sprouts, chick-peas, tofu, tuna, sardines, seeds, and nuts is perfect.

A brisk 10-minute walk for fresh air and sunshine at noon will also help clear your head and get the blood pumping.

Wheat Germ Booster

If all of your get-up-and-go seems to have gotten up and left, give wheat germ oil a try. It doesn't work overnight, but after four to five weeks of a teaspoon a day, you should feel the difference. (Wheat germ oil also comes in capsules and is often measured in "minims"; a daily dose is 60 minims.) It's best absorbed on a relatively empty stomach directly after exercise. According to a wheat germ oil expert, the oil is a kind of fuel that aids the production of energy in the muscle cells. In addition, it can stabilize the nervous system, lower the pulse, and increase the rest interval of the heart during work or exercise.

Wheat Germ for Stress

When under a lot of stress we feel bad and we usually look bad, too. We especially show the effects of stress in our hair, because stress preys on many of the vitamins and minerals needed to grow healthy hair. One beneficial thing we can do for ourselves when the going gets rough is to eat some wheat germ. It's a good source of the B-vitamins (except B_{12}) that our nerves need, plus protein and vitamin E. All these nutrients have proven successful in making hair healthy.

Exercise Can Elevate Your Mood

Exercise is the simple, effective answer to the blues, say many physicians. A brisk 1-hour walk three times a week gets rid of tension and aggression and breaks the inertia that typically accompanies depression. Scientists also believe that exercise can do the same thing that antidepressant drugs do: it can raise the level of certain brain chemicals that accompany a rise in spirits. And the only side effect you'll have is a healthier and trimmer body.

Sunlight Can Help

In order to give ourselves a chance at a healthy life—mentally and physically—we need plenty of natural outdoor sunlight. Scientists have found that the subtle vibratory energy of natural light seems to have profound effects on us. It works on the pineal, pituitary, and other glands and the many hormones they secrete. In addition, sunlight seems to increase the body's protective immune response. So if you are the typical American who spends most of the day walled in behind glass (which doesn't admit certain light wavelengths) and concrete, or trapped in a car, find an excuse to get out as often as you can.

Laughter Therapy

If you're a victim of depression, tension headaches, the common cold, or even a more serious illness, use a treatment some doctors use—a good belly laugh. Experts now recognize that humor is therapeutic, especially when it's positive and shows an appreciation of the paradoxes and absurdities of life. It enhances respiration and lowers carbon dioxide levels in the blood. It's a good exercise and a good stress reducer. And it helps you forget your problems and pain.

Stress May Make You More Accident-Prone

Driving doesn't mix with drinking. And it also doesn't mix well with problems with parents or in-laws, problems or pressure in school or on the job, or financial troubles. In studies these events were found to be the most likely to predict accidents because they produce physical stress responses, and stressed people can't think, act, or react in a normal, relaxed manner. So if you're under a lot of stress at home, at school, or at work, take a cab or a bus, or ask someone else to give you a ride.

Niacin for Nerves

A case of "nerves" may be triggered by a nutrient deficiency, specifically, niacin. So before you turn to a tranquilizer, try eating more foods rich in niacin. These include lean meats (not pork), poultry, fish, peanuts, brewer's yeast, wheat germ, and liver.

And Calcium for Nerves

During times of sudden, unexpected emotional stress, think calcium. When you are stressed, blood levels of calcium can dip, and even a tiny decrease of calcium in the blood can produce uncontrollable temper outbursts. So if you find yourself suddenly in the midst of an emotional upheaval, reach for some cheese, yogurt, or a good old-fashioned glass of warm milk.

Eyes

Vitamin A for Your Eyes . . .

If seeing at night seems to be a problem for you, your mother's old adage of eating your carrots, a rich source of vitamin A, is excellent advice. One of the classic signs of vitamin A deficiency is night blindness. That's because in dim light, the process we call seeing—actually chemical changes turned to electrical impulses turned to mental pictures—requires at one point a light-sensitive pigment known as rhodopsin, or "visual purple." And the primary source of rhodopsin is vitamin A.

. . . And Zinc, Too

Zinc is a mineral that could help return your poor night vision to normal.

Although you may already have increased your intake of vitamin A-rich foods, you may still find that seeing well in dim light is difficult. The missing element may be zinc, which the body needs to change vitamin A into a form that is usable in the retina. Liver is a good source of zinc, as are soybeans, sunflower seeds, and black-eyed peas.

Vitamin B2 for Cataract Prevention

Cheese, yogurt, and milk may help you see things clearly for a longer time. These foods are all good sources of the vitamin B_2 (also called riboflavin). Doctors at the Eye Foundation Hospital in Birmingham, Alabama, have found something very interesting about B_2. When they compared cataract patients to patients with clear vision, they discovered that the older people who had good eyes all had a lot of riboflavin in their systems. If you are in your later years, aim for 25 mg of B_2 daily.

First Aid

(See also Sportsmedicine in the chapter, Keeping Fit; and Burns and Sunburn, Aches and Pains, and Ear, Nose, Mouth, and Throat, all in this chapter.)

Sugar Heals

Sugar may be better *on* you than *in* you, because it is a very good wound healer for cuts, scrapes, and even burns (including burned tongues from hot foods). It seems that sugar may minimize the risks of infection by helping to keep wounds dry. Sugar tends to soak up the moisture from a wound, thus depriving bacteria of the fluids they need to survive. And sugar may actually supply some of the nourishment and calories that damaged tissues need for regrowth.

To make your own sugary wound healer, simply mix about 4 parts of table sugar with 1 part of Betadine ointment (an iodine-based salve that's available at drugstores). Make sure the wound has been thoroughly washed and has stopped bleeding (sugar will only make a bleeding wound bleed even more), then pack the sugar mixture on the wound and cover it lightly with a gauze dressing. Wounds can be "fed" as often as four times daily in the beginning, decreasing to once a day as healing progresses. Rinsing with hydrogen peroxide each time you replace the dressing is not essential, but it may help keep the wound extra clean.

Removing Tight Rings

When a ring gets stuck on your finger due to swelling, instead of using butter or margarine to slip it off, try this: Place the hand with the ring on it into a bowl of ice water. Soak the hand until the chill of the water contracts the ring finger enough that the ring just slips off.

Or try this: Insert a strong piece of string (3 to 4 feet in length) under the ring, with the loose ends facing toward your hand. A matchstick or a toothpick might help you get the string under the ring. Then start winding the string firmly around your finger, starting at the edge of the ring and winding toward your fingertip until you reach your nail. Keep the loops of wound string close together to prevent the swollen finger from bulging through. As soon as you've done this, unwind the string from the end closest to the ring and continue unwinding it toward your fingertip. The string will have compressed your finger enough that the ring will usually slide off easily. Don't hesitate to unwind the string and remove your ring; the tight string can stop circulation to your finger if the string is left in place for more than just a few seconds. And if the pain is too great or the finger is badly discolored or numb, don't attempt this; call or see your doctor immediately.

Cleaning Off Sticky Remains

If you don't want to use a harsh abrasive or a smelly cleaning fluid to clean off the remains of sticky bandages or Scotch tape from your skin (or from furniture finishes, for that matter) try using a household lubricant like WD-40.

Removing Splinters

When you know that you have a splinter but you can't see it, place a piece of adhesive tape over the sore spot, then pull up straight and sideways until the splinter is out. This simple technique won't work with all splinters, especially not those that have inflamed the surrounding skin, but it is often worth a try.

Poison Ivy Remedies

Juice from the leaf of the wild plant plantain will take the itch out of poison ivy and insect bites. Plantain, both the narrow- and the broad-leafed kinds, is a common sight in gardens and lawns. The best way to extract the juice is to wilt a leaf by holding it above (but not on) a lighted match and then rub the leaf between your fingers.

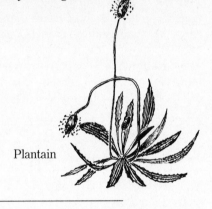

Plantain

You can also try catnip for poison ivy rash. Take several fresh catnip leaves, wilt them as for plantain, above, and squeeze out the juice. Dab the juice on the rash.

Very often the commonly known jewelweed can be found growing near poison ivy. Nature had a plan and many hikers know it. If you squeeze the juice from a jewelweed leaf over your annoying poison ivy rash, or simply rub in fresh jewelweed leaves, you might find yourself with an easy natural cure.

Jewelweed

Vitamin C may also work on poison ivy. Mix up a paste of ascorbic acid powder and water, or crushed vitamin C tablets and water, and apply it to the new poison ivy rash several times a day. The vitamin C may sting for a few minutes, but the itching will then stop, and you'll notice that in a few days the rash is dried up and healed. Use this treatment as soon as you realize you have the rash; it is not as effective if you came in contact with poison ivy many hours before. This same vitamin treatment can relieve the itching of insect bites as well.

Poison Ivy and Poison Oak Protection

If you are particularly sensitive to poison ivy and poison oak, you should know that you may avoid becoming affected by them if, within 1 to 3 minutes of exposure, you wash the affected area thoroughly with cold water. Use lots of water to wash away the irritating oil. Don't use soap because it will remove the skin's natural oil, which serves as a protection against the oil of the plant.

Even if you don't catch it in time and you begin to break out in a rash, wash the affected area with lots of cold water to remove any oil that hasn't yet penetrated the skin. And don't scratch—not because it will spread the infection, but because it will irritate your already sensitive skin. Then apply calamine lotion or one of the remedies mentioned here.

When you're working around poison ivy and poison oak, cover yourself as much as possible with clothing (gloves, snug sleeve cuffs, socks, and so on), and wash the clothing afterward. (It's disheartening to know, though, that the oils of poison ivy and poison oak can remain active on clothing and tools for more than a year!) Be careful not just of the leaves of these plants, but also of their roots and stems.

It may be somewhat comforting to know that you're not alone in your sensitivity. Half the population in this country is bothered by poison ivy, with about one-third of us sensitive some years but not others, and only 15% of us immune all the time.

Bleeding Heart for Stinging Nettle

If you rub against the stinging nettle plant, aptly named because it will sting and leave a rash on your skin, look for another wild plant, the bleeding heart, which, quite conveniently, often grows nearby. Grab a handful of leaves, mash them up in your hands so that the juices flow, and rub them on your rash. You'll find that the pain and redness disappear, as if by magic.

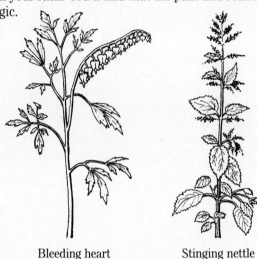

Bleeding heart   Stinging nettle

Bee Stings

The first step to taking the pain out of a bee sting is to get the stinger out of your skin. Scrape it out with your fingernail or carefully scrape it out with a knife. Don't try to pluck or squeeze the stinger out—you may just squirt more venom into the wound. Then make a poultice of activated charcoal or baking soda. Mixed as a paste and placed on a sting, the poultice absorbs and draws the venom out.

Pennyroyal Rub

To ease the discomfort of gnat and mosquito bites, rub your skin with pennyroyal.

Baby-Oil Barrier

If you're likely to encounter gnats while outside, rub a thin film of baby oil on all exposed skin before heading out. It forms a barrier against gnat bites.

Vitamin B Beats Bugs

Try taking B-vitamins to keep the bugs away. When the vitamins are excreted through perspiration, they give your skin an odor that insects such as mosquitoes and gnats seem to find offensive.

Comfrey Relieves Itch

For relief from itchy mosquito bites, try comfrey. Take a leaf from the plant, squeeze the leaf stem between your fingernails to release the juice, and rub the moist stem on the bites.

Mosquito Lures

If you're the person mosquitoes seek out in a crowd, even when you're wearing bug repellent, it could be because of something else on your skin. Suntan oils, creams, and lotions, as well as perfumes and colognes, all increase your chances of being bitten by a mosquito. Some products, particularly hair sprays, shaving lotions, and underarm deodorants, may have components that actually *attract* the bugs. When planning to put on some type of bug repellent, avoid using any other kind of hair or skin product.

Tenderize Those Stings

Meat tenderizer containing papain (papaya extract) can also take the sting out of mosquito and other insect bites. You can buy meat tenderizer in the grocery store. You can also take papaya extract pills, available at many natural foods stores.

Blisters

The best way to treat a blister is to drain it. First clean the entire area with rubbing alcohol. Then insert a sterile needle into the edge of the bubble and press gently. When the blister is completely drained, clean what remains with alcohol and then cover it with first-aid tape. If it bubbles again, repeat this draining procedure; you may have to do it several times on a particularly nasty blister. Should the blister break on its own, sterilize the area with an antibiotic ointment and then cover it with tape.

Storing Bandages

To keep an accumulation of elastic and gauze bandages clean and orderly, roll them up and wrap them tightly in self-sealing plastic food wrap.

Rx from Aloe Vera

With so many aloe vera products on the store shelves—hand creams, lotions, shampoos, and conditioners—you probably get the idea that aloe vera is beneficial. It is indeed. Aloe vera is a potent medicine with antimicrobial effects. What you also should know is that during the manufacturing of commercial preparations containing aloe vera all of its effectiveness may be eliminated. Your best bet is to grow your own plant. And when you burn or cut yourself, get an insect bite or acne, have detergent hands or other irritating skin problems, have a sunburn, or want to soothe baby's diaper rash, cut off from the aloe plant one of the thick rubbery leaves, squeeze out the juice, and rub the jellylike substance on your skin for quick, cooling relief.

Increasing Your Heat Tolerance

Studies on mine workers have shown that a 250-mg supplement of vitamin C can greatly improve heat tolerance during the hot summer months. The body throws off excess heat by sending blood to the surface of the skin; this requires more work from the heart. The body also loses fluid through perspiration; this means the blood may thicken. But with vitamin C added, blood volume is increased, perspiration rate is decreased, and circulation of blood close to the skin is improved. In other words, the body's natural control of its temperature is more efficient with a little more vitamin C in the summertime.

Increasing Your Cold Tolerance

If winter weather gives you the shivers, warm up by following these tips: Wear a hat; about 40% of body heat is lost through an uncovered head. Wear several layers of clothing, since air caught between the layers acts as insulation. Don't drink, because alcohol dilates blood vessels and leads to a loss of heat. And don't smoke; it decreases blood flow to the extremities, where you often feel the cold the most.

"Black Nails"

A blood blister under a toenail or fingernail can cause it to turn black. If you're careful, you can treat it yourself. Begin by heating one end of a paper clip with a match. While the paper clip is hot, place it in the center of the nail's outer surface. (Do not push it under the nail.) This will melt a hole in the nail and release the fluid beneath. Sometimes more than one hole is needed. Then cleanse the toe or finger with antiseptic and apply a bandage. Soak the toe or finger in warm water twice daily, 15 to 30 minutes each time, for several days. Don't use this treatment if there is any sign of infection; go to a doctor.

Emergency Treatment for Poisons

If a corrosive poison has been swallowed (such as acid or lye, gasoline, strychnine, turpentine, or cleaning fluid) do not induce vomiting. Rather, dilute the poison by swallowing milk, an egg white, a mixture of flour and water, or some oil. Go immediately to the hospital.

If another type of poison has been ingested, *do* initiate vomiting. Put a finger in the back of the mouth, or use a medicine sold just for the purpose. After vomiting, mix 1 to 2 tablespoons of activated charcoal powder in a glass of water and drink the solution. Although it looks horrible, it'll absorb just about any poison but cyanide in the stomach.

Feet and Legs

For Athlete's Foot

Should you suspect the beginnings of a case of athlete's foot, you can nip it in the bud by soaking your foot in a mild water and bleach solution. Mix 3 tablespoons of household bleach with each quart of boiled, luke-warm water. Use enough water to cover your foot completely when it is placed in a basin, then soak for 10 minutes. Dry thoroughly with a clean towel. If necessary, repeat in 3 or 4 days. If you don't notice results, then certainly see a doctor, and don't try this home treatment if your problem is an advanced one.

Warts, Corns, and Calluses

Vitamin E or vitamin A might be all you need to get rid of plantar warts, corns and calluses. Each night before you go to bed, empty the contents of the vitamin capsule on the sore spots and rub in the oil for several minutes. Wait a few minutes for it to penetrate before covering your feet with socks. Persevere for two weeks.

Varicose Vein Prevention

There's nothing like a great pair of legs—with no varicose veins. To help your legs keep their youthful appearance, elevate them for 20 minutes a day so that your feet are 3 to 4 inches higher than your heart. That counteracts gravity, which contributes to varicose veins, especially if you stand or sit in one spot for long periods of time. You also need to exercise the leg muscles by walking, running, bicycling, or swimming. Contracting the muscles helps the veins work efficiently, pushing the blood back up to the heart.

Food Supplements and Nutrition
(See also Weight Control, and Heart and Circulation, in this chapter.)

Don't Chew Vitamin C

We now know that taking your daily ration of vitamin C in a chewable tablet form can cause tooth enamel erosion, actually shortening your teeth. This is because vitamin C tablets are very acidic, like your stomach acid. So swallow your vitamin C supplements instead of letting them dissolve in your mouth.

Niacin Blush

Choosing a niacin supplement (which you know is a natural tranquilizer and a cleaner for your arteries) can be tricky. In fact, you may find yourself blushing—literally. Niacin comes in two forms: nicotinic acid, which lowers fats in the blood and calms you, and niacinamide, which calms you but doesn't lower blood fats. The harmless blushing, or really "flushing" as it is called, happens when you take more than about 50 mg of nicotinic acid and are not used to taking it every day. Nicotinic acid causes chemicals to be released into the bloodstream, widening your blood vessels so that blood rushes to your skin.

Check Your Vitamins' Shelf Lives

Vitamin supplements, like most anything else, age with time. Pay attention to the expiration date, and be aware that after that date the potency of the vitamins will be reduced.

Storing Vitamins

You can store your unopened vitamins in the refrigerator if you wish, but don't keep your opened bottles there. Condensation may build up inside the bottle, and moisture wears down vitamins' shelf lives. Better to keep your opened bottles tightly closed and in a dry cabinet or closet.

Maximum Benefits from Your Food Supplements

Vitamins and minerals are beneficial only when they are absorbed by the digestive system, in most cases, the small intestine. That happens most readily when they ride along with food, so make a habit of taking most of your food supplements with or right after a meal. Here are some other tips for taking your vitamins:

- The fat-soluble vitamins A, E, D, and K are absorbed most readily when they are taken with fat-rich foods like milk, butter, and oil; take them with the largest meal of the day if you can.

- Vitamins B, C, and others that are water soluble can be taken without food, but food slows the rate of absorption, ensuring that they are used more slowly and evenly by the body. If they are absorbed quickly, the body excretes what it can't use in a relatively short time.

- When taking large doses of vitamin C, take it little by little throughout the day, since your body can only absorb so much at a time.

- Some food supplements are good companions. For instance, taking vitamin C with calcium supplements increases calcium's absorption, thanks to the acid in the vitamin C. Vitamin C is also effective when taken with iron, because its acidity releases more iron to the body.

- Zinc and folate tablets also work well together.

- Take all your B-vitamins at the same time; they are most effective in combination.

- Watch out for black tea taken with thiamine and iron; the tannic acid in the tea will work against the food supplements.

Free Vitamin Containers

The plastic canisters that come with rolls of 35 mm film make good containers for traveling vitamins. Be sure to clean and dry them completely before you pop in those pills.

Some Nutrient-Depleting Activities

Some of the things we do undermine the beneficial effects of vitamins and minerals. For instance, heavy alcohol drinking can cause a zinc deficiency, as well as deplete thiamine, folate, riboflavin, vitamins B_6, B_{12}, A, C, and D, and calcium and magnesium. Smoking drains off vitamin C from the body, and birth control pills deplete your body's store of vitamin C and vitamin B_{12}.

Bioflavonoids

Don't peel the skin from apples and vegetables, and don't remove all the white membrane from citrus fruit. Both contain bioflavonoids, which strengthen the walls of capillaries, the tiny blood vessels that carry nutrients to individual cells. And bioflavonoids make vitamin C more absorbable by your body.

A Bonus from Iron Pots

Whenever possible, cook your foods in cast-iron pots and skillets. Some of the iron from the pan will be absorbed by the foods as they cook—and ultimately by you. Iron is an especially important mineral for women, who lose it during menstruation.

How Much Protein?

Most people in the United States get more protein than they actually need. We used to think that the more protein we consumed the better, but we now know differently. One 4-ounce serving of a high-quality protein, such as meat, fish, or poultry, in a daily diet that includes fruits, vegetables, dairy products, and grains is all that we really need. A large amount of protein can actually do harm because it gets stored as fat in our bodies. And some sources (red meats, luncheon meats, pork, cheeses) contain heavy doses of salt.

Brewer's vs Baker's Yeast

Don't confuse brewer's yeast with baker's yeast. Brewer's yeast is nutritional, inactive dry yeast that is particularly rich in vitamin B. On the other hand, active dry baker's yeast may actually eat up the B-vitamins you already have in your body.

Sodium in Vegetables

Vegetables are a good bet if you're watching your sodium intake, except for celery and spinach, which are surprisingly high in sodium.

Salt Substitutes

Spices and herbs, with the exception of chili powder and some commercial spice and herb seasoning blends, contain little or no sodium and can be used as salt substitutes.

Wash Away the Salt

You can reduce the amount of salt in some prepared foods merely by washing them. A team of researchers from Durham University found that rinsing food under tap water for 1 minute can cut its salt level by as much as 80%. The researchers rinsed canned green beans and found a 41% reduction; rinsing tuna fish yielded a 79% reduction, and rinsing cottage cheese, a 56% reduction. A 3-minute rinse cuts salt by even more.

Sodium-Laden Soy Sauce

Avoid soy sauce if you're watching your sodium; it's loaded with salt.

Getting the Most from Your Salad

Don't make the dinner salad too far ahead of time; you'll be losing important nutrients if you do. All the exposed cut surfaces allow oxidation to destroy vitamin C, folate, vitamin K, and several B-vitamins. Chopping also releases certain enzymes that can destroy some nutrients.

Not All Shellfish Are Harmful

While all shellfish have acquired a reputation for being high in cholesterol and bad for the heart, only crabs, lobster, and shrimp deserve the bad marks. Mollusk-type shellfish, like clams, oysters, and scallops, are actually fairly low in cholesterol, which should be good news for many people watching their cholesterol intake.

Nuts and Seeds—High-Nutrition Snacks

Nuts and seeds are excellent high-protein snacks, especially for those who skip meals. Although they're fairly high in calories, the nutrients and protein they contain make up for it. Most are good sources of thiamine and folate (both B-vitamins), magnesium, and zinc, and several contain good quantities of vitamin E, protein, and fiber.

Unroasted peanuts and almonds and sunflower, pumpkin, and sesame seeds are the best to snack on; cashews, pecans, and salted nuts are the worst; roasted almonds and peanuts, Brazil nuts, walnuts, filberts, and pistachios lie between the best and the worst.

Heart and Circulation

(See also Food Supplements and Nutrition, in this chapter, and Sports-medicine in the chapter, Keeping Fit.)

Coffee and Smoking Don't Mix

A team of English doctors tested 16 patients with high blood pressure who regularly smoked cigarettes and drank coffee. They found that when the patients smoked two cigarettes in the morning, their blood pressure rose slightly for 15 minutes. When they drank coffee, their blood pressure rose slightly for 2 hours. And when they had a cigarette *and* a cup of coffee together, their blood pressure shot up to its highest level. If you must smoke and drink coffee, be sure you don't do them together.

Potassium-Yes; Sodium-No

Hypertension, or high blood pressure, is surely a disease none of us wants. Genetically speaking, if both your parents have it, your chances of getting it are three in four. If one parent has it, your chances are one in two. But studies show that you can fight the odds by increasing your intake of potassium-rich foods (as well as cutting down on salt). Foods high in potassium include potatoes, blackstrap molasses, lima beans, flounder, orange juice, and winter squash.

Reducing Your Salt

About 10 to 20% of Americans have high blood pressure, but most of these people can control it if they keep their sodium intakes low, i.e., to 1,400 mg a day, which is about ¾ teaspoon of salt. This means not just forsaking the salt shaker, but also avoiding foods that are heavy in salt. Some obvious foods are ketchup and other condiments, pickles, olives, and soy sauce; some not-so-obvious ones include many cheeses, red meats, luncheon meats, butter, milk, and ice cream.

Even people who don't have high blood pressure would benefit from restricting salt. Because sodium occurs naturally in many foods, you get enough from just normal eating. In addition, salt makes you thirsty, so you tend to drink more calorie-containing beverages; salt is also an appetite stimulant, so you tend to eat more.

Inner Tract

(See also Allergies, in this chapter.)

If You Use a Laxative

Milk of magnesia and glycerine suppositories provide the gentlest relief of all the laxatives. Those that contain castor oil or senna are the harshest because they relieve constipation by highly stimulating the bowels. In so doing they can irritate the intestinal lining, causing cramping, gas, and, in some cases, dehydration. They can be especially harmful if taken over a long period of time because they may weaken the bowel muscles.

Natural Constipation Relief

One of the most effective constipation remedies is not a laxative at all, it's diet. If you suffer from irregularity, you might like to try this advice:

Limit milk and milk products, including cheese, ice cream, and yogurt. These foods are constipating. Eat only breads and cereals that are made from whole grains because they contain lots of fiber. Add more salads, fruits, and fruit juices to your diet, but leave out apple juice. Each day eat at least 2 tablespoons of unprocessed wheat or oat bran.

Hemorrhoids

Hemorrhoids are enlarged veins in or just outside the rectum that are particularly painful when they become inflamed, often the result of constipation and straining on the toilet. It's obvious, then, that one way to prevent the problem is to avoid becoming constipated. (See constipation earlier in this section.)

If hemorrhoids bother you, take as many warm baths as you can— several a day if possible—to relax and relieve the pain. Witch hazel compresses placed right on the affected area will also help.

Natural Diuretics

When you are in need of a mild diuretic, relief may be as close as your refrigerator. Some healthy foods that can flush excess water from your body are citrus fruits, watermelon, cranberry juice, and parsley.

For Indigestion Sufferers

There are several ways that you can work to prevent heartburn or indigestion:

- Chew your food, and then chew it again. The less work your stomach has to do, the less likelihood of indigestion.

- Watch the amount of food you eat; don't stuff yourself. When you overeat, you stretch the walls of your stomach, which then puts extra pressure on the esophageal muscle, causing food to back up into the esophagus.

- Try not to eat when you're tired or upset. Such stress can cause excess acid secretion in the stomach that results in a burning sensation.

- Avoid coffee, tea, alcohol, and spicy foods. They can trigger the release of extra hydrochloric acid in your stomach.

- Keep away from tobacco, which has been shown to decrease acid output to a point where your food is not digested. Smoking has also been shown to lower the sphincter pressure at the point where the stomach and esophagus join, thus making it easier for what little acid you do have to escape.

- Eat fewer meats and fatty foods and more unrefined carbohydrates. Meats and fatty foods are hard to digest, but carbohydrates are digested more easily. Look for your protein in the form of low-fat dairy products and chicken and fish instead of red meats. If you do eat meats, broil them, and pick the leanest cuts possible.

- Mix 1 tablespoon each of honey and vinegar in a cup of hot water, and take it about 20 minutes *before* your big meal.

Once you get indigestion, there are a number of remedies you might try to relieve it:

- Mix ¼ teaspoon of ground ginger in a cup of hot water, steep for 5 minutes, then sip slowly.

- Take peppermint, chamomile, or catnip tea about an hour after eating (it helps settle a rumbling stomach).

- Drink a glass of ice water. It helps relieve indigestion by washing acid from the surface of the esophagus back into the stomach.

Ginger for Nausea

Ginger can be surprisingly effective at relieving nausea from morning sickness, motion sickness, or an old-fashioned stomach ache. Take a few ground ginger capsules as soon as the queasy feeling starts, and repeat the dosage throughout the day as you need it. Or suck on a small piece of candied ginger. Ginger calms the inner tract, but it does not affect the central nervous system, as so many antinausea drugs do.

Irritable Bowel Syndrome

If you suffer from irritable bowel syndrome (IBS), which is a troublesome condition of diarrhea alternating with constipation and abdominal pain, you'll most likely find relief by making some changes in your diet. Keep a record of what you eat, and when irritation strikes, make note of it. You'll probably find that skipping spicy and fried foods, sauces, coffee, tea, and alcohol helps. In addition, eat high-fiber foods, avoid gas-producing foods (like cabbage, sodas, and beans), and stay away from milk products, especially if you suspect that you have a lactose intolerance.

Should such measures be ineffective, you may have something other than IBS. A research team from England found that two-thirds of the IBS patients they tested suffered because of food allergies. (See also Allergies, in this chapter.)

If You're Prone to Gas

Certain foods have a tendency to give people gas. If you're plagued by this annoyance (and embarrassment), then you will want to go lightly on fried foods, sweets, beans, cabbage, parsnips, and corn. Gas can also be the result of constipation. If you suspect this is your problem, then see the hints for constipation earlier in this section.

Sleep

Slow Down, Then Sleep

Have trouble sleeping? Don't do anything that requires too much mental activity immediately before going to bed. You're better off doing things that are boring and ritualistic late in the evening, like watering the plants, making tomorrow's lunch, straightening things up. The idea is to get your body used to a routine whereby you wind down slowly.

Calcium Can Put You to Sleep . . .

Calcium has a calming effect on our nerves and can therefore be a godsend for those insomniacs whose sleeplessness is due to a calcium deficiency. Despite a good diet, we can become calcium deficient under stress because our bodies produce excess amounts of lactic acid when we're pressured, and this acid "binds" up the calcium, making it difficult to assimilate.

If you suspect you have a deficiency, take calcium supplements along with vitamin D, which will help you to absorb the calcium more readily. Or bolster your diet with calcium-rich foods, like dairy products, eggs, filberts, almonds, artichokes, broccoli, and soybeans, to name the best.

. . . So Can Vitamin B

The B-vitamins, particularly B_6, are known to act as natural sedatives. Vitamin B-rich foods include organ meats, whole grains, lean beef, peanuts, whole milk, sunflower seeds, chicken (white meat), and brewer's yeast.

Smart Napping

Do you find yourself dragging through the day? Try taking a short nap in

---

Antisnoring Techniques

Snoring can really test the strength of a marriage. If you've consulted a doctor and found no serious physical problems, but your nightly session of "sawing logs" is keeping your spouse awake, give these simple tactics a chance:

- Elevate the head of your bed by putting a brick or two under its two back legs. This raises your head and keeps your airway open. Don't put extra pillows under your head—they only kink your airway.

- Wear a cervical collar, the kind that's prescribed for people with sprained necks. Most snoring occurs when you lie on your back with your chin resting on your chest; that the early afternoon, if your schedule permits. You'll find that it will do the most good between 1 and 4 P.M. If napping on the job jeopardizes your career, then grab a wink when you get home, before dinner. Taking a nap instead of a cocktail will make the rest of evening more relaxing and pleasant.

Early to Bed, Early to Rise?

Going to bed especially early before a big day may defeat the purpose. You might feel more groggy than ever in the morning because you've broken your natural sleep cycle.

Less Sleep When We're Older

Our need for sleep decreases as we get older, especially after our mid-50s, so don't be concerned if you find you're sleeping less as you get up there in age. It's really quite normal.

Bedwetting

This embarrassing problem has been linked not just to psychological problems, but to allergies and to scoliosis (curvature of the spine). So if your child seems to be an incurable bedwetter, try investigating the latter two areas.

---

narrows the windpipe. The cervical collar keeps the chin up and the windpipe open.

- Sew a small rubber ball or marble into the middle of the back of your pajama top. If you roll onto your back, where you're most likely to snore, the ball will cause you to turn back onto your side, usually without waking you.

- Keep a humidifier in the room. The extra moisture sometimes prevents snoring.

- Cut out smoking and drinking since they swell the tissues that cause snoring.

Weight Control

Don't Go It Alone

The best dieting tip of them all might be to lose weight with a friend. Tests show that diets are more successful when you have someone to share information and experiences with than when you just have support from your family or friends.

Buckle That Belt

Tightening your belt may literally help you lose weight. Before you sit down to the next meal, tighten your belt notch just so that it's a bit more snug, but not uncomfortable. You will find yourself being more conscious of the belt, and you'll feel full sooner.

Make Breakfast Your Biggest Meal

If you're dieting, try to eat your biggest meal in the morning to make sure it will metabolize quickly. Digestion of a meal doesn't reach its peak until about 7 hours after the last bite. Eating a heavy, fat-laden meal at 6:00 P.M. or later means that you will probably be asleep when your metabolism is at its slowest ebb and when most of that digested food hits your bloodstream.

Your breakfast will keep away late morning hunger pains if it contains plenty of protein. By maintaining your body's blood sugar at a high level, protein keeps you alert and interested in the world around you. Pick eggs, cheeses, and yogurt instead of Danish pastry.

No Extra Calories in Winter

Contrary to what a lot of people think, you don't need to eat more calories in winter, unless you spend a lot of active time out in the cold. Since winter days are shorter and weather conditions make most of us less active, we actually burn up fewer calories in winter than in summer.

Make Those Calories Complex Carbohydrates

Studies have shown that you will lose more weight, trim off more fat, and even feel better if your diet includes plenty of complex carbohydrates. That's because consuming a lot of complex carbohydrates, such as unrefined flours, grains, fruits, and vegetables—foods that are high in bulk but low in energy density—will result in a lower overall caloric intake; make you feel fuller; and even make you chew longer, giving you

Don't Eat Less, Eat Better

A diet centered on the following foods will have you cutting calories naturally.

- Vegetables: There are fewer calories in 30 1-cup servings of broccoli than there are in just one 12-ounce sirloin steak.

- Fruits: There are fewer calories in 10 peaches than there are in one piece of peach pie.

- Low-fat dairy products: There are fewer calories—and twice as much protein—in a pound of low-fat cottage cheese than there are in 4 ounces of most hard cheeses.

- Whole grains: There is three times as much fiber—and hence a lot more satisfaction—in a slice of whole wheat bread as there is in a slice of white. You might also be interested in knowing that plain popcorn is high in fiber *and* low in calories. There are just 6 calories in a butterless cup, compared to 114 calories in the same amount of potato chips.

- Poultry and fish: There are fewer calories—and almost four times as much protein—in the meat from four entire chickens (broiled) than in one beefy serving (16 ounces) of prime rib.

more "mouth sensation." And eating complex carbohydrates can actually rid you of calories. Researchers at Oregon State University found that their test group lost 18% more calories through their stools when they ate half an ounce of bran a day than when they did not.

Low-Calorie Salads

If you're dieting, keep the "chef" out of the salad. A salad topped with meats, cheeses, eggs, and olives can weigh in at about 1,000 calories, and that doesn't include the dressing, which can add a few hundred more. So, skip the weighty garnishes and load on the greens and raw vegetables. Choose French dressing (67 calories a tablespoon, compared with 69 for Italian, 76 for Russian, 77 for blue cheese, and 80 for Thousand Island), or play it really thin and sprinkle on just lemon juice or vinegar. You'll be rewarded with a slimming 400-calorie meal.

Fill Up, Not Out

If you are on a diet and you are looking for foods that fill you up but not out, keep these in mind:

asparagus	lettuce and other greens
green and wax beans	mushrooms
bean sprouts	okra
broccoli	red and green peppers
cabbage	radishes
cauliflower	sauerkraut
celery	seltzer and club soda
cucumbers	tomatoes and tomato juice
eggplant	zucchini

Start with Soup

Eating hot soup at the beginning of a meal can shrink your appetite. Have a cup to start out and maybe you won't crave second helpings.

Calorie-Conscious Dining Out

When dining out and watching your weight at the same time, the kind of restaurant you choose to go to can determine whether you'll have a high- or low-calorie meal. Italian, American, and French cuisines tend toward heavy foods with high fat contents, while Chinese, Japanese, Mexican, Middle Eastern, and African foods are lighter.

To save calories, choose a baked apple rather than apple pie; rye toast rather than a bagel; Manhattan clam chowder rather than New England clam chowder; skim milk rather than whole milk; popcorn rather than potato chips; pumpkin pie rather than pecan pie.

Light Wines Are Leanest

If you have to drink, make it a light rosé or a light Chablis. Light wines contain less than 60 calories per wine glass, compared with 85 for regular wine. The worst thing you can drink when you're cutting calories is a sweet liqueur, such as crème de menthe or crème de cacao, each adding up to about 100 calories an ounce.

Low-Calorie Mayonnaise

When you'd like mayonnaise on a sandwich but want to cut the fat and calories, try making your own low-calorie "mayonnaise." In a blender combine 1 cup of cottage cheese, 2 tablespoons of vegetable oil, 1 tablespoon of vinegar, ½ teaspoon of dry mustard, and ½ teaspoon of paprika and process until smooth. This slenderizing spread will keep for about 2 weeks in the refrigerator.

Low-Calorie Sour Cream

Make your own low-fat and low-calorie "sour cream" by processing low-fat cottage cheese in a blender; skim milk or lemon juice can be added if necessary for easier blending.

What's in Milk?

Did you know that milk contains more calories, measure for measure, than beer and soda? Of course, it's a lot better for you than beer and soda and even more beneficial if you drink a low-fat type. Compare the different kinds of milk with this chart:

Per 8-oz. serving	Cal-ories	Fat (g)	Pro-tein (g)	Cal-cium (mg)	Vit. A (I.U.)	Vit. D (I.U.)	Ribo-flavin (mg)
Whole milk	150	8	8	291	307	100	0.395
2% low-fat milk	121	5	8	297	500	100	0.403
1% low-fat milk	102	3	8	300	500	100	0.407
Skim milk	86	0.5	8	302	500	100	0.343
Nonfat dry milk (reconstituted)	82	0.2	8	280	539	100	0.400

Women's Health

Menstrual Cramps

The pain and discomfort of menstrual cramps have caused many women to refer to their monthly periods as "The Curse." That curse can be lifted, however, by a charm called magnesium. Magnesium plays a role in regulating female hormones and is also a natural diuretic. If you do have problems with cramps, boost your daily magnesium intake by eating more lima beans, kidney beans, wheat germ, whole wheat products, and nuts.

Another nutrient that can lift the curse of monthly menstrual cramps is vitamin E. It works in several ways. First, it inhibits prostaglandins, hormonelike substances that cause contractions of the uterus, which in turn cause cramps. It also increases circulation, which means that more oxygen-carrying blood goes to the uterus, thereby combating the cutoff of blood and oxygen during contractions that is partially responsible for cramps.

Exercise can be a great way to ease menstrual cramps. It relieves constipation by increasing intestinal contractions. If you work up a good sweat, it may even ease that bloated, heavy feeling. And because exercise makes you breathe deeply, it brings oxygen into the blood, which helps to alleviate depression and can actually give you a sense of elation.

Anything that exercises the major muscle groups, gets you breathing hard, and massages the pelvic area is great for preventing cramps: jogging, swimming, cycling, and fast walking will all do.

In addition to exercise, heat can soothe the pain of cramps by relaxing muscles and getting blood to flow. A heating pad is an obvious aid, but sipping warm herbal tea, soaking in a warm tub, or a massage can all work wonders.

PMS

Studies have illustrated that vitamin B_6 (pyridoxine) can be quite a blessing to women who suffer from premenstrual tension or syndrome (PMS). Some doctors recommend taking a daily dose of 50 mg, which is almost always enough to relieve tension.

The B-vitamins may help protect against the bloating and tension that some women experience right before they menstruate because B complex is essential to the health of the liver, and the liver plays a key role in neutralizing the excessive amounts of estrogen produced by the ovaries during this time. Vitamin B_6, in particular, can relieve that heavy, bloated, puffy feeling.

Relief for Vaginal Infections

The maddening itch of a vaginal infection (vaginitis) can drive any woman screaming into the night and probably to the gynecologist more often than any other complaint. But before you run anywhere, try these simple cures:

Take a salt water bath: Dissolve ½ cup of table salt in a bathtub of water and hop in. This saline solution works to clean the vaginal area much like your tears bathe and clean your eyes.

Try a vinegar sitz bath: To a few inches of warm (not hot) water, add ½ cup of white vinegar. Then sit with your feet propped up on the sides of the tub so that the water rushes in. Vinegar also acts as a gentle cleaner.

Sugar Can Promote Vaginal Infections

If you suffer from recurring vaginal infections, check your sugar intake. Doctors have found a direct correlation between high blood sugar and vaginitis. Women with a family history of diabetes, women who are prone to sugar binges, and women who are pregnant often have a higher concentration of infection-causing organisms in their bodies. Because excess sugar promotes the growth of organisms commonly found on the skin and in the vagina, a high-sugar diet or binging on chocolate or other sweets may foster yeast-type infections.

The Pill's Effect on Vitamins and Minerals

Researchers have found that many cases of Pill-induced depression are the result of the body's depletion of vitamin B_6. That's because the estrogen in the Pill prevents the body from absorbing this vitamin.

But B_6 isn't the only vitamin affected by the Pill. Thiamine (B_1), riboflavin (B_2), vitamin B_{12}, folate, zinc, and vitamins C and E can all be depleted by it.

Urinary Tract Infections

If you're prone to urinary tract infections, make sure you urinate as soon as you have the urge to do so. "Holding back" can put pressure on the bladder wall and make it more vulnerable to infection by increasing concentrations of bacteria.

Cutting down on sugars and other simple carbohydrates can also lower your chances of getting a urinary tract infection. That's because most disease-causing organisms thrive on sugar.

Bladder Infections

Cystitis is an infection or inflammation of the bladder. You'll know it if you get it, because you'll have to urinate frequently and it will burn intensely. You should see a doctor for this condition, but you can probably get some relief by drinking plenty of water and cranberry juice and avoiding coffee, tea, spices, and alcohol, which irritate the bladder. Treat yourself to hot baths as often as possible, even several times a day. Gentle heat on your pelvis from a heating pad or hot water bottle may ease any pain you have.

Lowering Risks of Breast Cancer

Evidence is mounting that the risk of breast cancer is tied to dietary fats. The greater the fat intake, the higher the amount of estrogen in the blood; an increase in estrogen may make a woman more likely to get breast cancer. You can cut dietary fat by skipping butter, margarine, mayonnaise, and ice cream, and eating only lean meats and poultry without their skins. Take in lots of fiber (by eating whole grains, bran, and fruits and vegetables with their skins), which helps the body excrete estrogen.

Health Miscellany

When Taking Antibiotics

When taking antibiotics for a few days or more, you should also take *Lactobacillus acidophilus,* or a yogurt that contains these "friendly germs." This will counteract the antibiotic treatment, which kills off the good germs with the bad, sometimes resulting in yeast infections in women and diarrhea in children.

Seasickness (and Motion Sickness) Relief

At the first sign of seasickness, stand up on the open deck beside an upright pole or doorway and hold on to it. Keep your feet about a foot apart and your eyes *on the horizon,* relax both knees, and adjust your position to the movement of the deck as it rises and falls with the waves so that your torso is always upright. Don't go below deck, and remember to keep your eyes on the horizon. Seeing the horizon can also help cure regular motion sickness. Look up and out of the car, and make sure little children are elevated when sitting so that they can do the same.

A Snack for a Traveling Break

If you start getting drowsy during a long car trip, have a snack. Tests have shown that a food break is more effective than a rest break for improving driving performance and keeping drivers awake. And there seems to be no difference in effect on driving performance between a rest break of 15 minutes and one of an hour.

Reducing Bone Loss

Ninety percent of postmenopausal women have a significant bone loss, called osteoporosis, that can start as early as age 25. Studies have shown that you can minimize this bone loss by taking calcium each day, along with vitamin D to aid its absorption, and exercising to increase bone density. Although many foods contain calcium, you'll need about 1,200 mg a day, which probably means you'll have to take supplements. The vitamin D you need is produced when sunlight comes in contact with your skin, so spend some time outside each day, preferably exercising.

12 Look and Feel Your Best

Bathing

An Oatmeal Bath for Sensitive Skin

If you love the way baths relax you, but your sensitive skin finds them irritating, try oatmeal in your bathwater. Pour some into a square of cheesecloth, close it with a rubber band or plastic twist, and hang it under the faucet as your bathwater is running. Once in the tub, use the cheesecloth bag of oatmeal as your sponge. The oatmeal softens and moisturizes your skin.

Softening Hard Water

Hard water baths can be made softer by adding ½ cup of either ordinary table salt or baking soda to the bathtub. Hard water has an over-abundance of certain minerals—chiefly calcium and magnesium. The sodium in salt and baking soda helps to offset the minerals.

Soaps for Hard Water

Synthetic soaps are also called detergent soaps. Don't confuse them with laundry and dishwasher detergents; they don't have the harshness. Synthetics are made from fatty acids derived from petrochemicals instead of the fatty acids found most often in tallow and coconut oil. They clean just like true soaps but they don't deposit a film when used in hard water. They also tend to be less alkaline than soaps.

Good Uses for Soap Ends

Save the last bits of your bars of soap and stuff them into the pockets in your loofah for an instant sudsy natural sponge.

You can also put those last slivers of soap into a plastic squeeze bottle (an old detergent bottle works fine) and add a little water. As the soap melts into the water you'll have your own liquid hand soap.

Keeping Bathroom Mirrors Clear

To prevent a mirror from fogging up while you're showering, go over it lightly first with a bar of soap.

Cosmetics

Removing Eye Makeup

Mineral oil, baby oil, or petroleum jelly remove mascara just as well as any fancy makeup remover. They are more effective and gentle than soap and water, and they leave behind a thin, protective film that moisturizes lids and lashes. When removing eye makeup wipe gently, don't rub; each eyelash you lose will take nine months to replace.

Vitamin E oil is also good for removing eye makeup. It doesn't sting and it's good for your skin.

Putting on Mascara If You Wear Contacts

Contact lens wearers who have trouble with smudging mascara should try the waterless, waterproof mascara (not just the water-resistant kind, which is neither waterless nor waterproof). Apply it *after* inserting your lenses and let it dry for about 3 minutes.

Maintenance for Makeup Brushes

Keep your makeup brushes soft by applying a bit of hair conditioner after washing them.

Emphasizing Eyelashes and Eyebrows

To make eyelashes and eyebrows appear thicker and darker, dab a little petroleum jelly on them.

Getting the Best from Your Perfume

Once you've found a perfume you like, use it, don't save it. Perfume contains alcohol and will evaporate with time. The older it is, the more likely its scent has changed just due to simple deterioration. If you want to store it with minimal deterioration or evaporation, keep it in the refrigerator.

Make your perfume scent last longer by mixing it with a dab of petroleum jelly and working it into your skin.

Lipstick Colors

Don't blame your lipstick if it changes color often. It's not the product that's to blame but the natural excess of acidity or alkalinity in your lips. Powdering your lips first is quite useless; lipstick fixers are very temporary. When lipsticks turn deep pink or red, you have extra acidity in your skin; orange tone changes indicate alkaline skin. The best solutions to the problem are to: (1) totally avoid lipsticks; (2) use only lip glosses since they contain little or no color pigment; (3) stay with orange-tone lipsticks and remove and reapply them often; or (4) use lipstick tones that are frosted.

Eyes

Itchy Eyes

For itchiness around the eyes, use cucumber slices. They help to relieve irritation.

Feet

Hangnails

Bothered by a hangnail? Before you go to bed rub petroleum jelly all around it. Hangnails are painful because they're all dried out, and they split dry skin. The jelly forms a seal around the dead skin so that your body fluids can moisten and soften it, and when it's softer, it's less painful.

Rubbing Off Dry Skin

You'll always have some rough, dry skin on your heels, regardless of how much cream you rub into them. Though cream won't remove it, a pumice stone or pumice brush, wetted and lightly soaped, will do the trick. Use it to scrub off dead skin. A half minute of this after every bath or shower will keep your feet smooth. Particularly bad heels will need some presoaking first.

Reducing Foot Odor

The key to keeping your feet smelling good is to keep them dry and well ventilated. Go shoeless or wear sandals when you can. Wear leather shoes rather than shoes made from synthetic material because leather "breathes" and the synthetics don't. For the same reason, choose cotton socks over acrylic and nylon ones. After bathing, dust your feet with talcum powder or plain cornstarch.

Homemade Foot Powder

Make your own foot powder to absorb moisture and odor by mixing 1 ounce of powdered orrisroot with 3 ounces of zinc oxide and 6 ounces of talc. One batch should last two weeks if you use 1 teaspoon per shoe per day.

Hair

Drying Bounce into Your Hair

If you don't curl your hair but still want some bounce to it, dry bounce into it. Lean forward so that your hair hangs down over your head. Blow the hair dry, aiming the hot air at the roots to avoid overdrying the fragile ends. Don't overdry; it's the last few minutes of drying that can make the difference between healthy hair and hair that's brittle and dull. When your hair is just dry, brush it back and notice its new body.

Comb, Don't Brush

Brittle hair that breaks easily and has many split ends may be the result of too much brushing. The 100-strokes-a-day-with-a-hairbrush rule that we all grew up with actually does more harm than good. Hard brushing strips away your hair's outer cells, exposing the soft inner core of the hair shaft to all kinds of possible damage. It is much better to gently comb your hair. Never brush your hair while it's wet because it stretches more easily then and more readily snaps and breaks, much like a rubber band that gets stretched too far.

The Right Kind of Comb and Brush

Plastic and metal combs can be harmful to your hair because both have sharp teeth. Plastic combs are often made in molds, and the molds can leave grooves down the center that grab and rip hair shafts. A sawcut comb, in which each tooth is cut into the comb and smoothed, is the best since it has no sharp edges. Never use a brush that has sharp, hard, short bristles or wire bristles. Inexpensive plastic bristle brushes may actually be better for your hair than expensive natural bristle brushes because they are softer and therefore gentler on your hair.

Washing Brushes and Combs

Wash hairbrushes and combs by soaking them for a few minutes in a sink of water to which has been added a tablespoon of baking soda and a drop or two of household bleach or other antiseptic. Swish a few times, then rinse.

A Homemade Dry Shampoo

You can make an easy homemade dry shampoo by mixing a tablespoon of baking soda into ½ cup of bran. Rub it into your hair when you don't have time for a wet shampoo, then brush it out.

Shampooing

Problem hair? It may need *more* shampooing, not less. Contrary to what most of us think, daily shampooing is good for your hair. Wash it with a mild shampoo and make sure you rinse it out well. If you shampoo each day, there is no need to lather a second time. Condition your hair as you would normally.

If the hard water that comes from your tap leaves your hair dull and dry, you can soften the water by acidifying it. Add the juice of half a lemon or 2 tablespoons of cider vinegar to your rinse water. You can also switch from soap-based shampoos to detergent shampoos. They work more effectively because they lather better in hard water, and they won't dry your hair out if you use them properly.

Don't throw away your empty shampoo bottle. Fill it part of the way with warm water, and shake. You now have "free" liquid soap.

"Dandruff" Problems

Before you try out all the dandruff shampoos, make sure what you have is actually dandruff. If you are out in the sun regularly you might really have a sunburned scalp. Try wearing a lightweight, light-colored hat. If you don't want to wear a hat, try applying an alcohol-based, high-SPF (sun protection factor) product, making sure to cover your hairline, part, and any other exposed scalp area.

Dry Hair Treatments

If you've got particularly dry hair and an itchy scalp, you might find relief from a rinse made with water to which a cup of vinegar has been added. Use the vinegar-water solution as your first rinse and then cool, clear water as a final rinse.

You can give yourself a hot oil treatment with plain vegetable oil. Choose a light one, like corn oil or sunflower oil. If you have especially dry hair you may want to try olive oil, which is heavier but also more difficult to wash out. Heat the oil to lukewarm and apply it with the palm of your hand. Make sure you coat the entire hair shaft and the scalp as well. Cover your hair with a plastic bag or a shower cap and leave it covered as long as you can stand it—overnight is best. When the time is up, wash your hair well with your regular shampoo, being sure to remove all the oil. A second lathering will probably be necessary, but skip the conditioner.

You can also try mayonnaise. Rub in just enough to soak the hair thoroughly, and then comb it through. Let it remain on your hair for 30 minutes, then shampoo thoroughly and rinse with water that has a bit of lemon juice mixed in. Give your hair a final rinse with clear water or rinse with lemon water again.

Conditioner for Oily Hair

To condition oily hair (and to treat common dandruff, which is caused by oily, not dry, hair), apply a scalp lotion after regular shampooing and conditioning. Mix 1 cup of witch hazel with 1 cup of distilled water (and squeeze in the juice of one lemon, if you want a lemony scent). Towel-dry your hair. Then pat your hair every inch or so with a cotton ball saturated with scalp lotion. There is no need to rinse it out; just dry your hair as usual. This lotion will clear and help to dry your scalp, as well as restore its natural acid balance.

Thickening Your Hair

Some hair conditioners make your hair *look* thicker by giving it a temporary coating that washes off with the next shampooing, but gelatin has been found to actually thicken individual hair strands. One study that tested the hair of 52 people who took 14 grams (that's about 7 teaspoons) of unflavored gelatin each day found that there was a definite increase in the diameter of their hair strands in about two months. And when the volunteers stopped taking gelatin, their hair returned to its normal thickness within six months.

Taming Frizzy Hair

Here's a good trick from a professional salon for people who are plagued with frizzy hair, especially in humid weather or after damp-drying it. Take a small section at a time and twist it into a spiral, then blow-dry the sections one by one, keeping the dryer moving. You'll find that your hair will be more manageable and will fall into a more natural shape.

Hair Can Change during Pregnancy

Hormonal changes that occur during pregnancy, especially during the first three months, can change the look and feel of your hair. It's best to wait until baby is born to make radical changes in your hair, such as perming it. (That might be the best time, too, to give yourself a new look, as you get out of your maternity clothes and back into shape.)

Keeping Cool and Fresh

Cool Cotton

To keep your cool, dress in natural fibers. Cotton absorbs perspiration and feels cool against your skin as it dries, while polyester, which is really a plastic, doesn't absorb perspiration but traps the moisture against your skin, making you feel sticky. What's more, cotton, unlike synthetic fabrics, lets air pass through and aids evaporation.

Reducing Body Odor

Embarrassing odor from perspiration can be more than a minor problem for some of us. If you are a strong-smelling perspirer, before you reach for another roll-on, add more zinc-rich foods to your diet. Clinical observations show that zinc can diminish perspiration odor. Foods high in zinc include liver, turkey, peas and beans, nuts, and whole grains.

Gently rubbing under your arms with a sudsy loofah while in the bath or shower is more effective than merely washing with a washcloth because the mild abrasiveness of the loofah removes more odor-causing bacteria. Be sure to rub gently, though.

Talcum Powder Substitute

Cornstarch is a very good substitute for talcum powder. It's cheap, odorless (which is good news for those of us whose skin gets irritated by perfumes in beauty care products), and as absorbent as talcum powder.

Face Fresheners

To freshen up your face while traveling, carry a small plastic bottle of astringent, like witch hazel, and some cotton balls. Then, when your face feels grimy but you can't give it a good wash, dampen a cotton ball with the witch hazel and wipe it over your face and neck. You can also dampen the cotton balls with witch hazel before you leave home, making sure to pack them in a travel container that has a good seal (otherwise the astringent will evaporate) or in a small plastic bag closed with a wire twist. You now have your own instant wipes.

Yogurt is a good face pick-me-up, especially when you're hot and tired. Just rub plain yogurt on your face, leave it on for 20 minutes, then rinse with cool water.

Mouth and Teeth

A Sweeter Breath

What's the best way to get rid of bad breath? Brush your teeth thoroughly, gently massaging the gums, with a soft toothbrush with rounded bristles. Floss every 24 to 36 hours. Bacteria that accumulate on teeth and around gums produce toxic waste products that not only weaken the gums but also create odors. If brushing and flossing don't work, try brushing your tongue as well. This might sound a bit odd, but a study carried out at a school of dentistry found that while brushing the teeth decreased mouth odor by 25%, brushing the teeth *and* the tongue cut it down by 85%. How do brushing the teeth and tongue compare with mouthwash in eliminating bad breath? These techniques can solve the problem; mouthwash just covers it up temporarily.

Don't Waste a Drop of Toothpaste

Get the last bit of toothpaste out by placing the almost-empty tube under hot water before rolling and squeezing it.

Nails

Polishing

To dry nail polish faster, use ice cubes. Apply each coat of polish, wait 30 seconds, then place your fingers in a bowl of ice water, being careful not to touch the bowl or the cubes.

Face it, your nail polish is going to chip, no matter what you do. Unless of course, you do absolutely nothing—with your hands, that is. Water is polish's nastiest adversary; wear vinyl gloves to protect your nails (and your skin, for that matter) whenever you put your hands in laundry water or dishwater. Choose clear and light-colored polishes and you won't have to remove and reapply them so often; chips will be less noticeable, and touch-ups won't show as readily. You also won't have to use moisture-robbing polish removers as frequently.

Store your nail polish in the refrigerator; it'll always go on smoothly and evenly.

Cuticle Care

If your nails have horizontal ridges, you're probably being too rough with them during your manicure. Push cuticles back very gently with an orange stick. Using a sharper tool or pushing back forcefully into the cuticle could mean that you're digging into the nail below the cuticle, where it's softest. You won't see the indentations you're creating until the nail grows beyond the cuticle, which could take four to five weeks.

Saturate your cuticles and fingernails in vitamin E squeezed from the capsule once a week, and dry skin, torn cuticles, and hangnails won't be nearly so bothersome.

Filing

Correct filing is the secret to preventing nail splits. Use long, sweeping strokes rather than back-and-forth sawing motions. And hold the file at a straight angle, rather than perpendicular to the nail, so that each layer of the nail is slightly longer than the one underneath and less likely to break on contact with objects you touch.

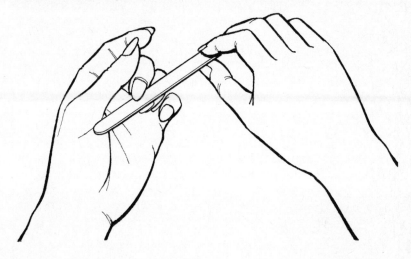

Skin
(See also Burns and Sunburn in the chapter, Here's to Your Health.)

Simple Astringents

Cider vinegar and lemon juice are inexpensive and handy astringents. And they don't contain the drying alcohol found in most commercial astringents. Pour a few tablespoons of vinegar or lemon juice into half a sink of cool water and splash the mixture onto your face after washing it to close pores, restore your skin's acid balance, and give your face a fresh, clean feeling.

Rx for Dry Skin

If you have dry skin, make sure you're drinking plenty of water. The more water you drink (within reason—six to eight glasses a day on the average) the more water your body has available to moisturize your skin. You can also *eat* some water, by including in your diet plenty of leafy vegetables, salad greens, and fruit—all foods with high water content.

Your dry skin is partially due to the drier inside environment thanks to central heating, particularly the forced-air type. Room humidifiers help provide moisture in especially dry rooms.

Dry skin is also due to the fact that our intake of vitamins A and D is lower in winter. We get less vitamin A because we usually eat vegetables that are not as fresh in winter as in the growing season. And we get less vitamin D because we spend more time indoors, reducing our exposure to sunshine.

Moisturizing Your Skin

Using a moisturizer during the day as well as overnight provides your skin with protection against dryness, temperature extremes, wind, sun, and air pollution. And a moisturizer will absorb your makeup so that your skin doesn't have to.

The most effective way to apply a moisturizer is to spread it on your wet face immediately after washing. The moisturizer will hold in this extra water as well as the water naturally found in your skin. And by the way, any moisturizer, so long as it doesn't irritate your skin, will do a good job. Don't assume that the most effective ones are those that cost the most. Here are three that cost a lot less than the fancy kinds you'll find at cosmetics counters:

- Plain old petroleum jelly will moisturize as well as, and sometimes better than, most of the fancy creams. That is, if you can tolerate the greasiness.

- Mayonnaise isn't just for tuna salad; you may find it just as good for your skin. You've got yourself an inexpensive and handy moisturizer in that mayonnaise jar. Use it as you would any of the fancy creams, but remember to keep it stored in the refrigerator after it's been opened.

- Mineral oil or baby oil is a good moisturizer when applied after every bath and shower, while your skin is still wet. (House brands are just as good as the fancy label that will cost you at least twice as much.) Then towel-dry as usual. The towel will remove the excess oil, but a thin layer will remain, holding in moisture. The oil will not stain your towels, but it will make the bottom of your tub slippery if it drips while you're putting it on. Baby oil is particularly good for dry legs, heels, and elbows.

Wearing What You Eat

Your diet shows. What you eat will affect your skin (and your hair). For lovelier, healthier skin and hair, lighten up on the heavy meats, oily foods, and sweets, as well as coffee, tea, and other caffeine-containing foods. And go heavy on the fruits and vegetables, salads, and nonmeat proteins, like grains, whole grain breads and cereals, and beans. These foods nourish from the inside out.

Fragrances and Sensitive Skin Don't Mix

You may be very careful about the cosmetics you wear on your sensitive skin, but have you considered your cologne as a source of irritation? Fragrance is the number one troublemaker for sensitive skin. But it's the easiest to steer clear of, even as an ingredient in other products. Should a product have a fragrance, your nose will know right away, even if it's not listed on the label.

Scrubbing Off Dead Skin

You can keep your complexion younger looking by removing dead skin regularly from your face. Men do this when they shave; the mild abrasion of the shaver does the trick. (And if they don't shave, no one knows the difference anyway!) Women can remove dead skin by mixing a bit of cornmeal in with their soap or cleansing cream or by washing with a paste of steel-cut oats (which are a bit rougher than rolled oats) and warm water. Use these preparations once a day (no more), or use commercial cleansing grains weekly.

A Warning about Freckles

Freckles cannot be faded by bleaching them with lemon juice and sunlight. Freckles are the result of pigment-producing cells that actually get darker when they are exposed to the sun. Lemon juice just makes the problem worse, because it heightens the skin's sensitivity to sunlight.

Shaving Cream Substitute

Out of shaving cream? Let baby oil fill in. It'll lubricate the razor, keep hair stubs standing up for a clean shave, and won't dry out sensitive skin, as will soap or shaving cream.

Keep Dry Hands Dry

If your hands are particularly dry, keep them out of water as much as possible. This is easily accomplished by putting on plastic or vinyl gloves

Homemade Facial Masks

Before applying a facial mask, smooth eye cream over the eye area and lids and massage a creamy moisturizer into the neck. Both areas lack oil glands and need all the moisturizer they can get.

- For oily or combination oily and normal skin: Mix 3 tablespoons of mineral water with 3 tablespoons of fuller's earth and work the mixture into a soft clay. Add more fuller's earth if necessary to get the proper texture. Apply the clay to your face and leave it on for 20 minutes. Remove with warm water.

- For normal and dry skin: Beat 1 egg yolk with a fork and add 3 tablespoons of clay powder. (This powder is gentler and less astringent than fuller's earth. Clay powder or mud powder, as it is sometimes called, can be purchased at most natural foods stores. Ask for a soft, porous clay with large grains.) Mix in 1 teaspoon of honey and enough mineral water to form a loose mud. Apply the mixture to your face and leave it on for 10 to 15 minutes. Remove with warm water.

- For problem skin: Mix 2 tablespoons of mineral water into 3 tablespoons of fuller's earth. Mix in 1 tablespoon of carrot juice, and add more fuller's earth as necessary to form a soft clay. Apply the clay to your face and leave it on for 20 minutes. Remove with warm water.

(not rubber, which can cause excessive sweating) before you do any washing chores. When through, hang them up by their fingers or place them right side up on a propped-up wooden spoon (that's standing in a tall glass, for instance) so that they dry out between wearings. If your hands are especially sensitive, wear cotton gloves underneath the plastic or vinyl ones to protect your hands from friction, to insulate them against hot water, and to make the gloves easy to remove.

Protecting Skin from Paint

When painting, protect your skin by rubbing moisturizer on your arms and hands first. You'll find that cleanup will be easier because the moisturizer prevents the paint from seeping into your pores.

Wear gloves when using oil-based paints instead of relying on turpentine, gasoline, or lacquer thinner to clean your hands. These solvents remove more than just paint. The skin relies on natural fats and oils to prevent liquids from seeping into the body and to keep body fluids from leaking out. Strong solvents "defeat" the skin and allow it to dry out and crack open. Then it becomes susceptible to damage by other substances, causing more drying out.

Preventing "Dishpan Hands"

"Dishpan hands," a form of dermatitis, may stem from contact with things other than just hot, soapy water. Frequent contact with such domestic items as bleaches, waxes, detergents, soiled diapers, or the juices of raw citrus fruits, potatoes, tomatoes, and garlic can severely irritate the skin of sensitive people as well.

Slowing Down Wrinkles

Wrinkling is caused by a breakdown of collagen (an elastic skin component) and general skin cell degeneration. It appears that exercise can slow down both these processes. This is because the skin is strengthened and made thicker by exercise. During exercise, skin sweats, excretes toxins, takes in oxygen, and undergoes increased circulation.

In addition to exercising, there are a few other things you can do to slow down the wrinkling process:

- Don't get sunburned, because lots of sun will accelerate wrinkling.

- Don't smoke, because smoking constricts blood vessels and impairs circulation—just the opposite effects of exercise.

- Keep your house humidified during the heating season because dry skin is the sure beginning to wrinkled skin.

- Use a moisturizer both at night and during the day.

For Acne Problems

If you're one of the unlucky people who are well past adolescence but find themselves stuck with acne so severe that permanent scars are created, you may want to ask your dermatologist about 13-cis retinoic acid, a synthetic cousin of vitamin A used with success by English and American scientists. Thirteen-cis retinoic acid, which is not to be confused with vitamin A or vitamin A acid, is used very efficiently by the body and, therefore, requires a physician's guidance. Like vitamin A, it normalizes all the epithelial tissues, including the skin.

In a study of acne patients, a physician discovered that zinc worked as well as tetracycline, an antibiotic commonly used to clear complexions. Although they are not sure exactly how zinc works, physicians believe that zinc may induce the release of vitamin A in the body, that it may have an anti-inflammatory effect, and that a deficiency of zinc causes an enlargement of the oil glands.

Don't aggravate an already troubled complexion. Avoid coffee, tea, and very hot or spicy foods because they may dilate blood vessels of the face.

While only a change in diet may clear up a teenager's complexion, one of the key factors in adult acne is stress. Reducing stress may therefore be the answer to eliminating your acne.

Vitamins A and D for a Clear Complexion

Your red, rough winter skin may develop a much prettier, healthier look if you take a fish liver oil supplement two or three times a day. That's because fish liver oil contains not only vitamin A but vitamin D, and vitamin D helps your body to absorb calcium. Calcium is a great quieter of skin problems.

You probably won't need these supplements in the summer because you are out in the sun a lot more. The sun turns a chemical that naturally occurs in your skin into vitamin D.

Itchy Skin?

Once you've ruled out a serious skin problem by checking with your doctor, try a few simple cures. A compress made with skim milk or reconstituted nonfat dry milk may bring soothing relief. And soaking the affected area in a colloidal bath made with ingredients such as oatmeal, cornstarch, or baking soda can often work wonders. Bland lotions such as calamine and milk of bismuth may also be very effective.

Epsom Salts for Psoriasis

Epsom salts can relieve psoriasis. Make a paste with a little bit of water and pat it onto the tender spots. Or pour about 1 cup of the salts into a tubful of lukewarm water and take a 30-minute soak.

No Treatment May Be Best Eczema Treatment

If you suffer from eczema or some other form of skin inflammation, the best treatment may be no treatment at all. Medicated creams that contain fragrances, coloring agents, and paraben preservatives can aggravate sensitive skin and make a bad problem worse. Also, avoid ointments containing drugs ending in "caine," such as benzocaine; they are common causes of allergic reactions.

13 Keeping Fit

General Advice

Getting Started

Feeling too tired to add exercise to your life? That's a sure sign that you need it. If you have trouble getting started, set yourself manageable short-term goals, and build up from there. Seeing results gives you the motivation to continue. A partner with similar goals helps, too.

Fitting Fitness into Your Office Routine

If you sit at a desk all day long, use every opportunity to exercise. Get up and get your own coffee or tea, rather than asking someone else to get it for you. Use the stairs and not the elevator. Get two 15-minute walks in a day. One way to accomplish this is to park your car in the parking space farthest from your office so that you're forced to walk more. It will wake you up in the morning, and at the end of the day it will help you to unwind physically and mentally.

Begin Slowly . . .

To avoid early fatigue and discomfort, ease into your exercise activity slowly. After 6 to 8 minutes you can pick the pace up and start working.

. . . And End Slowly

When your exercise session is over, don't stop all at once; slow down gradually to cool down. This will assist the return of blood to your heart and prevent it from settling in your legs.

Overcoming Stiffness

Feel sore and stiff the day after your exercise? Try 10 to 12 minutes of relaxed stretching immediately after you do your cool-down. If stretching

Rules of a Successful Fitness Program

- Listen to your body.
- Proceed slowly.
- Warm up with slow, nonresistance exercises.
- Cool down by decreasing the stress of your exercise program over the last 5 to 7 minutes of exercise.
- Stretch after you cool down with slow holding motions.
- Never increase duration and stress level at the same time.
- Use good footgear.

doesn't prevent your aches and pains, try a nice hot bath. If that doesn't work, your exercise program is too strenuous.

Talk to Test Your Exercising Level

To make sure you're not exercising too hard, try the "talk test." If you can't carry on a conversation without gasping, you'd better slow down.

Increase Your Level Slowly

You can gauge whether your exercise program is too strenuous by comparing your present activity with what you did last week. If you're exercising more than 10 minutes per day over last week's program, you may want to slow down.

If You Feel Discomfort around Your Heart

Every muscle in your body needs oxygen to keep it working, and your heart is no exception. Angina is pain or discomfort in (and around) the heart that tells you your heart isn't getting sufficient amounts of oxygen. If angina occurs, immediately decrease your activity to a slow walk and then rest. Make a note of what you were doing when you experienced the angina and schedule an appointment with your physician or a cardiologist prior to your next exercise session.

Exercise's Effects on Your Blood Pressure

Blood pressure (BP) is the amount of pressure created in your arteries by blood (like water in a hose). Systolic BP is the amount of pressure created when your heart contracts and forces blood through the arteries. Diastolic BP is the amount of pressure in the arteries when the heart is relaxed (between contractions). The immediate effects of exercise increase your systolic BP and decrease your diastolic BP, but the long-term results are a low resting blood pressure. A normal blood pressure reading is around 120/80.

Exercise with Music

To make your calisthenics (or any other indoor exercise) more enjoyable, turn on the radio or put on a record and move to the beat. Mini-cassettes or radios with headphones can get you really involved with the music because they cut out all other noises—including your own grunts and groans!

Good Reasons to Exercise

If you need good reasons to start exercising or to keep it up, consider the following:

- By exercising as little as 20 minutes a day, three days a week, you're enlarging and increasing the number of blood vessels responsible for feeding your heart blood, and you're improving its ability to pump more blood with fewer beats. All this adds up to a heart better able to resist a heart attack.

- Lungs themselves don't change much with exercise, but their capacity to take in and transmit oxygen does. This is due in part to the strengthening of the muscles responsible for breathing and also to an increased ability of the muscles of your arms and legs to use oxygen as an energy source.

- Scientific studies indicate that people who are physically active appear to absorb more of the good things from their food, like vitamins and minerals, while at the same time absorbing less of the bad, like cholesterol. Bowel regularity, too, is a benefit of regular physical activity.

- Your bones benefit from exercise. The stress of activity, it is theorized, sets off tiny electrical charges that encourage the buildup of bone tissue, resulting in greater bone size and density.

Skip a Day between Hard Workouts

We now know that well-worked muscles need about 48 hours to rest, which is why a heavy workout every other day is better than a workout every day.

Know When to Stop

Finish your exercise session before you try to squeeze out one more repetition, mile, or sit-up. An exercise session should leave you feeling tired but confident, not weak and worn out. You should finish feeling like you can do a little bit more. If you are totally exhausted, you've gone too far.

- The brain benefits, too. Studies are showing that people who exercise suffer less from depression, anxiety, headaches, uncontrollable appetite, and even age-related decline in intelligence. These good things happen not only because exercise keeps the brain richly supplied with blood, but also because it tends to promote the release of chemicals thought to elevate mood.

- Perhaps exercise's most healthful changes, however, occur in the blood. Exercise tends to reduce the fat content of blood, thus making it freer flowing and less apt to form artery-clogging clots. It also tends to alter the cholesterol content of the blood in a fashion capable of discouraging hardening of the arteries. It's known, too, to keep insulin levels where they should be, thus reducing the odds of maturity-onset diabetes. Finally, exercise has been shown to enhance the ability of the blood to "thin out" in times of emergency—during heart attacks and strokes, for example.

- Exercise has an additional advantage in controlling weight—it increases the rate at which you burn calories, even when you're not exercising. So work out once a day and burn extra calories all day and night.

Stretch It Out

Muscles shorten (in other words, tighten) as they age, and this is especially the case with people who get little exercise. Shortened muscles put pressure on the nerves that run through them, which results in aches and pains. Here are some things to remember about stretching out when exercising:

- You should stretch after you exercise, or after an 8- to 10-minute warm-up, but if you have to make a choice, it's better to stretch after you exercise than before. Spend a few minutes warming up and loosening your muscles before you start to stretch out in preparation for your exercise bout. Cold muscles are less flexible than warm ones that have blood rapidly circulating through them.

- Ease into your stretch slowly; never bounce to touch your toes, as many of us learned in school.

- It's better to stretch when sitting or lying down than it is when standing, because when standing you're supporting your body weight, and this pressure contracts your leg muscles.

How Many Days Can You Afford to Miss?

Once you're up to a regular level of fitness, you can afford to miss about three days of exercise before you start to lose some of the fitness you've gained. After that, the muscle strength and lung capacity you've built up begin to decrease.

A Stationary Bike for Inclement Weather

When the weather makes outdoor exercising anything but a pleasure for you, try moving inside with a stationary bike. It's great for runners, bikers, and skiers. Turn on your stereo or plug in your headphones and spend the same amount of time exercising inside as you usually do outside.

Many stationary bikes feel uncomfortable to the avid biker, but that's no excuse to stop cycling. You can put your own bike on rollers or on a turbo-trainer and peddle away. Look for them in your local bike shop, bike magazine, or equipment catalog.

Buying Shoes

When you buy a new pair of athletic shoes, regardless of the activity they're to be used for, take your old ones with you so that the salesperson can inspect them and make suggestions as to what you need. If you're just starting an exercise program and have no athletic shoes, take along a pair of old, well-worn casual shoes.

Dressing Right for Cold Weather

Four types of clothing are highly recommended for outdoor activity in cold temperatures:

1. Polypropylene pants and shirts; worn next to the skin, they will keep you dry and warm.

2. Nylon pants and jacket; they retain some heat and keep most of the cold out (not waterproof).

3. Gore-Tex pants and jacket; in the coldest weather, generally −5°F or less, Gore-Tex fabrics keep all of your body heat inside, and they're waterproof, too.

4. Gloves and mittens; use gloves until the temperature drops to 5°F, and when it gets below that switch to mittens for more warmth. Both gloves and mittens should be light-weight and wind resistant.

Give Your Shoes Priority

If you play tennis or basketball, run, or dance, your shoes are your most important piece of equipment. No matter how good they are they won't last forever. So, get new shoes if:

- You have used them for more than 600 miles.

- The heels tilt when you set the shoes on a table.

- You can see more than ⅜ to ½ inch of wear on the sole or heel.

- You can see the midsole through the outer sole.

- Your ankles, knees, or hips begin to ache for no apparent reason.

The Right Way to Do Sit-Ups

A proper sit-up is done with legs bent. Straight legs can lead to back problems, and feet anchored to the floor tighten hip muscles, which can lead to back problems and related aches and pains.

Exercising to Lose Weight
(See also Weight Control in the chapter, Here's to Your Health.)

Exercise in the A.M.

By performing your exercise routine first thing in the morning you will increase your metabolism for the day, thereby helping your body to burn more calories.

Exercising in the morning will also increase your blood sugar, which may help you cut down on breakfast and that mid-morning snack.

If you find yourself feeling hungry at times other than mealtime, try to take an exercise break (such as walking or doing calisthenics) right then and there for 10 to 15 minutes or more. This will elevate your blood sugar level naturally and do away with your appetite.

Aerobics Is Best

Aerobic exercise is your best calorie burner, but you'll need to do it for 30 to 40 minutes at a time, three to four times a week, to burn away body fat.

Take a Pinch Test

If you can pinch more than an inch of skin at your waistline, skip that second helping. Should you find less than an inch there, your body composition (lean-to-fat ratio) is right where it should be—probably about 20%.

Recommended Weight Charts Can Be Misleading

Don't try to judge your body composition by your size and weight alone. A large person who is fit may have a high muscle and low fat ratio, while a thin person who is out of shape may have too much fat and not enough muscle.

Exercise As You Diet

When trying to reduce your fat weight, don't count on diet alone. Diet by itself will decrease both lean and fat weight, but diet plus exercise will burn more fat and maintain or increase your lean weight.

Running and Aerobics

The *Good* Things about Morning Running

As hard as it might be to get going in the morning, try to do your running at the beginning of the day. It will give you a sense of confidence and satisfaction that will stay with you all day long, and you won't have to juggle a busy schedule around a run later on. If you have a bad day, you can be sure at least *something* went right.

Avoid Traffic-Heavy Streets

A study of runners who jogged through New York City's Central Park, which has roadways winding through it, found that they had moderate amounts of carbon monoxide in their lungs and blood. Carbon monoxide binds to red blood cells and hinders their ability to take up oxygen.

A Wet Hat for a Cooler Run

If summer's heat gets you down when you run, try wearing a terrycloth hat soaked in water.

"Running" in Place

You can get the benefits of a two-mile run right in your bedroom or motel room. Start out with 500 jumping jacks, which will do you about as much good as jogging a mile. If you're a runner, you should be able to do them in 8 minutes. Then do 60 sit-ups at a rate of 20 to 30 per minute, and finish with 30 push-ups, which you should try to do in 1 minute.

Alternate these exercises, but keep moving so that your heart is pumping at about the same rate as it would if you were jogging, cycling, swimming, or doing some other aerobic activity. Stretch out between exercises to catch your breath and stay limber. If you can keep yourself exercising for about 20 minutes, you've gotten activity equal to a two-mile run without leaving your room.

Getting in Shape for Aerobics

Do aerobic activities cause you a great deal of discomfort? If so, perhaps you should start your exercise program with body toning, such as weight lifting. This will help your muscles develop the strength they need to perform aerobic exercise.

Dressing Right for Running

- When running outside you should dress for a temperature 20°F higher than your outdoor thermometer reads. The right clothes for running are those that feel too light when you are standing still. The generally accepted level of discomfort is a thermometer reading of 90°F or higher while you're sitting or moving slowly, but this discomfort level drops to 70°F once you're running or exercising hard.

- On the other hand, when you're not working hard, anything below 50°F may seem "cold," but the cold-weather line drops to 30°F and under when you're running.

- Start dressing for your run with a foundation of socks, shoes, and underwear. The wardrobe builds up from here according to the way the day will feel:

  70°F and up—Add only the lightest top that modesty will allow.

  50° to 65°F—Add a T-shirt.

  35° to 45°F—Add long pants and a long-sleeve shirt or light jacket.

  30°F and under—Add a layer of protection for the hands and ears and perhaps another layer on the legs and face for extreme cold.

Lifting Weights

Building Up Body Tone, Not Muscle Mass

Are you concerned that weight lifting will make you a mass of muscle and bulk? It won't if you just make sure you're lifting weights light enough to complete eight repetitions with your arms and twelve with your legs.

Weight lifting won't have you weighing less, but it will increase your muscle-to-fat ratio, thereby toning and tightening your body in general.

Body Toning without Weights

If weights don't appeal to you, or you don't have them available, try calisthenics. Calisthenics are body exercises such as jumping jacks, sit-ups, squat thrusts, and back arches that tone your body without weights.

Mix Weights with Aerobics

As good as weight training is, don't expect it to be as good an aerobic exercise as running, cycling, swimming, hiking, and other aerobic activities are. For best results, alternate a weight training program with an aerobic one.

What's Best for Your Heart

Circuit weight training, in which you do several repetitious weight-lifting exercises one after the other in what is called a circuit, is better for the heart than doing any one weight-lifting exercise at a time with a rest between each. This is because circuit weight training is both strenuous and repetitive enough to give your heart a good workout. To get the maximum benefit from circuit weight training, do more repetitions with light weights, rather than a few repetitions with heavier weights. If you don't have weights, you'll find that repetitive pull-ups, push-ups, and chin-ups have similar upper-body benefits.

Warming Up to Weights

Do you always feel worn out and stiff when you first start weight lifting? Warm up first by running or riding a bike at an easy pace for 3 to 5 minutes and you'll feel great.

Weights Aren't Good for Boys

In general, weight lifting doesn't do much good for preteen boys who want to build up their muscles. Until a boy reaches puberty and starts producing more male hormones, there is very little that can be done to increase muscle strength or mass. Moreover, most young boys lack the coordination to handle heavy weights without hurting themselves.

Weight Training Is Beneficial for Women

Women don't develop muscles the way men do when they lift weights because men have more of the hormone testosterone, which promotes muscle enlargement. But weight training, especially circuit training, is an excellent exercise for women because it gives them increased muscular strength and endurance.

Bicycling

Dressing for Cool Mornings, Hot Afternoons

The early-morning start of a long ride on a summer day is often too chilly to go without a shirt. This is where your really old T-shirts come in handy: You can start the trip wearing one, and then merely take it off when you begin working up a sweat.

Removing Chain Grease

If while riding your bike you get some chain grease on your leg, simply rub a little butter or margarine on the spot with your hand until the black smear has dissolved into the fat. Then wipe the spot clean with a cloth or tissue. Vegetable oil or baby oil also works well.

Counting Cadence

Cadence is your pedaling rhythm. A lively cadence will make cycling more enjoyable and also keep your heart rate up for a good aerobic workout. If you have never counted cadence, it is easily done by counting the number of times per minute one of your feet goes full circle on the pedal. Strive for a pedaling cadence of 70 to 80 rpm at least; with training you may learn to favor 80 to 90, as many experienced riders do.

Drip-Dry Cycling Briefs

Swimsuit briefs make good underwear under hiker's shorts when bicycle touring. Because they are nylon, they wash and dry very easily. Two pair are all you'll need on even a two- or three-week trip, since you can wear one while the other is drying.

Keeping Panniers Dry

To keep items in your panniers clean and dry, line the panniers with plastic trash bags, then pack in your gear, and seal the plastic bags with wire twists. If you're going on a long trip, take along a couple of spare plastic bags.

Homemade Map Case

You can make a cheap and convenient map case by using a zip-lock plastic bag; a 6 × 9-inch bag is the perfect size to hold maps and letters. It keeps them dry, and you can read right through the plastic.

Why the Flat Tire?

The most common reason for a flat tire is the obvious: riding over glass, pebbles, or potholes. But there are other, more subtle things that will make your bike flat-tire prone.

- Lightweight, high-pressure tires are going to puncture a lot quicker than heavier ones that take less air pressure.

- Weak rims, most likely bent or sprung apart by running over a pothole or a pebble, don't give the tire itself the support it needs and can lead to a puncture.

- Overloading the bike with too much gear, underinflating the tires, or overinflating the tires can lead to a puncture as well.

Air-Drying Laundry

Wet laundry or rain-soaked clothing can air-dry while you're touring. Just fasten it with brass (that is, rust-free) safety pins to your bike packs.

A Winter Helmet Liner

You'll find an inexpensive winter helmet liner at the hardware or construction supply outlet. Purchase a winter hardhat liner and remove the external fasteners meant to attach it to the liner of a hardhat. It will now fit most bike helmets.

Ski Mask for Winter Cycling

Cold weather cycling can be made much more comfortable by a trip to your local ski shop. Ski gear is designed for breaking the cold wind you're likely to face when winter cycling. A knit ski mask with a vapor-permeable membrane will protect your face from icy winds but won't get soggy as you breathe hard during exertion. It should fit closely enough to allow you to wear your normal helmet on top.

Mittens for Winter Cycling

You *can* keep your hands warm while cycling in subfreezing weather. Get a pair of plain calfskin mittens and line them with a pair of plain knit

A Bike Tool Kit

Here are some essentials you'll want to have in your bicycle tool kit:

- Stamped steel wrenches with tire irons for handles.

- A 6-inch adjustable wrench, which works when the stamped-steel wrenches don't.

- A pocket knife, complete with an array of different blades.

- Needlenose pliers with a built-in wire cutter to cut cables and clamp a brake or derailleur cable.

- Pocket-size Channelock arc-joint pliers, for gripping all sorts of parts.

- A repair kit for flat tires.

wool mittens. The leather affords a sure grip on the handlebars and does a fine job of breaking the wind. All four fingers share a common wool-insulated pocket and help to keep each other warm. Both materials "breathe," keeping your hands from getting soggy.

Big Wheels for Rough Terrain

If you have to commute over rough roads with your "good" bike, get some insurance. Get a cheap set of rims and 1¼-inch tires that you can easily switch with your good wheels. The bigger tires will take much more abuse without being damaged, and even if you do damage them, they're cheaper to replace.

Other Sports

The Best Courts for Tennis

Tennis court surfaces that allow you to slide, rather than screech, to a halt, are easier on the legs, ankles, and knees. A survey of tennis court injuries found that roughly six times more mishaps had occurred on asphalt, felt carpet, and synthetic grill surfaces than had happened on clay courts or those of a loose, granular composition.

Cross-Country Ski Clothes

When dressing for a cross-country ski session, follow the guidelines for running (see the box, Dressing Right for Running, earlier in this chapter), and be sure to wear clothes that let you move freely.

How Long to Swim

Swimming can be a nice change from running or cycling. Don't plan to spend the same amount of time in the water as you spend on the pavement or on your bike, though. The rule of thumb for swimming time is one-third the time of running and one-sixth the time of riding.

Preventing Irritated Swimmer's Eyes

If your eyes get irritated when you're swimming, you might want to wear watertight goggles. Or try keeping your eyes closed for a little while after you come out of the water so that they have a chance to make tears and moisturize themselves.

Preventing Water-Clogged Ears

You can keep your ears from filling up with water when you swim by putting a few drops of baby oil into them before you go into the water. The oil will coat the ear canal, enabling water to run out more freely. If water does get trapped, many doctors recommend using a few drops of isopropyl alcohol to remedy the situation. Don't use alcohol, however, if you have any ear problems.

Sportsmedicine
(See also First Aid, and Aches and Pains, in the chapter, Here's to Your Health.)

Why Saunas and Steam Baths Feel So Good

The reason you feel good after a steam bath or a sauna is that the heat, be it dry or moist, gets your heart pumping more blood to your skin in an effort to cool off your body, and this has a stimulating effect. The heat also elevates the level of nerve stimulants in your blood. Finally, the coolness you experience after you leave the hot sauna or steam room brings welcome relief in itself, raising your spirits.

Preventing Blisters

Blisters are the most common foot problem for fitness and sports activists. To avoid blisters, make sure your shoes fit snugly, but allow a ⅜- to ½-inch space between your toes and the ends of your shoes, because your feet swell during exercise.

If you're plagued by blisters when running, make sure you've got shoes and socks that fit. Wear thick athletic socks. Don't go running in a brand-new pair of shoes without walking around in them for a few days to break them in first. Should your shoes rub against parts of your feet, protect your feet with moleskin.

Petroleum jelly can be very effective in preventing blisters. Before you slip on your socks, apply a thin coat of jelly to the areas of your foot that generally blister.

If you find yourself blistering in the same spot in just one pair of your shoes, dab some petroleum jelly inside those shoes at that spot.

Preventing Black Toe

Black toe can be avoided by making sure your shoes fit properly—and by placing a ½-inch strip of athletic tape over the top of your toe and nail and then another around the toe as an anchor.

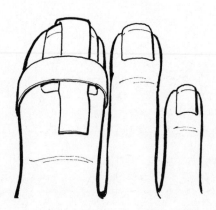

ICE for Discomfort

To ease discomfort in your Achilles tendon, knee, hip, or other muscles and tendons, the thing to remember is ICE: *I*ce, *C*ompression, and *E*levation. If the discomfort lasts for more than 24 hours, change that to RICE by adding *R*est.

Sprained Ankle

When you sprain (turn) your ankle, always leave your shoe on and keep it tied; this will decrease swelling. Next, elevate it and apply ice, which will keep swelling down and reduce the pain. Use ice as long as you need to, perhaps even for a few days. If the pain persists, see a doctor. Once the swelling is gone, a warm heating pad will increase blood circulation to the tender spot and promote healing.

Shin Splints

Runner's shin splints are usually caused by running on a hard surface; the constant impact on the legs produces the problem. It can also be caused by just plain overuse. To relieve the pain of shin splints, ice your shins and elevate them, then rest. To prevent shin splints from occurring again, avoid running on hills and paved surfaces. Make sure your shoes have good shock absorption qualities and superior heel and arch support.

Quick Relief for Big Cramps

To relieve a muscle cramp in your calf, continue bicycling or walking while pinching your upper lip between your index finger and your thumb. The onset of a cramp is usually due to a lack of fluids, so drink large amounts.

Avoiding Stomach Cramps

The cramping that some people get when they eat before exercising, especially running, is often due to the fact that the stomach isn't getting the large blood supply it needs to digest the food properly; exercising is diverting the blood supply to other parts of the body. To avoid cramping, wait an hour or more after you eat before you begin exercising.

If food isn't the reason you have a cramp or sidestitch, try starting your running or other exercise program slowly, easing up to your regular pace, so that your stomach muscles aren't pushed into quick and heavy use. Don't jostle or jump when you run, and make sure that you stretch out before you begin.

Replenishing Your Potassium

You sweat more when you exercise in hot weather. That's pretty obvious information, but perhaps not so obvious is the fact that you're not just sweating off water but also salts, including the important mineral, potassium. If you sweat a great deal when you exercise, no matter what the reason, replenish the potassium you're losing by eating more fresh fruits and vegetables.

14 Pets and Backyard Livestock

Cats

No Newspapers for Kitty

Avoid using newspapers in your kitty's litter box or letting your cat habitually sleep on newspapers. As your cat cleans himself, he may ingest toxic substances from the ink such as hydrocarbons or phenolic compounds.

Flea Control

Citrus oil (such as that from an orange) rubbed on a cat's fur can chase away fleas.

Since fleas don't like vitamin B_1, feeding your cats and dogs brewer's yeast, also called nutritional yeast, will give them a nice shiny coat of hair, as well as keep them flea free. Just mix in a tablespoon or so with your pet's dinner.

Flea Shampoo

To rid your cat of fleas, wash your pet in a bucket of warm water with a small amount of dandruff shampoo.

Flea Powder

Flea allergy is very common in cats, often causing severe itching and baldness. Sometimes the presence of a single flea on a sensitive cat can lead to a scratching fit. If your cat has such symptoms, even though fleas don't seem to be present, try dusting his fur weekly with 1% rotenone powder. Fleas come and go on cats and you may just be looking for them during the "off time."

Bathing Your Cat

If your cat gets into dirty places and picks up more oil or grime than he can lick off, bathe him. Cats don't mind a bath as much as they do a dirty coat! Use warm water and a mild shampoo. Towel-dry your pet, give him a snack treat afterward, and you will be forgiven. A dirty coat can make your kitty sick because he can ingest grime and hair as he strives to clean himself.

Bathing your cat can be a real hassle for you; you're bound to get scratched a lot unless you take special precautions. One special precaution is to slip your cat into a cotton gym bag and pull the drawstrings around his neck, being careful not to pull too tightly. Then gently place him in a bucket of warm soap and water, making sure not to get his head wet. Rub the bag so that you lather up his fur well, and then rinse him by placing him in a clean bucket of water or by gently spraying him with a kitchen or bathtub sprinkler hose. Finally, let the cat out of the bag and towel him dry.

Wheat Grass for Your Cat

If your cat is housebound, you can still let him enjoy the greenery that outdoor cats love to munch. You might even find that a houseplant-loving cat will stop gnawing at your spider plant if you give him the following treat.

Sprout wheat seeds just as you would when making sprouts for yourself. In five or six days, when you've got a mat of roots, place the sprouts, root mat down, in a flowerpot, and cover the roots with dirt. Water the sprouts, place them in a sunny window, and watch the wheat grass grow. Keep it where your cat has easy access to it. You'll be giving him the chlorophyll that he can't get in his cat food.

And Tuna Fish Oil

Save the liquid from canned tuna fish (especially the salt-free kind) for your cat (or dog). They like the taste of it poured over their dry food. It's good for them, too.

Pennyroyal Repellent

If your kitty decides to use the carpet instead of his litter box, sprinkle dried pennyroyal on the spot to keep him away from the carpet next time.

Cardboard Collar

To prevent your cat from scratching or licking his face because, for instance, there's an injury there you want to heal, fashion a wide collar out of cardboard.

Transporting Kitty

Does your cat get sick or excited when traveling by car? Try keeping him in a box, where he will feel secure. It will often do the trick.

When "cartoning" your cat to restrain or move him, put the weaker side of the box under him, since cats try to escape upward.

Moving an Injured Cat

A badly injured cat is carried safely by grasping the skin on the neck as closely to the ears as possible. You won't further hurt the cat by grasping injured parts, and he will not be able to twist and bite you. This carrying method works well in such emergencies but shouldn't be used to pick up your cat at any other time.

Keep Kitty Away from High Places

If you live in a high-rise building, don't let your cat climb or explore outside on a balcony or on windowsills. A New York City veterinarian noted that of all the feline cases he sees, most are victims of window and balcony falls.

Try Trimming before Declawing

Before you decide that declawing is the only way to save your furniture, try trimming your kitty's nails. Clip off the tiny, sharp hooks with a pair of dog nail trimmers or heavy-duty people nail trimmers.

Urinary Calculi

Adding a teaspoon of vinegar to your male cat's water daily will often help prevent the urinary calculi that often lead to urinary problems later in life. The vinegar helps keep the urine more acid, preventing the formation of stones. Feeding your cat low-ash cat food and making sure he has lots of fresh water available all the time will help, too.

Rx for Ear Mites

To effectively treat ear mites in your cat, simply drop a few drops of vegetable oil into his ear and massage. Then clean out all debris with a ball of cotton. Repeat daily for three days, and the mites should be gone. The oil soothes the cat's sensitive skin, smothers the mites, and promotes healing.

Eliminating Hair Balls

Hair balls are the plague of most adult long-haired cats. They're nasty because they can cause impaction, sometimes even death. At the least, they are troublesome. Adding a teaspoon of bacon fat or vegetable oil to your cat's food daily will usually enable him to pass the hair swallowed during grooming before it forms large balls. You can also use petroleum jelly. Just put a dab on your finger about once a week and let the cat lick it off. Do not feed your cat mineral oil; it robs the body of B-vitamins.

Keeping Cat Food Fresh

Cats hate stale canned cat food. Wouldn't you if your leftovers had little flavor and low quality? Avoid the quick deterioration of opened cat food that is stored in the refrigerator. When using large cans, divide the contents into smaller, meal-sized portions, place them in sandwich bags, tie tightly, and freeze. Defrosting and serving them one at a time will protect nutritional content and flavor. Portioning out a large can is also more economical than buying several small cans.

Keep Disinfectants Away

Avoid using phenol-based disinfectants and iodine on or around cats; it can kill them. This includes toilet bowl disinfectants. Either skip the disinfectant or make sure you keep the seat lid closed, since many cats love to drink out of the toilet.

Pills That Go Down Easily

Medication time will be a lot easier for your kitty *and* you if you coat tablets and capsules first with butter before giving them to your cat.

No Aspirin for Cats

Human medicine is not always good cat medicine. Aspirin and aspirin-free substitutes are good examples; both can cause toxic reactions. A cat can tolerate very little aspirin, and even small doses of an aspirin-free substitute can be lethal.

Feeding a Recuperating Cat

To encourage a cat that has been ill or has had surgery to eat, feed him *tiny* amounts of food, several hours apart. A few special dishes that should appeal to him are tuna, salmon, liver sausage, and boiled liver. If you offer a large amount of food to an ailing cat, he will usually lose his appetite right away. A teaspoonful is safer, until his appetite returns.

Special Feeding Care for Kittens

When bottle raising orphaned or abandoned kittens, remember to massage their bottoms and tummies after feeding. This stimulates them to urinate and defecate. Without such stimulation, they often become constipated and toxic.

Don't Feed Your Cat Dog Food

A cat will starve if fed a sole diet of dry dog food. It is too high in bulk, not giving the cat enough protein and vitamins.

Vitamin E for Cuts and Scratches

Small cuts and scratches on a cat's skin often heal well when treated with vitamin E. Simply trim the hair away, rinse the area well with warm, clear water, and dry. Then cut a vitamin E capsule open and squeeze the oily fluid onto the wound. Should the cat lick away the vitamin, there is no chance of a toxic or digestive upset; merely apply some more.

Paw Protection

If your cat injures his paw and it needs to be protected, the plastic cover of a 12-cc syringe works very effectively. It is light and strong and can be easily taped into place, immobilizing the foot and lower leg.

Dogs

Getting Rid of Lice

If you suspect your dog has lice, you can kill the eggs or "nits" by bathing the dog every other week in a 5% vinegar solution.

Rx for Mange

A mild solution of household bleach and water—about ½ cup of bleach to a shallow tub of water—makes a good bath for a dog with mange.

Two Rinses to Combat Skunk Odor

Rinsing your dog in tomato juice is the old tried-and-true method of getting rid of skunk odor, but a mixture of vinegar and water does the trick, too. Just be careful of his eyes.

Separating Fighting Dogs

A full hose with a high-pressure nozzle aimed right at dogs locked in combat breaks them apart and scatters them in a matter of seconds.

Keeping Your Dog Clean

To clean your dog, brush him rather than bathe him. Brushing or combing will remove the dirt and help to keep your animal's natural flow of skin oils active. It also cuts down on the amount of scratching he will do and lessens the amount of loose hair you'll have around the house.

Don't bathe your dog unless he's unusually dirty because bathing can remove the natural oils that act as a skin lubricant and may result in unpleasant skin irritations.

Removing Mats in Hair

Small areas of matted hair can often be removed from a long-coated dog by bathing the animal with shampoo, followed by a cream rinse. Then, when the dog is dry, dust the mats with baby powder and tease them apart with a slicker or stiff brush. Heavier mats may be cut lengthwise and pulled gently apart, aided by frequent dustings of baby powder.

Keeping Fleas Away

There are about as many ways to prevent or minimize these nasty pests as there are fleas on a dirty dog's back. Here are some of the most popular:

- Pennyroyal oil can keep fleas and ticks away from pets. Spread some on the underside of your pet's collar; then put a few drops on your hands, rub the palms together, and rub your hands over your pet's fur.

- Green walnut leaves may also keep fleas away. Put a heap of them in your dog's house to ward off the little pests.

- Fleas will generally go elsewhere if the dog's bed is made up of cedar chips or if cedar wood is used for its flooring. A pillow stuffed with cedar chips or cedar sawdust works equally well.

- Eucalyptus seeds can be strung together into a natural flea control collar for your dog. Shaped like stubby teepees, they are about an inch long and quite hard. Since you won't be able to puncture them with a needle, you'll need to drill or bore a hole into them before you can thread them on a string. Your dog won't care for them too much, but the fleas will like them even less.

  You can also sprinkle some eucalyptus seeds on a bed, sofa, or anywhere where you don't want your dog to sit; the seeds will keep him away.

- Another kind of homemade flea collar can be made by fashioning a tube of material and stuffing it with crushed tansy and catnip. Sew up the ends and tie this around your dog's neck. Rubbing the collar between your hands daily will activate the aroma of the herbs and keep the collar repelling fleas for a long time.

Removing Road Tar

When your dog comes in splattered with sticky road tar, don't despair. It can be safely taken off by soaking it with mineral oil. After the tar is removed, the oil can easily be washed out with warm water and shampoo.

Cleaning Your Dog's Teeth

A dog who eats a lot of soft foods will often have teeth caked with tartar. If left alone, these teeth usually become loose and the gums infected, resulting in tooth loss and illness. A dime and an old toothbrush are all that are needed to keep your dog's teeth white and clean. Use the dime occasionally as a scraper, hooking the edge over the tartar at the gum line and scraping the caked grime off cleanly, often in one chunk. After the teeth are cleaned, go over them with a toothbrush and baking soda. Done regularly, and gently, scraping and brushing will keep the dog's teeth healthy and strong. An added bonus will be fresh-smelling breath.

Belly Rash

Dust your dog's belly rash with cornstarch. It will keep the area dry, and because it's a natural product, it won't make your dog sick if he licks it off.

Sure-Fire Pill Tricks

If you have trouble giving your dog a pill, make three bite-size balls of meat, one containing the pill. Feed him first a plain meatball, then the one with the pill, and finally, a plain one again. He'll be so anxious to eat more meat he probably won't notice that the second contains medication.

You can also try cutting a piece of liver sausage and wrapping the medication in it. Not only will its seasoning prevent him from smelling it, but its sticky consistency will hold the pill in place.

Keeping Fido Off the Sofa

Sprinkle pepper on your couch or any other surface you want your dog to stay away from. One good sniff (and dogs *always* sniff around) should be unpleasant enough to keep him off the forbidden place in the future.

Protecting Paws in Cold Weather

Put a little petroleum jelly on your dog's paws before he goes outside on cold winter days. The petroleum jelly will protect his paws from rough ice and rock salt. But be sure to check your animal before he comes back in.

You may want to wipe off any remaining petroleum jelly to save your carpets and furniture from grease stains.

Foxtails May Injure Floppy-Eared Dogs

Foxtails are a problem for floppy-eared dogs, whose ears hang down and trap the plants and sometimes even direct them right down into the ear canal. What you should do after your dog has been out running is immediately check his ears (and between his toes). If you see any foxtails, pull them out. Should you suspect that a foxtail is further down in the ear, don't try to remove it; take your dog to a veterinarian. If seeing a vet involves some delay, put a small amount of warm olive oil into the ear. This will soften the plant material and make it less irritating.

Soothing Skin Irritations with Tea

"Hot spots" are wet, red skin eruptions that unfortunately plague many dogs. If your dog has hot spots, take him for medical help. But in the meantime, give your pooch some relief by fixing him a poultice of black or green tea bags. The tannic acid in the tea leaves works to reduce secretions, and that means less sensitivity and itching.

Treating Inflamed Eyes

One of your dog's favorite activities may be riding in the car with his head hanging out the window. Unfortunately, it can produce an uncomfortable side effect: mildly inflamed eyes. If this happens to your canine, first clean his eyes gently with a damp tissue. Then put a drop of olive oil or cod-liver oil on the surface of each eye. Treat the eyes twice a day until they look normal.

Use Caution When Clipping

If you clip your dog's nails yourself, you know that clipping too close can cause bleeding. To stop the bleeding, insert the cut nail into a bar of soap.

Diarrhea Relief

Mild to severe diarrhea in dogs may be caused by the coccidium, a one-celled animal that can be picked up from other dogs and lives in the dog's intestinal tract. Coccidia are actually a common problem, and your dog's immune system will eventually build up a resistance to them. In the meantime, your dog should get some fresh natural foods and adequate amounts of vitamins A and C during the early stages of the disease. Until the problem is eliminated, you may also want to try feeding him fresh, grated, or crushed garlic with every meal.

Clearing Up Diarrhea in Pups

Cottage cheese, fed as the sole diet for two days, will usually clear up even the most severe case of coccidiosis, which causes diarrhea in puppies. It seems to change the pH in the bowel, making it inhospitable to the organisms.

Feeding too much milk to pups often causes diarrhea, which is produced both by overeating and a lactose intolerance that makes the milk difficult to digest. Substitute broth or cottage cheese to moisten dry foods.

Watch That Garbage

Dogs can become the victims of their own adventures through the neighbors' garbage cans. Spoiled food, or just too much food, can spell trouble. So don't let Fido roam unattended, and keep your own garbage and waste cans well sealed and out of reach. Don't put meat scraps in your compost pile, and keep it well tended or even fenced off.

Inducing Vomiting

To make a dog vomit after eating a poison or another inedible substance, pour hydrogen peroxide down his throat, slowly, so as not to choke him.

Garlic for Coughs

Help for dogs with a cough due to allergy or bronchitis can be found in oil of garlic capsules. Give your animal one to two capsules every 3 hours, or more often in severe cases.

Impacted Anal Glands

Anal glands, the scent glands near a dog's rectum, often become impacted, causing symptoms ranging from itching to tonsillitis, vomiting, and lameness in the hind legs. Expressing these glands is easily learned. Using a handful of cotton or tissue, hold the tail up and press firmly on either side of the rectum, drawing outward, toward you. A foul-smelling, greyish matter will attest to your skill. If this is done at least every two months, your dog should never suffer impaction.

Feeding an Orphaned Puppy

A puppy that has been rejected by his mother is often weak from chilling and starvation. He can sometimes be saved by warming with a heating pad, set on medium, and tube-feeding 3½ cc's of warmed milk (depending on the breed and size of the dog). Tube-feeding is not difficult. Obtain the correct size tube from your vet. (They are very inexpensive.) Moisten the tube with milk, draw the right amount of milk up through the tube into the syringe, and slip the tube slowly down the pup's throat. It should go into the stomach, so judge the distance before inserting it. If the pup struggles excessively, or coughs, withdraw the tube and repeat the procedure. When the tube is in place, deposit the milk slowly to avoid giving the pup cramps. Once the pup is fed and active, try returning it to mom if she's available.

Treating for Vomiting

When a dog is vomiting, cut out all solid food and milk and give him an electrolyte solution, such as Lytren (found in the baby care department of the drug store) or Gatorade. If he has a case of simple indigestion, it should be cleared up in 24 hours. If it isn't, see your vet.

Clearing Up Dark Tear Stains

Light-colored dogs with dark tear stains below their eyes can often be helped by adding 25 mg of oral tetracycline to their food daily, until the problem clears up.

Preventing Ear Infections

Ear infections in poodles and other small, long-haired dogs can often be prevented by keeping the hair plucked inside the ear. This hair blocks the ear canal, making it moist and warm, the perfect incubator for bacteria and fungi.

Transporting an Injured Dog

When a dog has been injured, the safest method of transport is to pick him up by the skin on the back of the neck and back and lay him in a strong box or car seat. He will struggle less if so confined and will be afforded little chance of doing more damage should he have broken bones or internal injuries.

Pets in General

Watch Your Pet's Toys

Provide your pet with a rawhide toy or bone so that he won't chew and eat things like plastic toys, newspapers, or books. Cats, in particular, have barbed tongues that make it difficult for them to spit objects out. Once they start swallowing they may be unable to stop. This means that they shouldn't be allowed to play with yarn, string, or rubber bands. The consequences are sometimes fatal.

Natural Light for All Living Things

Natural light is a necessity for a healthy, normal pet. Sunlight affects the neuroendocrine system and many other body processes. So get your pet out in the sunlight as much as possible. You can, however, approximate natural light indoors if need be. One way is to install a special tube in a fluorescent light fixture called "Full Spectrum," which mimics natural sunlight. You could also install an ultraviolet-admitting plastic window that would admit more of the sun's natural rays than glass does.

Like Owner, Like Pet

You are having problems, and then your pet gets sick, too. Any connection? Some veterinarians say that there is. They have found that in certain stubborn cases an animal finally gets well only after its owner resolves emotional stresses that had been rubbing off on the pet. So if your pet is not up to par, look at your own and the pet's surroundings. Is it too noisy? Have you recently moved? Has a change in routine prevented you from paying as much attention to your dog or cat as the animal is used to? Kitty or Rover may be a lot better when you're a lot better.

Oil to Stop Bleeding

When using a bandage on an injured animal just isn't practical, try some vegetable oil. Swabbed generously on the wound, the oil can effectively control bleeding.

Relief for Itchy Skin

A pet with a mild skin irritation can be given relief until you can see a veterinarian. Dab on apple-cider vinegar to stop itching and burning. Use it full strength on small areas. For large areas, dilute 1 part of vinegar with 3 parts of water. A covering of petroleum jelly will also provide temporary relief from inflamed, scabby, and itching skin.

Olive Oil Remedy

Olive oil is a handy healer for your pet's minor skin injuries. Dabbed on the skin, it eases the pain and promotes the healing of burns. It can also reduce the inflammation and itching of mosquito and flea bites.

Keep Toxins Out of Reach

Toxic household products are dangerous for curious pets as well as young children—so keep the drugs and cleaners out of reach. Automotive products, too, can spell disaster. Antifreeze, for example, tastes sweet, so pets will lap it up if they get a chance. Antifreeze poisoning, which produces vomiting, depression, and coma, is a persistent problem in veterinary medicine.

Garlic for What Ails Them

A clove or two of crushed garlic added to your pet's daily food can be quite a versatile remedy for some common problems. For the following conditions, give garlic a try:

- intestinal worms
- indigestion
- constipation
- coughing spells and bronchitis
- fleas

Disguising Strange Water

If you're going to travel with a pet and are worried that he will refuse strange-smelling water, add a few drops of peppermint to his regular water for a few days before the trip. Take the peppermint along and add a few drops to the drinking water along the way; he won't know the difference.

Treatment for Heat Prostration

Heatstroke is common in animals during the hottest days of the summer. A short period of extreme heat, such as when a tethered animal is exposed to direct sun or a pet is left in a closed car, can bring about panting, unconsciousness, and, ultimately, death. Should such an animal be discovered, quick action can save his life. Immediately immerse the animal's body, except his head, in cool water, until he seems revived. Then keep him in a shaded, cool area until you're certain he has recovered.

General Livestock

Homemade Flypaper

You can make homemade flypaper for your animal shelter by mixing pine tar with molasses and brushing the sticky substance on a piece of heavy material or cardboard.

Squash Leaves for Repelling Flies

A highly effective fly repellent can be made by adding a handful of squash leaves to some water and then processing it in a blender until well mixed. Strain the mixture and rub it onto your animals' coats with a piece of terrycloth. Its potency lasts as long as most commercial products, and it's free and nontoxic.

Keep Flies Away from Injured and Sick Animals

Any injury or diarrhea in livestock should be checked carefully, especially during the summer months, when flies are a problem. Flies lay their eggs in any foul, damp spot, and the maggots, which quickly hatch, can almost instantly eat their way into an animal's flesh. Keep the affected areas clean and dry at all times.

Homemade Salve for Cuts

The North American Indians discovered the healing powers of a salve made from the swollen spring buds of the poplar tree. Simply heat some vegetable shortening or lard until very warm, and add enough of the sticky buds to thicken the mixture. Cook over low heat until the buds are soft and cooked down. Then quickly strain the hot salve through a piece of cheesecloth to remove the particles of the buds that are left. When cooled, this salve works miracles on all types of cuts and abrasions on pets or livestock.

Treating Burns and Abrasions with Tea

A cooled tea bag makes a ready dressing for burns and minor abrasions on all animals. Not only does it help clean and soothe the area, but the tannic acid toughens the skin and promotes quick healing.

Treatment for Bee Stings and Insect Bites

Bee stings or other insect-bite reactions can be treated with the crushed, moistened flower of bee balm, or bergamot. In minutes, the swelling and

Bee balm

pain will be gone. And this pretty summer-flowering plant is a great addition to any flower bed.

Ringworm Cure

A safe, nontoxic ringworm treatment can be found in most kitchens. Take the white from one large egg, and mix with it a dime-size pinch of alum powder. Soak and clean the ringworm area well, then dry it. Apply the alum and egg white, and let it dry. Repeat daily. This is very effective, and it works extremely well on cats and rabbits, who are highly sensitive to other antifungals, such as iodine and copper naphthenate.

Removing Porcupine Quills

Porcupines are common in many areas of the country, and sooner or later, most domestic animals come in contact with these prickly creatures. If your animal is attacked and winds up with many quills in his body or quills deep in his throat, take him at once to your veterinarian. But, if there are only a few quills, they may be pulled at home. The trick to extracting these barbed quills is to grasp them firmly, and pull *very* slowly, so that the flesh releases its grip on the barbs. If you are hasty, the quills will shatter and break off, only to cause infection later.

Sick Signals

Body language is usually the first clue to a sick animal. By watching carefully, you can soon learn the normal actions of your healthy animals and be more aware of health changes that can be discovered by slightly depressed appetites, inactivity, or a sudden "puffed up" look to the coat.

Any animal with a lowered body temperature, whether from the shock of an accident, illness, or chilling, is close to death. The most important treatment is to get that temperature back up into the normal range, using artificial heat from a heat lamp, space heater, electric blanket, or warm water. Placing a blanket on a chilled animal does no good, as the weak animal has already lost the ability to raise its own body temperature.

Water Is Critical

Water is the most important of all feed. Not only does it make up over 80% of the body weight, but it also carries off body wastes and impurities. Don't neglect to give ample fresh water to your animals every day.

Handy Medication Syringe

A disposable plastic syringe makes a convenient dose syringe for small animals. Liquid medications are easily administered with little resistance.

Cleaning a Wound Rather Than Bandaging It

Trim the hair around an animal's wound rather than bandaging it. The hair holds many, many bacteria, as well as trapping dirt, exudate, and debris, which slow natural healing. Clipping the hair to allow air drying does much more good than a bandage, which only causes foulness and dampness in the area.

Cleaning Eyes

Before treating an animal's eyes, rinse them with a warm solution of boric acid. This will wash away the exudate, soothe the eyes, and make any treatment more effective.

Cold First, Heat Later

When an injury, such as a sprain or bruise, first occurs, soak the area with cold water and ice packs. When the injury is hours old, switch to hot packs and soaks. The cold water constricts blood vessels and prevents swelling, whereas the heat increases circulation and promotes healing.

Keeping Notes

A blackboard is an invaluable tool in any barn. On it you can keep track of medication given, breeding dates, feed used for different animals, and instructions from your veterinarian, horseshoer, or trusted mentor.

Recording Normal Temperatures

Write down the normal temperatures of all of your animals, taken when they are well. Each animal has a slightly different normal temperature, and it is vital to know the temperature of an animal before you give it any treatment. This way, you'll know whether your animal has a slightly abnormal elevated temperature or just a higher normal temperature.

Chickens

Fresh Greens for Your Birds

To keep your chickens in healthful greens without having them eat the plants to the ground, securely anchor a sturdy bottomless wire cage over a prolific plant. The birds will nip off the savory greens that polk through the wire, while leaving enough of the plant intact to continue its vigorous growth.

Sunflower Seeds Are Good for Chickens

Sunflower seeds are easy to grow and are a good dry-weather crop. They are also a wonderful source of protein for poultry. Hang ripe sunflower heads within easy reach of your chickens so that they can peck out the seeds and eat them at will.

Growing Fresh Greens from Sprouted Oats

When greens for the flock are hard to obtain, treat the birds to sprouted oats. Soak the oats in warm water for 24 hours, then drain them and spread them on a tray that has a bottom made from window screening, in a layer no more than 1 inch thick. Keep them moist, watering daily if necessary. After about seven days, the oats will reach a length of 1 inch and be at their peak of nutritional value. Have enough trays to feed sprouts to the flock at least every other day, stacking the trays to reduce the amount of water needed.

Encourage Drinking in Warm Weather

Chickens prefer their drinking water at temperatures between 50° and 55°F. During hot summer weather, their requirement for water increases, but the warmer the water, the less of it they'll drink. If insulated pipes and shaded troughs are insufficient to keep their water cool, change it frequently during hot spells to encourage the flock to drink enough to remain in the peak of health.

Nesting Habits of Guinea Hens and Bantams

Guinea hens and barnyard bantams persistently "steal" others' nests, and hunting for them can make daily egg collection a time-consuming chore. Often several banties will lay in a single nest, and in the case of guineas, an entire flock may take advantage of a choice nesting site. Once you've located the nest, disturb it as little as possible and leave one or two eggs, or a decoy egg, in the nest to simplify future egg collection by encouraging the hens to continue laying there.

More Attention Means Bigger Appetites

For more rapid fattening of fryers or broilers, visit them often with a little extra feed, or simply stir up the feed remaining in their trough whenever you pass by. The extra attention seems to stimulate their appetites.

Scaly Leg Mite Control

Raised scales and limping may be the result of scaly leg mites that burrow under the scales on a chicken's feet and legs. If your chickens are bothered by them, dip their legs in mineral oil three times at ten-day intervals, working the oil under the scales with a soft toothbrush in severe cases, and thoroughly clean and disinfect the coop to prevent reinfestation.

Using Chickens for Fly Control

Summer flies around the rabbitry can be reduced by allowing a few chickens to run beneath the cages. The chickens obtain a healthful supplement to their diet while controlling the fly population and also gain nutrients by consuming spilled rabbit feed and an occasional rabbit dropping.

Tobacco Mite Control

Should your chickens be bothered by mites, scatter some tobacco leaves in their nests.

Guinea Fowl Security Alarm

If predators are a frequent problem around the barnyard, keep a few guinea fowl to sound the nighttime alarm whenever your protective services might be needed. The frightful hue and cry they raise is often sufficient to frighten off the would-be marauder.

Lights Out

When using artificial light for egg production, you can save money by reducing the number of hours the henhouse is traditionally lighted at night and still preserve laying efficiency. Cornell University researchers have found that a 10-hour period of darkness followed by only 2 hours of light triggers the egg-laying mechanism. Exactly how light induces this phenomenon is not yet known.

Eliminating Sticky Bottoms

Sticky bottoms in chicks are caused by moist droppings that cling to the fluff, a condition that can eventually stop up the birds and cause their deaths. If your chicks develop sticky bottoms, reduce their rich starter mixture by adding an equal portion of cornmeal, and feed it to the chicks until the problem clears up, usually in about 24 hours.

Fuel for Long, Cold Nights

To help your birds stay cozy during winter nights, feed them their ration of scratch in the evening. They will then go to roost with a crop full of grains that will produce energy for them while it's digesting overnight.

Introduce Additions to Your Flock Slowly

Each population of chickens develops a unique set of immunities, making it unwise to introduce new chickens into an established flock. But when this becomes necessary, insure against bringing in pathogens for which your birds have developed no defenses by placing the newly acquired birds in a holding pen with two or three from your flock. If your established birds remain healthy for at least two weeks, they may be reunited with the flock along with the new ones. But if your old birds show signs of illness, remove them along with the newly acquired carriers. When bringing in new birds, it's far safer to sacrifice a few from your flock than to endanger the entire population.

Signs of a Contented Flock

You can tell by its sound how content your flock is. Happy chickens are active and noisy, the hens loudly crooning throughout the day and the cocks enticing them repeatedly with excited staccato cries. If your flock is quiet, check for symptoms of diseases, parasites, or other causes of distress.

Use Roosters to Prevent Squabbles

To reduce fighting among surplus cockerels raised as broilers, place an older rooster in the pen with them. The presence of an authority figure tends to reduce squabbles that otherwise result in injuries that show up as blemishes on finished birds.

How to Move a Brooding Hen

If it becomes necessary to move a brooding hen, enhance the chances that she'll remain on the nest by moving her during the dark of night. If at all possible, move the entire nest along with the hen to minimize the degree of disturbance.

Introducing Adopted Chicks

You can enhance the chances that a brooding hen will accept foster chicks. Give her only day-old hatchlings and slip them under her during the night. By morning chicks and mom will have become accustomed to the sounds of one another, reducing the shock of a face-to-face meeting.

Baby Powder May Stop Picking

If you know the delight of hatching out your own chicks, you also know the distress of seeing the chicks being pecked by those slightly older, when the little ones are introduced. Since they are guided to a large extent by their sense of smell, try dusting the older chicks with baby powder, then do the same with the new ones as you put them in with the rest.

Separating a Hen from Her Chicks

To prevent a hen from leading her chicks through vegetation wet with dew or recent rain, and to keep her from eating their special starter ration, place the birds in a cage with wire spacing just large enough for the chicks to get through. Feed and water the hen inside the wire, but feed the chicks just outside it. They may roam a bit, but they won't stray far from the hen's continuous clucking. If she sounds the danger alarm, they'll pop safely to her side. When the chicks become too large to move quickly in and out, the cage is no longer needed.

Sure Footing for Baby Chicks

Newly hatched birds can be helped to rapidly gain sure footing by lining the brooder bottom with clean, rough material such as burlap, from which loose strings that the little ones might be tempted to swallow have been removed. If you must use newspaper, coat it with a good layer of sand for the first few days after the hatch. Slipping on a slick surface can cause serious injury to undeveloped little legs.

Sanitizing Incubators

Improve incubation success by reducing bacterial populations within the warm, moist unit. Clean the incubator thoroughly after each hatch, and with each new setting of eggs, fill the humidity pan with a solution of common household bleach and warm water mixed at a rate of 2 tablespoons per gallon. Thereafter, add only plain warm water as the solution evaporates, until the next setting, when the pan should again be filled with the weak bleach solution.

Reducing Picking by Brooder Chicks

When chicks in a brooder pick at one another, it may be a sign that they are being kept too warm. Reduce the brooder temperature 5° each week until 70°F is reached. Lighting a red bulb inside the unit, which causes everything to appear the same color, may also minimize the temptation to pick. Keep direct sunlight from striking the brooder and neutralizing the red glow.

Introduce Mail-Order Chicks to Water

If you get your little chicks by mail, dip their beaks in water immediately after they arrive. They are generally a bit dehydrated when they come, and this will show them right away where the water is.

Keeping Your Birds Cool

Chickens do not have sweat glands and so suffer, often seriously, during long periods of intense heat. When summer temperatures soar, use a hose attachment called a fogger to sprinkle the birds, as well as the interior and roof of their housing. The slight cooling effect resulting from evaporation may be all that is necessary to prevent overheating.

Getting Your Hens to Lay Again

If your birds are not laying when they should be, force moult them. Do this by blocking out their light and withdrawing their food for three days, but be sure to give them water during this time. Then, provide them with bulky feed, like oats, for two weeks. Once your birds' feathers fall out, resume their normal feeding. Their feathers will grow back and they'll start laying again.

Free Grit

You can get your chickens' grit for free. In the summer, dig sand out of ditches and creeks and then spread it on boards to dry before storing. In the wintertime, when the chickens can't scratch outside, place some of the sand that you've collected in their feeders.

A Dust Box

A dust box is a must for poultry that are kept inside in the winter. Any size box within reason will work, as long as it has sides that are about 8 inches high. Place a mixture made up of 2 parts of sand to 6 parts of wood ashes to 2 parts of lime in the box, and let your chickens go to it.

Corn-Cob Bedding

Corn cobs can be used for bedding in your chicken coop. They are free at most feedmills and they won't soak up water like shavings or straw will, making muddy floors.

Chicken Catcher

A large fishnet with long handle makes a good chicken catcher. It doesn't hurt the chickens and means less running around for you.

Turkeys, Ducks, and Geese

Training Young Turkeys to Eat

If you have trouble teaching your baby turkeys to eat, try this tip. Mix hard-cooked eggs and green onion tops into their dinner. Sometimes just a sprinkling of green onion tops is enough to attract the little birds' attention to the main course.

Natural-Born Meteorologists

Ducks and geese are often more reliable at predicting weather changes than the official weather service—they tend to become restless and noisy when a storm is brewing, signaling a change in the weather as yet undetectable by their keeper.

Ménage à Trois

Geese can be fussy about the company they choose to keep, so that attempting to create a breeding trio from a mated pair may simply result in ostracism of the new female. But the pair will rarely rebuff a new goose if she is one of their own young, which they themselves have raised to maturity.

Securing Muscovies

When carrying a Muscovy drake, get a good tight hold of the wings and keep the claws aimed away from yourself. Muscovies have incredibly sharp nails and are strong enough to inflict a serious wound when struggling to get away.

Showing a Goose Who's Boss

Geese are notoriously aggressive and should be given wide berth during the breeding season. But at other times it's best to call the bluff of a bully goose, for if you simply turn and run he'll try to catch you and slap you with his strong, outstretched wings. Instead, rush back at the goose, waving your arms. He should retreat with one eye guarding his rear flank. If he continues toward you, give his bill a sharp downward smack; this will not hurt him but it should injure his dignity sufficiently to deter the attack.

A rambunctious young male goose can sometimes be trained not to attack if you squirt him in the face with a water pistol each time he threatens you. But don't try this with a battle veteran; it may make him angrier and more vicious.

A Nest for Geese

A simple nest for geese can be made from a 55-gallon barrel or oil drum laid down horizontally and anchored by bricks along each side. Leave a pile of straw nearby, and your goose will soon be arranging it, along with her own feathers and fluff, at the closed back end of the barrel.

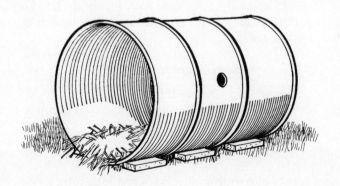

For the Water Dish

Keep newly hatched ducklings and goslings from splashing in an open dish of water by floating in it a circular piece of wood slightly smaller than the dish. The wood will ride down with the water level, providing a constant rim around the edges from which the little ones may drink without becoming overly wet and chilled.

No Small, Shiny Objects for Geese

Keep the gooseyard free of shiny nails, broken bits of glass, and aluminum pop-tops. Geese are attracted to such small, bright objects, and consuming them causes "hardware disease," involving infection and possibly death due to punctures in the digestive tract.

Goats

Fly Control

Give your goat about ¼ cup of vinegar with his feed each day. The goat should like the vinegar but the flies probably won't, and many will stay away from your animal.

Giving Medications

Goat-size boluses and pills can more easily be given if they are first coated with shortening. The medication slides down more easily, helping to prevent choking, and tastes better, so that your goat will more readily accept it.

Better Control While Leading

When trying to lead a fractious large goat, tip up his chin, keeping his head as high as possible. This position limits the amount of pull the animal is capable of.

Garden Leftovers for Your Goats

Don't forget your goats during the garden harvest. They love and greatly benefit from pumpkins, squash, carrots, corn, rutabagas, and even onions.

Storing Colostrum

Freeze a supply of colostrum (the doe's first milk after kidding) in ice cube trays. When frozen, empty the cubes into a plastic bag and keep them ready for an emergency. There is no substitute for colostrum, and the kids will not do well without at least four feedings of it. One or two cubes, thawed and warmed, make a handy-size meal.

Catching Mastitis Early

One of the most useful treatments for noninfectious mastitis is the gentle milking of the udder at least four times daily. This simple remedy can usually clear up the problem, often caused by a bang or bruise, before bacteria take over. Once there's an infection, antibiotics are necessary.

Minimizing Buck Odor

Clip buck goats twice a year, in the spring and fall, to keep "buck odor" down to a minimum. Be sure to also remove their beards.

Scours

At the first sign of scours (diarrhea) in kid goats, cut out a feeding of milk, and cut the next feeding in half. In the place of the missed feeding, supply electrolytes (available in the baby care departments of drug stores). Scours is often simply the result of overeating or eating too fast and, if stopped quickly, will not cause serious problems.

Special Care for Weak Newborns

Most newborn baby goats that are weak at birth die due to chilling and starvation. A good number of these can be saved by a warm-water soak followed by thorough drying with a blow dryer or heat lamp and a feeding of 30 cc's of warmed colostrum every 2 hours until they are active.

Good-Tasting Milk

Goat's milk picks up outside odors very quickly, especially if unpasteurized. The flavor of raw milk is best during the first 24 hours following milking. For good-tasting milk, try not to mix fresh milk with that of the last milking.

Restraining Your Goat for a Vaccination

When giving vaccinations and other medications by needle without the benefit of a stanchion, you can hold your goat still by straddling the animal's neck, facing the tail. Squeeze your legs together, holding his neck firmly. Animals are not frightened by this position, and they are effectively restrained.

Trim Hoofs While They're Soft

Trimming the feet is most easily done after goats have been outdoors after a rain or even a dewy morning. The moisture in the ground and grass softens the hardest of feet, making trimming an easier chore.

Increasing Milk Production

Molasses in their drinking water (1 cup for every 30 to 90 gallons) during the winter or cider vinegar in their water during the summer (molasses tends to ferment in warm weather) will encourage your goats to drink, resulting in more milk production and better health. (These additions are also useful, when traveling with your animals, to mask the strange taste of different water.)

Preventing Urinary Calculi

Goats prone to urinary calculi should be switched to distilled or other mineral-free water, as the problem is often made worse by minerals precipitating out of the water in their bladders. Artificially softened water is another culprit.

When Labor Is Difficult

You can help a doe having a difficult labor by lubricating the birth canal with a small amount of mild dishwashing detergent, infused by means of a 12-cc syringe minus the needle. The extra "slip" often is all that is necessary to allow a large kid to be born without complications.

Let Your Goats Brush Themselves

You don't have to spend a lot of time brushing your goats—simply mount two to four stiff, inexpensive floor-scrubbing brushes on a leaning post. The goats will soon learn to lean against them and rub in pleasure. During fly and mosquito season, sponge oil of citronella onto the brushes to ward off biting pests.

Garbage-Can Watering Trough

A small, goat-size watering trough can be made from a cheap, aluminum garbage can. It can be set a foot into the ground for short-legged goats, and it is small enough to replenish with fresh water, being easily drained and cleaned.

Simple Worm Prevention

Eighty percent of goat worms are "recycled," as the animals pick up worm eggs by eating the manure dust that settles on their feed and water. This can be drastically cut down, and the goats protected, by feeding and watering the animals *outside* the pen, by means of a keyhole (8 inches in diameter, with a slot 12 inches long × 5 inches wide) for the hay manger and a circle 10 inches in diameter for the watering trough. This prevents contamination of the feed and water by feces and hooves. It also makes hay last twice as long, with very little waste.

A Better Delouser

Rotenone, a safe, inexpensive, and effective organic delousing powder, can be found in most garden supply stores during the summer. Keep it on the shelf until wintertime, when lice plague the cleanest of goats.

Softening Chapped Teats

Should your milker be prone to dry or chapped teats, simply rub a dab of unscented lanolin on your hands as you finish milking, then massage the udder and teats. In a few days, the skin will be smooth and soft, and so will yours!

A Goat Wash-and-Dry Cloth

A terrycloth bath towel, cut into a 10-inch square, makes an excellent wash-and-dry cloth for goat udders. In addition to being soft and absorbent, it's easy to launder and will last for years.

Horses

Handy Leg Bandages

Save all your old socks! They make effective bandages for hard-to-dress areas on horses' (and dogs') legs.

The Playing Dead Trick

To catch an elusive horse in a pasture, just lie down in the middle of the field. Most horses are so curious they'll have to come over just to see what you're up to.

Homemade Remedy for Ringworm or Thrush

To relieve ringworm or thrush, mix about one capful of household bleach in ½ gallon of water and sponge it on the fungus-affected area.

A Clever Gate Latch

Discarded seatbelts make great latches. Just nail one strap to the post and the other to the gate, and buckle up. Even the smartest horse won't figure how to open it up.

Warm Up the Bit First

For your horse's comfort, and your ease of bridling, warm the bit with your hand before placing it in the animal's mouth. This will prevent his tongue from sticking to the cold iron.

Proper Use of the Hoof Pick

It's easy to avoid bruising your horse's heel when cleaning his feet by using the hoof pick from heel to toe, rather than toe to heel. Then, should your hand slip, the point of the hoof pick will slide harmlessly off the sole of the foot.

A Simple Restraint

If your horse has to be kept from licking, chewing, or rubbing a wound or treated area, make a simple restraint from an old broom handle with holes drilled in each end. Wire a snap to each hole. Then run the stick between the horse's front legs, snapping one end to the bottom halter ring and the other to a light rope around the body, like a surcingle. The horse will be able to eat, drink, and move about, but he won't be able to reach the wound.

Scratching Is a Good Distraction

To distract a horse while giving an injection or another unpleasant treatment, scratch his neck down where it joins the chest. It's the one place a horse can't reach, and the feeling produces total bliss.

Have Doors and Gates Open Outward

Stall doors and gates that open out are safest because there is less chance that a horse will catch his hip on a corner as he rushes past. Many horses suffer broken hips and internal injuries from doing just this on a door that opens toward them.

Making the Medicine Go Down

Worming a horse will be less of a chore if you use the sprinkle-on-the-feed-grain crystals. Refrigerate them overnight to eliminate their odor, then mix them with half of the horse's grain (preferably a mix containing molasses to provide adhesion and mask flavor). Finally, cover the medicated grain completely with the "good" grain. It will be eaten unhesitatingly.

If you use a paste wormer, dip the end of the syringe one-third of the way into a jar of molasses. Open your horse's mouth as if slipping in the bit, and deposit the paste quickly, as far back on the tongue as possible. The molasses on the syringe will make the medicine go down more easily and will make the procedure more acceptable to the horse.

An inexpensive squirt gun makes a good tool for getting liquid wound medicine into place, especially under the belly or in other hard-to-reach places.

Slowing Down a Fast Eater

When a horse eats its grain too quickly, place several fist-size rocks in the feed tub. The animal will have to interrupt his eating to push the rocks aside. This remedy will help protect a greedy horse from colic.

Discouraging Your Horse from Chewing Wood

Some horses chew wood out of boredom or habit, a dangerous activity that can wear teeth badly and cause digestive troubles. A quick remedy is to mix an ounce of cayenne pepper with a jar of petroleum jelly and brush this mixture on any area that shows chew marks. It won't wash away in the rain or stain the fence or stall, and it will stop the chewing at the next bite.

Hairbrush for Horses

A people's hairbrush makes a good mane and tail brush. It pulls out far less hair than a comb, and it enables you to massage your horse's hair all the way down to the roots, making it healthy and lustrous.

Tick Prevention

If ticks are a problem in the forelock and mane area, dusting the spots with a little rotenone powder every morning will provide nearly total protection.

Hoof Care

Hooves can be kept flexible and healthy by brushing on a mixture of 1 part of pine oil and 1 part of pine tar. If the dryness comes from grazing in a dry pasture, water the horse from a tank that overflows onto clay. The horse will treat his own feet to a clay pack every time he comes to drink!

Sweating Off Swollen Legs

A very effective sweat for swollen legs can be made by painting them with linament, then wrapping them lightly with plastic wrap. This can be a strong treatment, however, so don't use it for a prolonged time until you check the reaction of your horse. Some horses have more sensitive skin than others.

Removing Warts

Many warts on your horse's skin can be neatly and permanently removed by simply tying them off tightly with a piece of clean, strong carpet thread. In a week or so they will strangulate and drop off, usually with no scar at all.

An Ice Pack for Your Horse

A handy ice pack or cold soak can be made with a blown-out truck inner tube. Slide it over the horse's foot and leg, then tie it up loosely. It is easy to fill with crushed ice and cold water.

Securing the Feed Tub

An outside feed tub can be kept right side up by placing it in the opening in the center of an old tire.

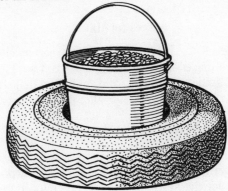

Cleaning Puncture Wounds

Puncture wounds can effectively be flushed with a 12-cc syringe (minus the needle) full of hydrogen peroxide. The tip can usually be pressed into the opening of the wound and the peroxide delivered with some force.

Trailering

To prevent accidents while hauling a single horse in a two-horse trailer, load the horse into the left side of the trailer so that he rides over the crown in the road. If the horse is loaded into the right side over the road shoulder, his weight, when coupled with a swerve or blowout, could topple the trailer, rolling it into the ditch.

Rabbits

Cold Water for Hot Days

Extremely hot weather causes many healthy rabbits to have any number of problems, from heat prostration to sterility. Bring them relief by freezing blocks of ice in old milk cartons or plastic jugs. One 8-inch block, taken from its mold and placed on the wire inside the hutch, will effectively cool and protect the rabbits during the hottest part of the day.

Trimming Nails of Caged Rabbits

Since domestic rabbits have limited opportunities to dig, their toenails grow too long, catching on cracks and the cage wire. Much rabbit lameness can be prevented by keeping the toenails trimmed with a pair of dog nail trimmers.

Successful Mating

Many hard-to-breed does can be encouraged to accept a buck's service if the buck's cage is placed next to hers for a day or two. This will give her time to get used to the buck slowly, and you'll find that she'll often mate the first time she is placed in his cage after such a courtship.

Weatherizing Nestboxes

In hot weather, remove most of the hair from the nestbox to prevent bunnies from overheating and dying. In cool weather, provide a simple cardboard liner for the nestbox; this can be changed, as needed, and thrown away between litters to prevent the growth of bacteria.

Nestbox Cleaning Tools

A whisk broom and wet/dry vacuum are invaluable tools in cleaning rabbit cages. The whisk broom loosens hair and dirt. The vacuum conveniently sucks the debris away, thereby preventing the dust from blowing in the air and possibly causing respiratory problems in the rabbits.

Food Booster for Nursing Does

Does that are thin after nursing a litter can usually be brought into shape quickly by adding a small amount of Carnation's Calf Manna to their pellets daily.

Pellet Scoops

Small quart plastic jugs with handles, such as those that fabric softeners come in, make great small-size scoops for rabbit pellets when cut down. They're especially handy when you have to reach inside the hutch to feed the animals.

Hanging Cages

Hang rabbit cages from screw eyes on the ceiling, on chains and snaps, rather than supporting them on legs or benches. They can then be moved around to different locations as needed. What's more, cleaning under them is a breeze, and rodents cannot get into the cages by climbing the legs.

Soothing a Nervous Doe

There's help for a doe that seems distressed, either dragging her bunnies out of the nestbox or killing them. Try playing a radio near her cage before and after she kindles next time. Soothing music (not rock and roll!) masks the outside sounds that may be making her nervous.

Living Shade for Cages

In hot areas, plant vine crops, such as squash, pumpkins, and melons, at the edge of a simple wire trellis around and over rabbit hutches. Not only will it provide shade with good air flow, but it will also provide the rabbits with extra nutrients.

Ventilation for Disease Prevention

Most rabbit diseases and deaths can be prevented if you're careful not to overcrowd the prolific animals. Stale air carries over 100 times as many harmful bacteria as fresh air does.

Foster Does

Try to have two or more does kindle at the same time. That way you can switch a few babies from an overprolific mother to one that has fewer bunnies, saving the larger litter and making the lesser producing doe pay her way. Dab a dot of Vicks or menthol on each bunny in the nest; if the doe cannot distinguish a difference in their odor, the fostering process will go more smoothly.

Manure Management

Barn lime, mixed with dry sawdust and laid in a 3-inch bed under rabbit hutches, absorbs urine, cuts down odors, and makes cleanup easier if manure removal cannot be done daily. It also makes great garden compost!

Rx for Ear Mites

Ear mites in a rabbit can usually be eliminated by simply putting a few drops of mineral oil into the animal's ear, wiping out the excess wax and dirt, and then repeating the treatment. The oil suffocates the mites and removes the debris in which they hide.

Index

Page references in italics indicate illustrations.
Boldfaced page references indicate tables.

Rodale Press, Inc., publishes RODALE'S ORGANIC GARDENING®,
the all-time favorite gardening magazine.
For information on how to order your subscription,
write to RODALE'S ORGANIC GARDENING®, Emmaus, PA 18049.